LEARNING *Privilege*

LEARNING *Privilege*

LESSONS OF POWER AND IDENTITY IN AFFLUENT SCHOOLING

ADAM HOWARD

Routledge
Taylor & Francis Group
New York London

Routledge
Taylor & Francis Group
711 Third Avenue
New York, NY 10017

Routledge
Taylor & Francis Group
2 Park Square
Milton Park, Abingdon
Oxon OX14 4RN

International Standard Book Number-13: 978-0-415-96082-3 (Softcover) 978-0-415-96081-6 (Hardcover)

Library of Congress Cataloging-in-Publication Data

Howard, Adam.
Learning privilege : lessons of power and identity in affluent schooling / Adam Howard.
p. cm.
Includes bibliographical references and index.
ISBN 978-0-415-96081-6 (hb) -- ISBN 978-0-415-96082-3 (pb) 1. Upper class--Education--United States. 2. Children of the rich--Education--United States. 3. Social status--United States. I. Title.

LC4941.H69 2008
371.96'20973--dc22 2007009023

Visit the Taylor & Francis Web site at
http://www.taylorandfrancis.com

and the Routledge Web site at
http://www.routledge.com

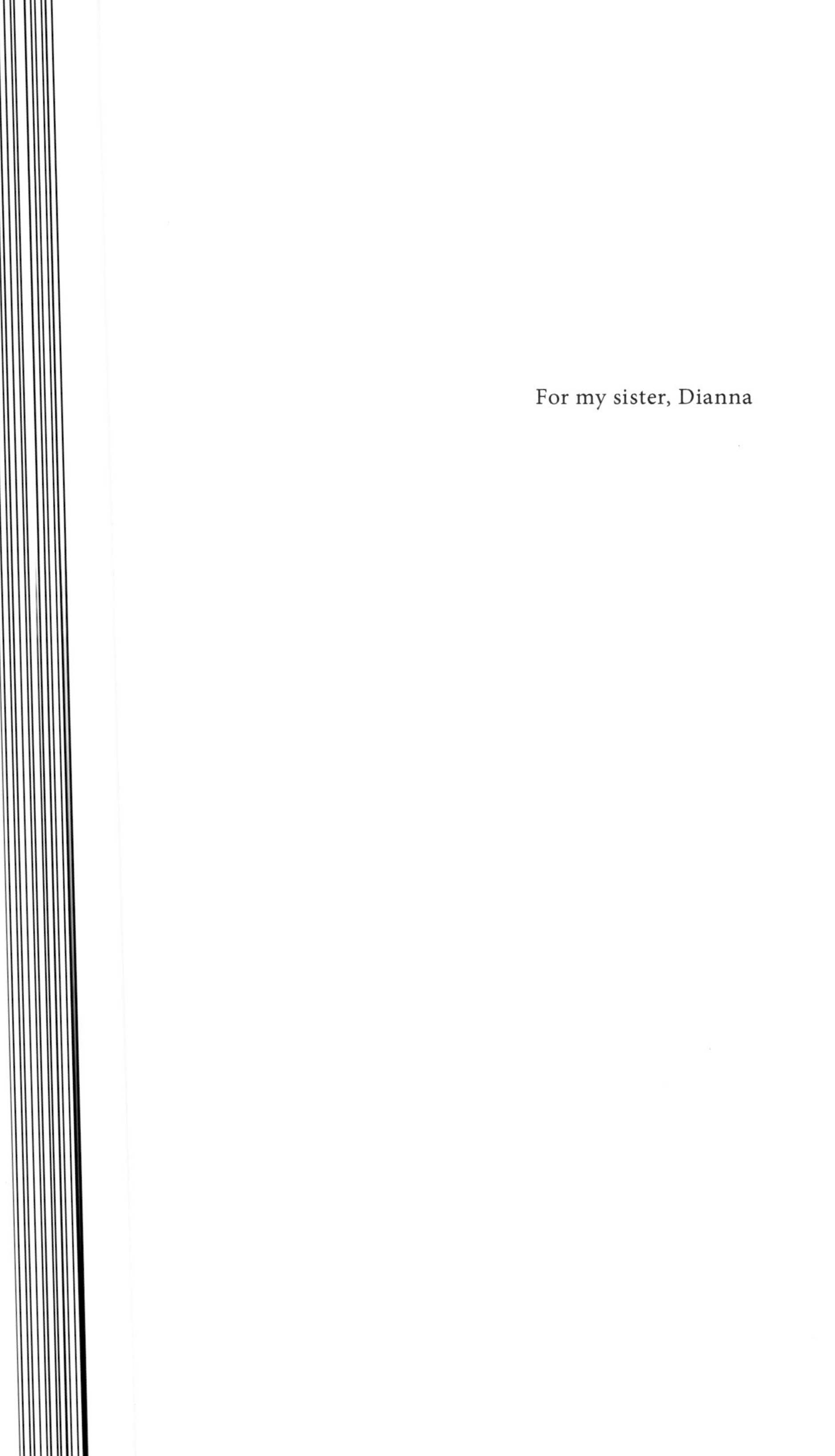

For my sister, Dianna

Contents

Preface

ntered kindergarten, my family lived without a home but was not . We lived in a church basement located in a small, poor community cky. My dad preached at this church when he felt well enough, but eived pay because the congregation was nearly as poor as we were. ny parents were unable to work on a regular basis because of poor d disabilities. My dad had been sick since he was a child. I never ctly what was wrong with him; all I knew was that he had stomach and every once in a while he had a "spell" that nearly took his life. afford proper health care, he received medical treatment only when e of these spells. Even then, we could not afford the proper medical he needed. Most of the time during these spells, he remained bedrid-d in a fetal position for days, and at times, for weeks. Dad was never d at hiding his pain from us. We knew how much pain he experi-illness engulfed our living space.

d met my mom as a traveling evangelist. He began preaching at 13 led from one small town to another across Kentucky and Tennes-ning everywhere he could. One year he was invited to be one of the at a weeklong tent revival meeting in a small town about 40 miles ouisville. My mom lived with her mother, stepfather, and six broth-sters in a three-room house located just outside this town. She was hurchgoing Christian in her family and went to church as often as it was the only time when she escaped the everyday realities of her abusive stepfather and her responsibilities as the oldest child to raise rs and sisters.

m was 16 and my dad was 20 when they met at the revival. Mom had o attend only the first night but met my dad and stayed the entire he end of that week, they were dating, and 5 months later they were They had my sister, Dianna, 11 months later. After Dianna was born, ld my parents they would never be able to have other children. My ears later, therefore, was a surprise—to say nothing of Jason's arrival r I was born.

people I have met in my life were more opposite than my parents. dad was not at the pulpit preaching about hell and fire and brim-vas a quiet, small man. His lifetime of illness had left him thin and barely spoke, and when he did you could barely hear him. Quite te, my mom was large, sassy, and loud. She was also confident in a y. The reason that I say strange is because she spent her life battling an untreated, undiagnosed psychological illness that revealed itself, in one way, by her inability to be around people. Mom rarely left the basement. "I just want to keep to myself," she told us. With windows covered with aluminum foil, it was always dark in that basement. She spent most days and nights in bed. Dad and the rest of us did not worry that much about my mom sleeping so much, because when she was awake, she seemed so alive and present. Mom was also a diabetic and had developed heart disease as a result, which she eventually died from in her early forties.

Mom was not one of those parents who kept the details of living in poverty from us. My sister, brother, and I knew how difficult it was for my parents to make ends at least come close enough to each other for us to have clothes on our backs and food on the table. We also were aware of how difficult it was for them to deal with their health problems enough to take care of us. These early experiences taught me to survive on as little as possible, to be a child of parents who were ill, and to become accustomed to uncertainty. These lessons that I learned from living in poverty, however, did not prepare me adequately for a school environment. Similar to what has been reflected in years of research on emergent literacy (e.g., Clay, 1975, 1991; Dyson, 1983; Heath, 1983; Purcell-Gates, 1988, 1995), I had not been exposed before I entered schooling to the many critical ways in which young children learn about reading and writing by being a part of a literate home environment where people (e.g., parental figures) read and write for various reasons. Therefore, I had not developed the necessary preliterate behaviors or skills to make a smooth transition to schooling.

Ignoring the fact that most adults in our community could barely read or write, the school, even at the kindergarten level, expected us to be able, for example, to recite the alphabet, count up to a certain point, be able to write our names, and hold books the right way. Although my parents had a higher level of literacy than most in the community—that is, my dad had graduated from high school and my mom had completed 10 years of formal schooling—they did not read to us and did not spend time with us rehearsing the alphabet or teaching us our numbers. Although reports commissioned by government agencies published around that time (e.g., *A Nation at Risk*) would claim that my parents were not doing their job at parenting, they taught us different lessons about knowing and doing. They taught us lessons about life that come from living in poverty. These learning experiences had no value in transitioning to formal schooling. At school I was known as the kid from a poor family without the intellectual abilities or family support to learn what they thought I needed to learn: I was labeled unable to learn.

The lessons that I had learned from my family also consistently conflicted with the lessons I was taught at my school. One moment of being caught between these conflicting lessons occurred during kindergarten. I do not remember much about my teacher other than her giving us a lot of opportunities to paint. The other students in my class loved painting. None of us lies to do art projects at home, so this was considered a special treat However, I thought it was messy. I was never one of those kids who et dirty, and painting seemed way too messy. But beyond my natural to avoid getting dirty, I worried about getting paint on my clothes. ıe previous summer, my brother and I "helped" my grandfather, who "Papaw," paint his barn. Before we started on the barn, Papaw told be "foolin' around" because the paint would ruin our clothing. My ıs usual, did not listen, and by the time we finished, he had paint all . "Y'all's momma gonna kill me," Papaw told us. "You never listen." I did not have one speck of paint on me. I even avoided getting paint ıile my brother was "foolin' around." When we arrived home, Mom paw have it, and then she punished my brother for not doing what he o do. I did not get in trouble because I had listened to Papaw, and I istening when the teacher asked us to paint. I felt like my teacher was e to do something that Papaw had warned me not to do and Mom ;hed my brother for doing.

acher gave us a white piece of paper, brushes, and small cups filled t and then assigned us various things to draw—a house, a cat, and ɔst of my classmates jumped right into the assignment. Holding a ɔrush, I just stared at the blank sheet of paper. The paint beside me ntouched. I refused to follow my teacher's instructions. My protest il Mom asked me to paint her a picture for her birthday. I later found ıy teacher had sent a note home informing Mom that I would not ım never told me this part of the story. I found out years after she d away. But Mom did what she needed to for me to begin painting at e gave me permission.

the first, but not the only, memory I have of the conflict between the at I learned from my family about living in poverty—in this case, ı your clothes because we don't have money to buy new ones—and s I learned at school—in this assignment, Don't worry about getting ⁄our clothes. I did have to worry because I knew that my parents afford to buy me new clothes if I ruined what I had. I was well aware .rd it was for them to make sure we had clothing on our backs. I at what we had could not be easily replaced. I learned that from my ɛs living in poverty and the everyday realities my family faced in ;gle to make ends meet.

time, my understanding of the world was profoundly defined by l seen and experienced living in poverty and shaped by the lessons lults in my family and community had taught me about who I was, ıld live and relate to others, what to do and not to do, what to value, was important in life. I had developed particular ways of knowing and certain habits of the heart and mind. These habits, actions, and : were shut out of my experiences in formal schooling. My school, instead, fostered a different community, both physically and culturally, that encouraged different expectations, rules, and behaviors. At home I was taught that in order to survive, you must work together. At school I was taught that in order to be successful, I had to be engaged in competition with others. At school I was also forced to read without using my own voice and to write without using my own words; I was denied the richness of my family's oral traditions. I was urged to abandon these traditions for the printed word. In the school environment, I was excluded and singled out; and in my family, I was part of a network of people working together to survive poverty. I found school strangely unfamiliar from what I knew and held to be true.

This unfamiliarity made it impossible for me to connect with my experiences in formal schooling and, in fact, kept me from becoming literate. After kindergarten, I was placed in the remedial track because I had been diagnosed with a learning disability.[1] Part of this diagnosis came from my noticeable lack of preliterate skills and behaviors. I also struggled with oral language. Mom assured me that when people could not understand what I was saying, I had not grown out of my "baby talk." My parents did not worry about my problems with speech, because they thought I would learn how to work on those problems at school. Instead, the way I spoke became another indicator of what skills and knowledge I did not possess.

The remedial classes at my elementary school were housed in the lower level of the school alongside the classes for students with so-called behavior disorders and for mentally and physically challenged students in special education. This floor of the school was mostly open, with some partitions separating the classes. Students with learning disabilities and behavior problems were placed together according to grade level. With few exceptions, we stayed separated from the rest of the school throughout the day. I have few memories of my experiences at school during these years.

Unlike several of my classmates who graduated from high school functionally illiterate despite the incessant focus on mastering the basics of a "pedagogy of poverty" (Haberman, 1991) that guided most of our educational experiences, for me this course of education would change once I arrived in Mr. Mattingly's seventh-grade English class. It did not take Mr. Mattingly long to realize that I was unable to read or write. My previous teachers had probably noticed this inability as well but had refused or had not known how to address it. Mr. Mattingly asked me to stay after class early in the year and spoke what had never been spoken. He had discovered my secret; my poverty had been misdiagnosed as a learning disability. Until then, my illiteracy had been a secret; I did not keep it a secret, I just did not know how to be literate or did not know I was supposed to be literate. I acted as everyone in my community acted. My family and others in my community were too consumed with living in poverty to think about much else other than what it took to put food on the table, a roof over our heads, and clothes on our backs. Disconnected from

nowing and doing of our community and the everyday realities we all
' teachers and other school officials mistook poverty for stupidity.
:periences at school changed after seventh grade. Mr. Mattingly
vith me individually—even when I was no longer enrolled in his
help me reach a sufficient level of academic proficiency for college.
enth grade until I graduated from high school, he often stayed after
th me to provide additional instruction and to offer guidance about
es that confronted me. As I reflect on this period of my life, I realize
faced with many opportunities to make decisions that would have
n poverty. Many of my peers had dropped out of school and were
On the surface, they seemed happier than when they had attended
some ways they probably were. But for most, the choice to work
bout being happier. Their families needed the income earned from
r. Some classmates also abused or sold drugs, and some had already
rcerated. Successes in school were rare, and few of us anticipated
lure in school was treated as the norm. Mr. Mattingly provided me
ive to this standard. He provided me with the support and guid-
parents could not provide. My parents wanted me to be successful
they just did not know how to help me become successful. Through
ngly's mentoring,[2] college attendance became a reality for me, and I
ay out of poverty.

attingly's advice, guidance, and example all were important parts
:ionship with me. I knew more than anything that he cared for me;
ed me and my experiences and knowledge. He did not grow up in
id did not fully understand my family and community, but he did
d that my poverty meant more than just where my family stood
ılly. He understood that my experiences living in poverty had deter-
ues, standpoints, and interests, and he realized that these experi-
e often in conflict with what I encountered in formal schooling.
iimself accessible and in so doing, helped me make the unfamiliar
:hool more understandable. He responded sensitively and lovingly
est realities of my life at that time. His relationship stimulated me
ore about a world not limited and defined by poverty.

rest in becoming a teacher emerged from my relationship with Mr.
I wanted to have the same influence on the lives of students as he
ı my life. When I made the decision to become a teacher, I never
at I would begin my career at an elite private school. Instead, I had
hat I would spend my career teaching students from a similar class
d as my own. Strangely enough, my interest in working with poor
d me to an elite school. The school sponsored an educational out-
ram for poor students, and I came to the school as the director of
m. In addition to coordinating this program, I was a teacher at
In these two positions, I had the unique experience of working

simultaneously with both poor and affluent students. I spent my workdays split between two very different worlds. I taught at the private school in the morning and then worked in urban public schools in the afternoon. Although I recognized that my own educational experiences were influenced by poverty, I did not truly understand social class distinctions in schooling until I moved between and worked within these two worlds on a daily basis.

Although I faced many struggles in my work at urban schools, I soon discovered that my life and educational experiences had prepared me less for the difficulties that I faced as a private school teacher. Similar to what I experienced as a child when I entered formal schooling, I found the culture of this school disconnected from what I knew and held to be true. Unfamiliar with this educational landscape of privilege and abundance, I struggled to be the kind of teacher that I wanted to be, a teacher committed to preparing my students to live critically, justly, and meaningfully. To begin working toward bridging the gap between my commitments and practice, I realized that I needed to learn more about the social and cultural particularities of this school context.

I began conducting the studies reported in this book to become more familiar with this world. In these studies, I explore the questions that I began developing as a teacher about the concept of privilege itself and the cultural and social processes in schooling that reinforce and regenerate it. More specifically, I examine the ways that privileged identities are constructed by the lessons affluent students are taught in their schooling about their place in the world, their relationships with others, and who they are. This book offers an overview of how these lessons and the values behind them assist students in constructing privilege as a central component of their identities.

In chapter 1, I describe my experiences teaching affluent students and how these experiences led me to specific questions about privilege and the advantages of elite schooling. I also describe the methods used in the studies reported in the book. In chapter 2, I provide an overview of the literature on social class influences in schooling and explore the concept of privilege as identity that provides the grounding for the studies of affluent schools included in this book. To explore this way of thinking about privilege, I articulate a sociocultural conception of identity formation, based on the concept of mediated action (Wertsch, 1998). My conceptualization is informed by recent scholarship on racial identity development, with a particular focus on whiteness as a privileged (racial) identity, and by recent scholarship on the role that position-centered ideology plays in reinforcing and reproducing dominance and power (Thompson, 1990).

In chapters 3 through 7, I explore what educators, students, and families at the schools in these studies value most in education, which are academic excellence, ambition, trust, traditions, and service. I explore how these values are expressed in a variety of ways and contexts and guide ways of knowing g that both create high standards for their educational programs and the privilege of their students. Although these values relate to all four situate my exploration of each value in one or two of the schools. In pters, I also describe the context of each school and the members chool communities. In chapters 8 and 9, I explore the overarching Othering in my research. In chapter 8, I examine the narratives of merican parents as they articulate the experiences of their children ninantly white and affluent schools and their reasons for wanting dren to attend these schools. In chapter 9, I examine the narra- vo affluent students to explore the ways they understand and justify ntages in life and the disadvantages of those outside of their milieu they use particular ideological operations and frames to construct l identities. In chapter 10, I summarize the findings of the research n this book and explore the lessons students learn about their place ·ld, who they are and should be, and their relations with others that and regenerate privilege. I conclude the book with some reflections fic examples on the ways that individuals can work toward critical in order to create institutional settings that interrupt privilege.

Acknowledgments

begin by thanking the students, teachers, administrators, and par-
participated in the studies described in this book. They welcomed
;htfully responded to my questions, and generously and graciously
eir time with me. I am indebted to them all.

;hout the process of researching and writing this book, I have been
th the invaluable support of many individuals. I am especially grate-
eral colleagues and friends who gave helpful suggestions along the
ll as asking hard questions. Their suggestions helped me to reach a
ded sense of perspective at the right times during my fieldwork and
extend my sincere thanks to Paul Dobelhoff, Robert Burroughs, Janet
Chris Bortz, Tamara Brown, Cheryl Keen, Patricia Linn, Thomas
Elizabeth EnglandKennedy, Ann Filemyr, Karen Kusiak, Lyn Mikel
illiam Pinar, Erik Malewski, Judy Roberts, and Kay Williams.

ery fortunate to have the following mentors who encouraged and
l me: Deborah Meier and Ellen Brantlinger. I am thankful for their
nd critical judgment. I am especially grateful for Deb's critical feed-
iapter 5, and Ellen's feedback on sections of chapters 2 and 9.

ncredibly indebted to Mark Tappan, an extraordinary colleague
, for his insights and encouragement. Our work together has been
in shaping many of the ideas and perspectives found in this book. I
debted to Jenn McLean, who provided me feedback and great ideas
beginning. I also thank Bruce Parker for his ongoing support and
ment. And I am thankful for the gentle patience and unwavering
Omar Haddad. Their intellect, generosity, and enthusiasm were
ble in helping me complete this project.

;h the research reported in this book was not funded, I received
nding from Antioch College (1998–2005), Colby College (2003–
Hanover College (2005–2006) to hire the following researcher
Jacqueline Shepherd, Bruce Parker, James Thompson, Jennifer San-
Adam Stevenson. I am grateful for all the support that I received
institutions and individuals in making different parts of this proj-
e.

like to thank the publishers for permission to make use of
ng materials: a version of the Preface appeared in Howard, A.
sson from poverty: Towards a literacy of survival, *Journal of
ı Theorizing, 21*(4), 73–82; and parts of chapter 6 in Howard, A.,
Kennedy, E. (2006) Breaking the silence: Power, conflict, and

contested frames within an affluent high school, *Anthropology & Education Quarterly, 37*(4), 347–365 (© American Anthropological Association). I would also like to thank Mark Tappan for allowing me to use a slightly modified version of our paper in chapter 2: Howard, A., & Tappan, M. (2007, April) *Privilege as identity,* presented at the annual meeting of the American Educational Research Association, Chicago, Illinois.

Finally, I am eternally grateful for the support and encouragement of my sister, Dianna, whose guidance has had a profound impact on my life, thinking, and work. The lessons that she has taught me are reflected throughout this book.

1
Teaching the Affluent

ɾard, why are we learning about those people? This isn't about social ose people are just bad business people," Jonas,[1] one of my seventh-isees, insisted during a discussion about homelessness.

discussing it because homelessness is a big problem in our country ın our city. It's an important issue for us to be aware of instead of just t," I responded.

ˈeplied, "Yeah, but it's because they don't spend their money right get jobs to get them out of their situation."

ɛr boy sitting across from Jonas added, "It's a problem because they just t to work so they can live in a house. They're too lazy to get a job."

k it's because they don't make the good decisions in life and it's got-where they're at," another boy told us.

do you think they don't make the right decisions?" I asked. "What ɔple not make good decisions?"

k Jonas said it. They're bad businesspeople," one of the boys replied.

ly, the bell rang, because I did not know how to respond to their ; at the time. It was one of those moments as a teacher when I ɔme up with the right response or the perfect question to challenge :hinking. Their beliefs about homeless people represented a world-position to what I held to be true. I was speechless.

my first year of teaching, I met with 10 seventh-grade boys for ɛs 2 days a week to cover a broad range of issues—everything from larger societal concerns. It was a designated time for them to feel rls around) to discuss personal and societal issues openly.[2] On this day, I started our discussion by asking them if they had ever seen ; person in our city. At first, all of them declared that they had not. our city did not have a large homeless population, a visible number lived on our downtown streets. To probe further, I asked them if ıttended sporting or other events downtown. Finally, one advisee ɛ had seen two homeless men sitting outside the entrance of a sport-ısking for money. "I wasn't about to give them money, and nobody ing to either, because they were drinking and would have just spent g drunk," he reported. After he gave this example, most of the boys ıey also had seen a homeless person at some point in their lives. I discovered that the reason they hadn't remembered coming across a homeless person at the beginning of our conversation was because they ignored them. We continued to talk about homelessness in a very general sense until Jonas questioned the value of "learning about those people."

Later that same year, with another group of students, a discussion of the welfare system emerged from an assigned reading in my sophomore English class. The majority of the students in the class argued that the system did not work, that their parents should not be forced to "support" the poor through their taxes, and that those who were receiving government assistance should just get a job. For the sake of exploring the issue further and sharing my own beliefs, I proposed an opposing argument to them that supported the welfare system: "Some people are forced to rely on the government to survive. They are put in situations where they don't see alternative options for providing for their families. Their circumstances in life are very different than what we take for granted," I argued. My response provoked a debate that eventually spread to the various issues relating to poverty.

The importance of this class discussion for me was in learning my students' perceptions of poor people. One of my students commented, "Our parents have worked hard for what we have. We shouldn't be forced to give it to people who don't do anything." Another student intensely argued, "Those people just want a free ride and want everything handed to them without working for it." The central point of their argument was that since their parents had worked hard, they deserved their wealth and were not obligated to share it with the poor. In their perspectives, wealth meant working hard and poverty meant laziness. The discussion concluded with a student pointing out, "Besides, we don't have to worry about them. Don't you know that's the reason why we have woods around [our neighborhood]? It blocks the view of [the adjacent poor community] so we don't have to see them." Again, the students posed the question, "Why are we discussing those people?"

These two exchanges with my students made me realize that I was not being the type of teacher that I wanted to be. At the right moments, I was not asking the necessary questions to challenge their privileged assumptions of how the world works. I was not engaging my students in the types of conversations that were essential to teach them important lessons about living more justly and meaningfully. Frustrated, I spent the summer after my first year of teaching trying to figure out how to become a better educator. I came to some new understandings that summer—new understandings about privilege and new understandings about myself and my work as a teacher. I came to new understandings of what types of relationships I wanted to form with my students in order to understand their understandings (Duckworth, 1987). I entered my second year of teaching more prepared and more determined to challenge their privileged ways of knowing and doing.

ing Privilege

r I taught at the school, the more I realized that my students did not o make mistakes in their competitive pursuit of academic success. were understood mostly as weaknesses and not as part of what it be human. My students did not know how to work through failure. ntly, they dodged failure at all costs, which led to behaviors such as ind other forms of dishonesty. They were willing to do whatever it the best but were not willing to form independent meanings or to ɛ.

lenging privilege, I needed to create an environment in the class- ıcourage my students to be more honest and to take risks. In work- l this goal, I first allowed myself to become more open and honest . I shared with them what I found important, even when my val- t correspond with the conservative nature of the larger educational y. I allowed my strengths and weaknesses to surface. Unlike the I put on during my first year, I let them know that I did not have wers. "I don't know, but let's find out," was a response that I was no id to give my students. By showing them that I didn't have all the ıey got to know me as more than just one who provided them with , but also as a human being who struggled to understand and who akes. They began to gradually understand that if I as their teacher l learning and teaching in this way—a noncompetitive, honest at least in my classes they had the freedom to do the same.

ssroom practice that I introduced as a way to establish this hon- ment was sharing my writing with students. I gave them not only idered to be my best work, but also pieces of writing (e.g., poetry, s) that I wanted to improve. When I began to do this, they did not o respond honestly, because they had been taught not to challenge rs at this level. I was even going a step further by asking them not llenge me but also to give me suggestions for improving my work. have my students break through what they had been taught not eir teachers, I set up a process for them to critique my writing—a required them to be critical. They eventually became willing to type of feedback that I was asking from them. They also began to mfortable with receiving critical feedback about their own work. ch as peer editing and working in writing groups were more effec- oping my students' writing skills, because they understood why ies were important in their becoming better writers. They came nd the importance of working together and became a little less ith trying to outdo each other to be the best. They were not as as they had previously been with each other.

In creating an open and honest environment, my students had to learn how to offer and exchange feedback in a respectful way, which was different from how feedback was typically provided by the adults in their lives. Their parents' feedback, for example, had more to do with control and economic power than a process of their working with school officials to improve their children's education. As a parent frankly told me soon after I started teaching at this school, "We pay a lot of money for our kids to go here, and we should have a say in how things are run." They wanted to make sure that they were getting their money's worth. The school was forced to "listen" to parents' feedback but rarely engaged in thoughtful dialogue with families. Parents and educators rarely had the types of conversations that would have allowed them to learn from each other. For the most part, parents engaged in conversations about the school as consumers who wanted to get their money's worth. In my classroom, I attempted to model a different way of giving feedback—a way that was not connected to privilege. I devised methods to generate respectful, collaborative, and honest feedback from my students. For example, students and I worked collaboratively to determine what activities, methods of assessment, and assignments were educationally effective. My students also wrote evaluations and provided verbal feedback about my teaching throughout the year. This free exchange of respectful and mutual feedback gave opportunities for my students to work with me in constructing the best environment for their learning. It also allowed them to see the value of working with, instead of working against, others.

This collaboration between my students and me was essential in establishing a classroom community. The school placed a theoretical emphasis on building such a community. For example, teachers attended numerous in-service workshops on the characteristics of a respectful and collaborative school community, and we were introduced to various methods of building community in our classrooms and during school activities. But as a community, we never worked toward this respect and collaboration. We just talked about it. We did not try to make our school community less competitive so that connections could be formed. The school's competitive environment disrupted connection, making closeness among members of the community impossible. In facilitating a community-building process, I encouraged students to be active rather than passive in their learning. They needed to do the work it took to build a community. Everyone needed to participate in class discussions and activities so that each person was contributing to what we were doing. I recognized, though, that each student could share his/her opinion and contribute in his/her own way. I wanted students not only to participate, but also to contribute their own uniqueness to the process. For example, I had one student who did not want to speak during class discussions. I tried various methods to urge him to share his understandings verbally with the class, but none of my approaches worked, until I discovered his love for drawing. I then

:nded that he draw as a way to communicate his understandings. He :tically accepted this suggestion and created drawings to share with : class for the rest of the school year. His drawings allowed his voice ·d and served as an alternative model for communicating ideas to the ss, which encouraged others to find their voices in various ways.

ıgh at first my students on the whole resisted being more honest and st of them eventually felt safe and comfortable enough to share their beliefs with the class, to share their understandings even when they 'e everything figured out, and to let me know when they needed 'or something different to form an understanding. In this classroom :y, my students and I could make mistakes and work through them pendently and collectively. They formed better working relation- others and me and came to understand more deeply what it meant an.

vith facilitating ways for students to have better relationships with , I expanded the curricular scope of my classes to present diverse es, experiences, and contributions, particularly those that had been ly omitted from the school's official curriculum, which outlined ıtent that was considered essential for college preparation. I under- curriculum—and how it was defined—was political because it was n through which consciousness was formed in students (Sleeter, inar's (2004) words, "The school curriculum communicates what to remember about our past, what we believe about the present, pe for the future" (p. 20). As a teacher who was required to imple- :hool's official curriculum in my classes, I negotiated the "givens" ific books, structuring tests to resemble the SAT and other college ams, and so on) to include subject matter that represented experi- deas of diverse cultural groups and women. Keeping the require- ind, I used a variety of curricular materials to teach my students essons about life, such as relating to others, living meaningfully nd being open to diverse perspectives. I presented this content in lowed my students to connect with what they were learning on a el, instead of only on an intellectual level.

ple, in my history course for seniors, I developed a framework for h to history and the process of understanding the past from the spective that Susan Griffin (1992) provides in *A Chorus of Stones*. ınderstanding, history is not a record of isolated events that hap- particular groups of people in particular places, but instead "is ıch that, when we hear any secret revealed … our lives are made arer to us, as the unnatural heaviness of unspoken truth is dis- erhaps we are like stones; our own history and the history of the ded in us, we hold a sorrow deep within and cannot weep until ; sung" (p. 8). To develop this framework, my students and I spent the first part of the year wrestling with this nontraditional perspective of history. This coming-to-understand process provided the necessary means for us to establish a questioning tone for our study of history throughout the year. By "tone," I mean a norm for both our approach to subject matter and our discussions of that subject matter.

In this class, I also used texts such as Howard Zinn's (1980) *A People's History of the United States* to provide stories and interpretations of history different from those in the required textbook. We read both traditional and alternative works to identify the differences and similarities in their interpretations of historical accounts. During the Civil War unit, we watched parts of *Birth of a Nation* and *Gone with the Wind* to understand how films have contributed to the perpetuation of a racist understanding of history. It is important for students to know, for example, that *Birth of a Nation* influenced the rebirth of the KKK, and films since then have constructed a particular history that supports white supremacy.

Our analysis of films and texts provided a means for my students to locate the political, economic, and social forces at work in constructing understandings of history. Most importantly, examining conflicting stories of our past and the influences of our past on our present further provoked students to question. For the most part, students no longer readily accepted dominant, official perspectives, but instead understood learning as a questioning process and knowledge as politically and socially constructed. This also provided students the opportunity to question me and for me to challenge them in their assumptions about the world beyond the walls of our school. The act of mutual questioning facilitated a classroom community wherein we were all teachers and learners and were all struggling for understanding.

This questioning approach to studying history initially frustrated most of my students. They wanted certainty that couldn't be found through this critical approach. This learning and teaching process recognized that knowledge did not come in a neat, convenient package to be opened and discovered. Coming to understand is a messy, not always direct process and requires us to become more critical of what we study and what we hold to be true. Most students eventually worked through their frustrations and began to ask important questions that challenged dominant forms of knowledge. My students also applied this critical approach to their daily lives outside the classroom. For example, a student told the class that he was at the movies with a group of friends and, as he explained, "couldn't stop thinking" as he watched the film. Another student reported, "Everything we read and watch seems to be giving us messages about society and people. I was watching the news with my parents the other night and wondered what the reporter was leaving out so that we think a certain way." Throughout our class discussions, other students shared similar stories of moments when they applied critical analysis to the world around them.

uestioning process frustrated my students because it also challenged :hink and talk about their privilege. It challenged their privileged nowing and doing. My students had been socialized to speak and act ılar ways that protected their privileged assumptions of the world ıg challenged. They knew what to say and what not to say and when d be honest about their beliefs and when they needed to not disclose ıions. Their socialized behaviors prevented them from genuinely ing in classroom discussions and activities. Therefore, although certain unpleasant assumptions about those different from them, really good at knowing what not to say.

ffort to encourage my students to be honest, I created a classroom ent where students could voice their ideas and beliefs even when :rstandings were not "socially acceptable." I recognized that I could nge them to think beyond their privilege without surfacing their assumptions. Initially, students tried to find out how far they could king outrageous comments, which really didn't represent their They wanted me to say, "OK, the game is over. We can go back to safe and pretending we don't believe certain things." I responded, ›y continuing to provide them a space for free expression of their ıtually, students used this "free expression space" as an opportunity more aware of how their understandings influenced their actions. ıness also provided opportunities for their ideas to be challenged ›r them to think differently about, and to become more critically of, the world around them. This genuine exchange provided stu- ›pportunity to struggle with their current and eventual positions in l challenged them to extend beyond privilege.

pen and honest discussions, however, did not always provide the ıeans for my students to step outside their privilege in order to form derstandings. In one of my classes, after the students had reached ed the *philosophizing without association zone* during a discussion m, I realized that my students were not engaged in the discussion ways. They felt no relationship between the subject and their own ›onded to their lack of connection with the subject by creating an ıilar to the controversial classroom exercise Jane Elliott devised in she segregated her all-white third grade class in Iowa based on eye ıch them about discrimination (see Bloom, 2005). In my activity, nts who were chosen based on criteria the entire class developed ivilege" of sitting while the others stood during class. After I gave ıctions, the students hurriedly developed criteria in hopes that would end and everyone could sit down to begin discussing the ght's reading. When they realized that they had to remain stand- facilitated a discussion, they became frustrated with the activity and me. They wanted to know what I was trying to demonstrate through this activity. I didn't answer their questions.

I directed my attention toward the sitting students during our discussion and ignored the standing students. I made negative comments about the standing students and praised the sitting students even when they provided inaccurate responses to my questions. At this point in the exercise, they no longer wanted to know about the activity but instead wanted to know why I was treating them this way. "Mr. Howard, you're acting different today," a standing student commented. I replied by telling the sitting students, "That's typical isn't it? The standing students are always complaining and are never satisfied." The standing students eventually disengaged themselves entirely from what was occurring in class. When the bell rang I dismissed the class. I didn't process the activity with them to answer their initial questions about the purpose of this exercise. I wanted them to think about it and have the time to do so.

The next day I entered class intentionally late to find most of the students standing. As I entered the classroom, one student said that his mother gave him permission to sit and if I had any questions, then I could call her at home. I then told the students that they could sit, and we had a discussion about the activity. We surfaced their anger and tried to understand how this activity reflected the larger society. Our discussions about who had rights in our country and about discrimination, assimilation, oppression, and our association with others had more meaning for my students because we had the shared experience of this activity to refer to when discussing these issues. Could they fully understand the lived experiences of African Americans and the poor through this classroom exercise? No. But experiences like this one contextualized that which was difficult for my students to make sense of and provided the "necessary conditions where learning can most deeply and intimately begin" (hooks, 1994, p. 13).

A few weeks after this activity, a group of students initiated a class discussion about the perpetuation of racism through films after they went to a movie rental store and noticed that Shirley Temple movies were classified as "family" movies. One of the students explained, "They make people believe that the movies are family friendly when they really send racist messages about African Americans." Another student recommended, "They should put a parental advisory on those movies: 'If you're going to watch this with your kids, you need to have a conversation with them about how African Americans are represented in this movie.' They put warnings on other movies and need to do the same with these racist ones." During this discussion, the class decided to write a letter of complaint to the business, and when we didn't receive a response from them after several weeks, some of the students decided to boycott the establishment. Their engagement in what we were doing in the classroom led to political action against racism outside the classroom context.

Responses

responded in various ways to what I was trying to do as a teacher. e accustomed to their teachers lecturing and their learning based on ıory and predictable assignments. They came to my class more inter- <nowing what they needed to do to acquire the best grade, instead interested in learning. In my classes, I offered them an alternative ıat required them to be active rather than passive and to work with king decisions about their learning. I also challenged them to think about the world around them and to step outside their privilege. ginning, my students were frustrated and resisted change because good at, and felt comfortable with, regurgitating subject matter so achieved high grades and being passive consumers in their learning ather than being actively involved. Most of my students eventually l this different approach to teaching and learning and became educa- vailable in meaningful ways. They were willing to think outside their n order to gain new understandings and to develop a more critical of the world around them.

er, there were a few students who never accepted a notion of educa- rent from the standard for the larger school community. In these understandings, what we were doing in the classroom was not y preparing them for college. They believed that my classes lacked rigor, because I used nonstandardized methods for assessment and cus entirely on the particulars of the subject matter. They wanted ure instead of facilitate classroom discussions. Beyond their wants s, I came to realize that their educational needs were not being met ıis approach to teaching and learning.

school, a student's persistent discontent with any teacher eventually student being switched to another teacher's class. Because of this ome students and I were not given opportunities to work together ing solutions and to find ways that I could better meet their needs. told their parents that they were not happy with me, their parents ame to the school and demanded that I change my teaching to their n. I responded to their demands by explaining why I was doing what g as a teacher and by assuring them that my students were learning needed to learn to be successful in their future classes. I had even ata to "prove" to parents that my students did as well as, if not bet- udents in other teachers' classes on the department's end-of-semes- nd at the next level of study. Some of the parents did not accept my n or my data and persuaded the principal to transfer their child to ıcher's class.

this educational context, I did not feel that I had failed these stu- teacher. I sincerely wanted to work with them in constructing experiences that met their educational needs and welcomed their resistance to my teaching approach. I believed that their resistance demonstrated an act of taking ownership of their education, which was what I wanted from them. I worked with some of the resisting students to develop individualized educational programs around their own particular style of learning. But my efforts were not enough for some of my students and their parents. I felt, of course, frustrated and disappointed by these situations, but maintained my commitment to teach in a way that challenged my students to think critically about the world around them and their place in that world.

Coming to Understandings of Privilege

I was in graduate school when I was offered a teaching position at this school. I had taught the summer before in the school's program for disadvantaged middle school students and came recommended to the headmaster as a progressive educator. During the interview, the headmaster told me that he wanted to "spice things up" on the faculty by hiring a few teachers who were different than most of the faculty—different in approaches, different in ways of thinking about students, curriculum, and the teaching and learning process, and different in life experiences. He thought this "difference" would be good for students and would better prepare them for the diversity of approaches they would find in their college careers. I would later find out that we were not that different from others, and most of us didn't have that much trouble fitting into and being accepted by the established culture of the faculty. All of us new progressive teachers were white, had credentials from prestigious colleges and universities, and except for me, were private-school educated. The headmaster's attempts to spice up the faculty eventually had little effect on faculty culture and the overall educational program at the school. In fact, within a couple of years, most of us were less progressive and provided students little difference from the school's traditional approaches to teaching and learning.

I struggled with the decision whether to accept this teaching position. I felt that I would be losing sight of my equity-seeking commitment to education and getting too far removed from what led me to become a teacher if I taught the affluent. What helped me eventually to accept this position were words of advice from Paulo Freire, the late Brazilian educator and philosopher. At the time, I was taking a class, Anti-Racist Multicultural Education, with Donaldo Macedo. During this course, several leading scholars in the fields of multicultural education and critical pedagogy spent a week or two as guest instructors/speakers, and Freire was one of these scholars. Outside class time, Macedo arranged more intimate conversations between these scholars and his students at a local coffee shop.

Sitting around a table in this coffee shop with Freire, Macedo, and a few of my classmates, we had a free-flowing conversation. There was no set agenda; we could ask whatever questions we had. I shared how uncertain I was about the affluent and the struggle I was having with my decision. Looking n't believe that I used this opportunity to ask Paulo Freire anything and I asked him for career advice, but his response helped me more ı my pressing concerns; his words became a part of my understand- ı educator. There were two main points in his response that stuck Affluent students need educators committed to working toward onsciousness as much as do poor students (the oppressed), and no ıere we teach we must remain committed to liberatory learning. His urged me to develop a larger scope for my commitments to social vould eventually understand that my commitment to equity-seeking education was a commitment to the education of the affluent as well education of the poor.

oo inexperienced as a teacher to understand the difficulties I would ng my commitments into practice when they conflicted with the d school culture. I spent my first year doing "business as usual" : Grant, 2003) and, consequently, did not effectively challenge my o think critically about their place in the world. When I began teach- nt students, I was not prepared to create the types of instructional ıat urged them to think critically about themselves and the world ıem because I was unfamiliar with the cultural script of privilege. ıts' worldviews seemed too different from my own assumptions for he kind of teacher I wanted to be—a teacher committed to preparing ıts to live critically, justly, and meaningfully.

king toward my goals and bridging the gap between my commit- d practice, I realized that I needed to develop honest and open ips with my students to form a better understanding of what they portant, who they were inside and outside the classroom context, ideas they had about themselves, their purposes in life, others, and ol. I situated my approaches and the content I was teaching in the e context of my students' lives. From the knowledge I gained of my hrough this approach and my relationships with them, I developed rstandings of privilege. I began to understand privilege more in n identity—a sense of self—than in terms of what advantages some d over others. As an identity, privilege is a lens through which one ds not only oneself, but also oneself in relation to others. Values, ıs, thoughts, feelings, and actions are shaped, created, re-created, ained through this lens of privilege. From this perspective of privi- ame less concerned with the advantages that my students had than they understood themselves and their place in the world. I came and that to think about privilege in this way was not to deny or he importance of advantages that individuals and groups had over t it was, in fact, to underline the relationship between advantages ty formation.

Guided by this understanding of privilege, I focused my efforts as a teacher on creating instructional settings that interrupted privilege in order for my students to step outside their privileged ways of knowing and doing to work toward a critical awareness of self and self in relation to others and to learn new ways that provided alternatives to privilege. I wanted my students to begin forming, as Peter McLaren (1995) describes, "hybrid and hyphenated identities in order to rethink the relationship of self to society, of self to other, and to deepen the moral vision of the social order" (p. 22). After my first year, there was evidence that some of my students were developing a more critical consciousness. For example, they no longer asked questions like, "Why are we discussing those people?" but instead, they asked, "What can be done?" The majority of my students understood themselves and their relations with others differently.

The understanding of privilege as identity that I developed as a teacher guides my inquiry as a researcher. In the studies reported in this book, I further explore the questions I began to develop as a teacher about the concept of privilege itself and the cultural and social processes in schooling that reinforce and regenerate privilege. More specifically, I explore the ways that privileged identities are constructed by investigating the *lessons* that affluent students are taught about their place in the world, their relationships with others, and who they are.

A Critical Interpretative Study of Privilege

I offer my graduate students a few words of advice before they begin their research projects. I tell them that although even the best-laid research plans often go awry, it is essential for researchers to work their way through a series of questions beforehand to develop a "blueprint" for their study. I did not exactly follow my own advice. I began my research as a teacher who had "burning questions" (Hubbard & Power, 1999) about my students and the educational landscape of privilege and abundance that I was entering. I did not exactly have everything figured out and did not really know where I was going. I used ethnographic methods to explore the questions I had, and my plan for the research and additional questions emerged "from an immersion in the data, a sifting and resifting of the evidence" (MacLeod, 1987, p. 173).

Also similar to MacLeod (1987), my methods "were not applied objectively in a manner devoid of human limitations and values" (p. 173). Before my research, I knew virtually nothing about privileged schools. I grew up in a different world and attended schools in poor communities in Kentucky. My understandings of the world that I was researching were limited by, and often conflicted with, the realities and assumptions of how things were and worked that developed from my own class background. I recognized from the beginning and throughout my research that knowledge, interpretations, and viewpoints are culturally constructed and therefore are partial, positioned, mplete (Magolda, 2000), and are susceptible to misinterpretation and interpretations.[3] I acknowledged that I had a lot to learn about afflu- ›ling and much to examine about my own *sense of self* before I could ming critical understandings of that which I planned to study.

›ut fully mapping out my research beforehand, I ended up tak- us routes and side trips along my 6-year research journey of afflu- ›ls. I began this journey by conducting a small-scale ethnographic ⁄IcLean Academy, a private high school located in a suburb of a large tern city.[4] My research at McLean explored questions I'd had before I ching affluent students. What were the everyday experiences of stu- hat were their prevailing ways of knowing and doing? What were the styles and substances of classes? What were the qualities of school e were some of the questions that guided my inquiry. During this ıade half-day visits to the school every week for 2 months. During I observed classes, assemblies, sporting events, and all-school gath- ›nducted interviews with three teachers and the headmaster; and classroom documents (e.g., assignments, examinations) and school ns (e.g., brochures, catalogues, school newspapers). This study gave er sense of the social and cultural particularities of school life at a private school.

›eriences teaching the affluent led me to additional and more spe- ions about privilege and the advantages of elite schooling. By this as familiar enough with affluent schooling both as a teacher and as er to form critical questions about privilege itself and the processes ures that reinforced and regenerated it. I extended the scope of the hat I began at McLean to explore questions about the structures, ınderstandings, and practices that influenced the educational expe- affluent students and what students learned about their place in the ir relationships with others, and who they were from these experi- interest in understanding the processes involved in reinforcing and ng privilege as an identity led me to a critical interpretative approach er, 1993, 2003), which drew from the interpretative (e.g., Gilligan, Rogers, 1989; Mehan, 1992) and critical ethnography (Anderson 1993; Carspecken & Apple, 1992) traditions. Mehan claims that ive studies can take a closer examination of the processes by which ification is generated and, therefore, as Brantlinger (2003) explains, eans to understand the complexities[,] … conflicted views" (p. 29), ld add, experiences of a dominant class. Interpretative studies do follow a critical perspective; however, in my approach, I applied oretical positions (e.g., Apple, 1996, 1999; Arnowitz, 1980, 1992; 81, 1992; Leistyna, 1999; McLaren, 1989) to interpret participants' lings and actions. Similar to Brantlinger (2003), I used a criti- ɔ situate affluent schooling and privilege in the larger context of "unequal power relationships among people" and "the nature of power differentials" (p. 29) in American schooling.

From 1997 to 2001, I conducted studies at two private high schools located in a midsize Midwestern city, Parker Day School and Bredvik School, and at a public school located in a small, affluent town in the Midwest, Oakley High School.[5] During these studies, I observed primarily one teacher's class at each of the three schools.[6] I observed each class approximately 30 times during a school year. I also observed other classes, assemblies, sporting events, and faculty meetings. Additionally, I conducted three interviews with the teacher whom I primarily observed and two students in the teacher's class (one male and one female), who were selected from the students who agreed to participate in the study. I also conducted an interview with the senior administrator at each school. In total, I conducted approximately 40 hours of interviews with administrators, teachers, and students at each of the three schools. Finally, as I did in my research at McLean, I collected classroom and school artifacts to gather additional facts about school policies and classroom practices.

In addition to these ethnographic studies at the four schools, I collaborated and facilitated a discussion with a group of African American parents whose children attended or had attended schools with predominantly white and affluent student populations. Nine parents, two men and seven women, from seven households collaborated with me to develop questions to guide our discussion and participated in the focus group. As a whole, the parents' children attended or had attended six of the seven private schools located in a midsize Midwestern city. The primary purpose of the focus group was to further explore the disadvantages, discrimination, cultural conflicts, and struggles that African American students confronted in predominantly white and affluent schools that data generated from my research at the four schools documented.

During the course of my research, I also visited 12 private schools in different parts of the country.[7] During my visits, which lasted 1 to 2 days at each school, I talked with administrators, teachers, students, and sometimes parents; observed classes and all-school gatherings; and gathered school publications. The main purpose of my visits was to learn more about the social and cultural particularities of schools with mostly affluent students. Although my discussions with individuals and observations at these schools are not reported in this book, my visits were influential in guiding my research and gaining new insights.

2
Revisioning Privilege

d States is the most highly stratified society in the industrialized ss distinctions operate in virtually all aspects of American life. iillion people in the United States live in poverty;[1] school success ıked tightly with a student's social class status; most Americans live gregated communities; and even with all the advances in medicine ears, the differences in health and lifespan are widening between ıd the affluent (Scott & Leonhardt, 2005). Moreover, since the 1970s,) of households has doubled their share of the national wealth to the total net worth of the median American household has fallen. now has more wealth than the entire bottom 95% (Sklar, Collins, -Wright, 2003). According to the U.S. Census Bureau (2004), the come of the poorest one fifth of households dropped from 4.2% to ywhere people turn in the United States they are confronted with ng gap between rich and poor (Anyon, 2000; Sleeter, 2005). Even considerable class distinctions, we, as a nation, remarkably hold ɔns about living in an egalitarian society.

mericans believe that the contours of social class have become blurɔme argue that they have even disappeared in recent years (Scott & , 2005). Today, most Americans hold tightly to the "rags to riches" s, they believe it is possible to start out poor, work hard, and become rding to a *New York Times*[2] poll (Leonhardt, 2005), 75% of Ameri- e that chances of moving up from one class to another have risen ıst 3 decades, a period in which social class has played a greater, not in shaping the everyday realities of Americans. Class awareness anguage are receding in the United States at a time when the gap ch and poor in the country has widened (hooks, 2000).

inst American principles for people to belong to a social class group. the general public recognizes that people occupy different class he prevailing belief is that these arrangements are not fixed. Any- orks hard enough can realize the "American dream," and mobil- , the movement of families up and down the economic ladder—is e that lies at the heart of this dream. Poverty, therefore, is an aber- ıis promise and of the American way of life. Surveys indicate that the American public believe "that lack of effort by the poor was the principle reason for poverty, or a reason at least equal to any that was beyond a person's control. ... Popular majorities did not consider any other factor to be a very important cause of poverty—not low wages, or a scarcity of jobs, or discrimination, or even sickness" (Schwarz & Volgy, 1992, p. 11). Poverty is seen as unfortunate but temporary and as an end product of the poor themselves. The prominent belief held in the United States is that the poor have brought their "predicament" upon themselves (Mantsios, 2003), and their conditions will change when they change.

The wealthy, on the other hand, are admired for their smart choices and moves and their talent and skill. Most people gawk at the excesses of the wealthy that they see on television and read about in print media. Society pages, gossip columns, news shows, articles on the private and corporate lives of industrialists, and reality shows on the extravagant lifestyles of the rich and famous not only provide people an insider's view of the lives of the wealthy but also help to keep the American dream alive (Mantsios, 2003). These reports of individuals' capital accumulation serve as examples of what is possible and there for the taking in our country. The lines between most Americans and the wealthy are blurred by the illusion that affluence is attainable and achieved mostly on the merits of individuals and through hard work. Unlike the despised poor, most celebrate the wealthy for living the American promise. The wealthy as a class do not exist but instead are understood as the most talented, most ambitious, and most successful individuals. For most, American society is divided between the inferior poor and everyone else.

The egalitarian myth, and the rhetoric that Americans hear from public leaders, the media, and other everyday sources that support it, comforts American middle classes while offering hope to the poor (Boudon, 1990/1994) and "allows the dominant class to appear not as a class but as representative of the whole society" (Larrain, 1992, p. 52). These fantasies of egalitarianism, moreover, steer us away from talking about social class and from revealing the taken-for-granted realities of different class positions. Social class has been and remains a taboo subject in American culture (Fussell, 1983). As Ortner (1991) points out, "American natives almost never speak of themselves or their society in class terms. In other words, class is not a central category of cultural discourse in America" (p. 169). Rosenblum and Travis (2003) add, "Because social class is so seldom discussed, the vocabulary for talking about it is not well developed" (p. 22). Without this vocabulary, the general American public is ill-equipped to engage in the type of complicated conversation that is needed to understand the evasive nature of social class in American society.

Another difficulty that prevents most people from talking about social class is that this concept means different things to different people; as Brantlinger (2003) points out, "class is an amorphous and ambiguous construct" (p. 9). For most, however, social class means just how much money one has or doesn't have. Social class is understood as something we *have*, rather than being y connected to who we are. Education, income, occupation, and e common criteria for gauging social class. Although these factors e significantly to one's social class, they do not define it.

d, social class is a lived, developing process (Anyon, 1980) that is con- by a particular form of socialized knowledge conditioned in a specific Bourdieu, 1984); that is, a system of dispositions that develops from ning and past experience (Reed-Danahay, 2005). The habitus "could ered as a subjective but not individual system of internalized struc- emes of perception, conception, and action common to all members ne group or class" (Bourdieu, 1977, p. 86). Bourdieu (1984) argues encompasses individuals who share homogeneous conditions of and sets of dispositions and preferences and are capable of generat- ır practices in social settings. Every aspect of an individual's social contributes to the development of the habitus and class member- individual's class position is homologous to others whose lives are affected by social conditions. Therefore, social class is defined by the ıditions of lived experience and the intrinsic rules of an individual's rld. Individuals form particular ways of knowing and doing, values, sumptions, and relations with others and the world around them t their social class positionality. Social class is an important part of le are and their identity, not just about what they have or don't have. nding the role of social class in schooling, therefore, is not only about ents have or do not have, but also about the lived, developing process ences their ways of knowing and doing.

ss and Schooling

lly, Americans believe that the best way to ensure equality is to enable en, regardless of their cultural, political, and social background, to ool with skills and knowledge that position them to contribute pro- in the nation's democratic governance and occupational structure. n and faith in the "American dream" are firmly linked in the public d have been since the days of Horace Mann, who declared, "Educa- , beyond all other devices of human origin, is a great equalizer of tions of men" (as quoted in Nieto, 2005, p. 43). According to Dewey hooling could not only serve to level the playing field, but also serve renticeship of civic life. More specifically, the common perception Americans is that education is a viable weapon against poverty and quality (Lee & Bowen, 2006). However, the fact that children's skills ledge can so clearly be predicted by the social class of their family challenge to these democratic ideals of American schooling (Roth- 4). In fact, as Nieto (1999) points out, "schools tend to reproduce sistently the inequalities that exist in society" (p. 24).

The argument that schools reproduce the economic and social relations in society and therefore tend to serve the interests of the dominant classes was first articulated during the 1970s (e.g., Bourdieu & Passeron, 1977; Bowles & Gintis, 1976; Jencks, 1972; Spring, 1972). These theoretical works placed schools within a political framework and explained the principal role of schooling as reproducing the class divisions in our society by teaching the poor the appropriate attitudes and behaviors for becoming good workers and by teaching the affluent the skills that prepare them to manage and control the working class. According to this analysis, school life is almost completely subordinated to the needs of the economy.

Schools therefore not only reflected structural inequalities of the larger society but also maintained them. Katz (1975), for example, demonstrated that from the beginning, public schooling was "universal, tax-supported, free, compulsory, bureaucratically arranged, class-biased, and racist" (p. 106). According to Katz, these conflicting features derived from the primary purpose of public schooling, which was to prepare and train different groups of people for different roles in society. Bowles and Gintis' (1976) *correspondence principle*—that is, "the close correspondence between the social relationships which govern personal interaction in the work place and the social relationships of the educational system" (p. 12)—explains that this function of schools is apparent, from their physical and organizational structures to their curricula and instruction. Schools with mostly poor students, for example, are generally factory-like fortresses that operate with controlling mechanisms, whereas schools with mostly affluent students provide the space for students to be more autonomous. Moreover, relations between poor students and their teachers reflect more dominant/dominated relationships than exist between affluent students and their teachers (McDermott, 1977). According to this theoretical position, "it is through instruction and social relationships in the school that students learn a way of being in the world and a view of reality" (Weiler, 1988, p. 7).

Similarly, Bourdieu and Passeron's (1977) analysis of the French education system demonstrates how students are socialized through their interactions with and within the school system through testing, subject matter, student/teacher relationships, tracking, and linguistic conventions to maintain a system that inscribes students to various social positions. They argue that schooling is "characterized by a functional duplicity which is actualized in full in the case of traditional systems, where the tendency toward conservation of the system of the culture it conserves encounters an external demand for social conversation" (p. 199). According to their analysis, schooling is the instrument in the duplicitous inculcation of members in the reproduction and maintenance of social hierarchies. Other scholars such as Katz, Bowles, and Gintis similarly claimed, as Nieto (2005) describes, that "schools reproduced the status quo and not only reflected structural inequalities based on class, gender, but also helped to create and maintain these inequalities"

ıgh the arguments of social reproduction theorists like Bowles and ve been criticized for being too simplistic and overdetermined (e.g., Weiss, 1983; Giroux, 1992; Morrow & Torres, 1994), their theories a tremendous impact on educational thinking since the 1970s. The rpose of schooling to serve as an "equalizer" was questioned criti- hese works, which established a solid argument that "schools had ly been engaged in the service of a dominant class to control not only ut even the ideas of dominated groups" and "school failure became y understandable by-product of this control" (Nieto, 1996, p. 234). orists expanded on the tenets of social reproduction to explore the olitical nature of schooling and to offer a wide range of explanations ys that schools tend to reproduce rather consistently the inequali- xist in society (e.g., Apple, 1982; Arnowitz, 1980; Fay, 1987; Giroux,). These theories also laid the groundwork to challenge the explana- attributed cultural and intelligence deficits of the poor to lesser edu- utcomes, which gained great momentum in the 1960s (Bereiter & n, 1966; Jensen, 1969; Riessman, 1962) and had tremendous impact ınd educational policymaking in the following years (Nieto, 2005). gh disagreements arise in explaining school achievement dispari- en poor and affluent students, with relatively few exceptions (e.g., Luthar, 2000; Seyfried, 1998) there is a fair amount of agreement onal research that there is a high correlation between student class school achievement and attainment (e.g., Brantlinger, 2003; Cole- ; McLoyd, 1998; Metz, 1998; Nieto, 2005). Consistently, research ocument the differences in school circumstances and outcomes oor and affluent students (e.g., Burton, 1999; Oakes, 1988; Orfield, ell, 1997). A variety of issues and questions relating to social class explored in this body of literature, such as achievement patterns unn & Duncan, 1997; De Civita, Pagani, Vitaro, & Tremblay, 2004; mmons, & Pager, 2000; Kao, Tienda, & Schneider, 1996), funding rces (Education Trust, 2001; Ingersoll, 1999; Kozol, 1991; Oakes, king (Ansalone, 2001; Oakes, 1985; Oakes & Guiton, 1995; Varenne nott, 1998), disadvantages of poor children as they enter formal (Phillips, Brooks-Gunn, Duncan, Klevanov, & Crane, 1998; Stipic 997), the overrepresentation of poor students in special education Trent, 1994; Barton & Oliver, 1997; Connor & Boskin, 2001), and g of students' aspirations (MacLeod, 1987; Willis, 1977). This exten- of research has documented the various ways that schools reflect class divisions of the larger society fairly consistently through their practices, and policies and the lived experiences of, and the inter- ong, those within schools.

Although these strong links between social class and schooling are widely acknowledged, there is remarkable silence in this body of scholarship as well as in the mass media about how practices and structures give advantages to affluent students and reinforce the inequalities that exist in the larger society (Brantlinger, 2003). Public leaders, mass media, and educational researchers are willing to be critical of schools with mostly poor students in efforts to explain the disproportionate failure of their students (Mortimore & Mortimore, 1999) but do not apply the same critical investigation to systems, practices, and policies that work to reinforce the social, political, cultural, and economic privilege of affluent students. Compared with the large body of research on the schooling of the poor, the schooling of affluent students has remained virtually unmapped terrain.

A few researchers have investigated the education of affluent students (e.g., Brantlinger, 1993; Eder, 1995). This body of literature addresses a variety of topics, including legal issues (Devins, 1989), tuition tax credits and governance structures (James & Levin, 1988), the economic advantages of students (Bills, 1988; Collins, 1979; Kingston, 1981), identity formation (Proweller, 1998, 1999), pedagogical issues (A. Powell, 1996), moral traditions (Hays, 1994; Peshkin, 2001), substance abuse and depression (Bogard, 2005; Luthar & Becker, 2002), and the educational experiences of minority students (Banks, 1984; Doyle, 1981; Ogbu, 2003; Zweigenhaft & Domhoff, 1991). Although a wide range of issues has been explored, with few exceptions (e.g., Brantlinger, 1993, 2003; Cookson & Persell, 1985; Kingston & Lewis, 1990; Peshkin, 2001) this body of literature avoids critical investigation of the processes of affluent schooling that reproduce and regenerate privilege.

For example, Arthur Powell's (1996) study explores "the education that privileged schools provide and not privilege itself" (p. 6) and the lessons that private schooling could offer public education in reform efforts. He provides a thorough study of schooling experience offered at privileged schools but separates this investigation from the privileged systems that provide such experience for students.[3] Similarly, Pope's (2001) study of five students' perspectives of their educational experiences attending a school located in a wealthy California suburb altogether avoids an examination of privilege. Although her study provides useful insight into the ways students at an affluent high school "do school" in their pursuits of academic success, she makes only a fleeting reference to the affluence of the school and its students. In so doing, she disregards the influence of the students' school and life advantages on their educational experiences. Again, privileged schooling and affluent students are researched, but privilege goes unexamined and remains unexplored.

One could assume that the need for this critical research on affluent students' schooling is not widely recognized because, as is evident throughout educational research, affluent students on the whole academically achieve in school. Affluent students' records of academic success have led many ıal researchers and writers (e.g., A. Powell, 1996) to conclude that ools have better teachers, provide the necessary conditions for stu-earn, and provide an overall better education. Beyond not recogniz-d for researching schools where evidence of success is everywhere, be argued that the reluctance to engage in critical examination of nt is ideologically and politically motivated. As Brantlinger (2003) "It is reasonable to assume that what gets studied and announced ı and silenced is a product of influential groups' intentions and is their desire to sustain their own personal (class) interests. ... [I]t is t to keep in mind that dominant groups are constantly energized ıp with new theories to support their hegemony" (p. 21). Similarly, 000) argues that "researchers from dominant groups have a long his-roducing knowledge about oppressed groups that legitimates their ation" (p. 10).

esearchers have focused their research and explained the class-cor-stinctions in American schooling in ways that divert attention from g systems. Even with the recent increase of social class distinctions ing and the larger society, most scholars do not focus on the social ral processes that reinforce and regenerate these distinctions. They end time trying to figure out how the success and advantages of te to the failure and disadvantages of many. More comprehensive al analysis of affluent students' education is necessary if we are to nd more fully the impact that privileging systems and the cultural l processes involved in creating and re-creating these systems have productive nature of American schooling. We also need to develop ical frameworks for that which is at the heart of these systems and —privilege.

ndings of Privilege[4]

past several decades, scholars writing about privilege have made great increasing general understanding of how privilege works, both in nd in society at large, to shape lived experience and human practice. of work has examined the ways in which so-called "naturalized" such as race, gender, and sexuality are intimately and inextricably with issues of power and power differences. Privilege, then, has been as consisting of the advantages that some individuals have over oth-h have been granted to them not because of what they have done ne, but because of the social category (or categories) to which they ee Goodman, 2001; Jensen, 2005; Johnson, 2001; Kimmel & Ferber, henberg, 2002; Wise, 2005).

McIntosh's (1988) groundbreaking work on white and male privi-htly celebrated, because she provides both a personal narrative and ical framework to encourage reflection on and conversation about the difficult topic of privilege. In her well-known essay on what she calls the "invisible knapsack" of privilege, McIntosh argues that one way of understanding how privilege works—and how it is kept invisible—is to examine the way we think about inequality. She claims that we typically think of inequality from the perspective of the one who suffers the consequences of the subordination or oppression, not the one who receives the benefits; hence, those who receive privilege are not in our focus. As she goes against this common way of thinking about inequality, McIntosh challenges the privileged to "open their invisible knapsacks," which contain all of the benefits that come to them from their social, cultural, and economic positionality. She challenges them to take a critical look at all the various (and often unconscious) ways they enjoy benefits and advantages that others do not.

McIntosh (1990) identifies two types of privilege. The first is "unearned entitlements," which are rights that all people should have, such as feeling safe, being respected, having access to all the opportunities that life offers. Unearned entitlements become a form of privilege—what McIntosh calls "unearned advantages"—when they are restricted to certain groups of people. Unearned advantages give members of dominant groups a competitive edge that they are reluctant to acknowledge or give up. The other form of privilege is "conferred dominance," which occurs when one group has power over another. Cultural assumptions related to people's social positions help to determine assumptions about which group is supposed to dominate another group. Conferred dominance is entrenched in cultural assumptions that establish patterns of control and maintain hierarchies in our society.

We begin to confront privilege, according to McIntosh, by becoming aware of unearned advantage and conferred dominance and by understanding how social locations (e.g., schools, workplaces, even communities) create and maintain privilege for certain groups (e.g., white/heterosexual/male/affluent). McIntosh (1990) argues that the more aware people are of their privilege, the more they can contribute to changing themselves and the privileged locations they occupy (see also Johnson, 2001). Because privilege is rooted primarily in social systems, change does not happen only when individuals change; locations that support privilege must change as well. Certain people, of course, need to change in order to do the work necessary to bring about change, but it is not enough for individuals simply to change (see Bishop, 2002; Goodman, 2001; Hardiman & Jackson, 1997; Tappan, 2006).

McIntosh (1990) paved the way for others to examine the complex and complicated ways that privilege works through memberships, representations, actions, and language to regenerate and re-create itself, thereby perpetuating structures of domination and subordination (e.g., Jensen, 2005; Kimmel & Ferber, 2003; Wise, 2005). This body of work established a critical foundation for making systems of privilege visible and for illuminating the ways privilege works to construct social relations in everyday life. Slowly but surely, has entered scholarly discourse as a useful and analytical concept. enomenon on which both scholars and practitioners have focused fforts to address the dynamics of power and oppression to achieve :ice.

are, however, significant limitations in the current understanding ge. By and large, what might be called the "first generation" scholars tructed *commodified* notions of privilege. Privilege, in other words, understood extrinsically, as something individuals *have* or *possess* s something that can fit into a "knapsack"—invisible or otherwise) ning they *experience*, rather than as something more intrinsic, as g that reveals who they *are* or who they have *become* in a fundamen- This commodified conception of privilege, moreover, while having a useful understanding of privilege as a source of the advantage of r others, has ultimately fallen short in providing a comprehensive k for understanding the pervasive nature of privilege as it is woven abric of people's lived experience.

:o move beyond this commodified conception of privilege to articu- ception of *privilege as identity*—as a particular sense of self-under- As an identity (or an aspect of identity), privilege is a lens through individual understands self and self in relation to others. This means es, perceptions, appreciations, and actions are shaped, created, re- nd maintained through this lens of privilege. Social systems func- ays that support and validate the social construction of a privileged or some while limiting and discouraging its construction for others. d by this understanding of privilege, my focus is on how individuals nd themselves and their place in the world, with a particular focus class privilege (i.e., the privileged identity of the affluent). Although n important connection between what advantages individuals have identity (that is, how their advantages in life fashion a particu- of self), I situate privilege in a more comprehensive framework by the process by which privilege is constructed and reconstructed as y across an individual's lifespan. Understanding privilege as part of as more potential for interrupting this malicious phenomenon.

'ormation

y 20 years, scholars have increasingly challenged the dominant dis- n identity formation to reflect more fully the complex and subtle of meaning making in school contexts.[5] Studies of youth identity n have recounted the various strategies that youth use in accom- of and/or resistance to prevailing institutional arrangements 000; Proweller, 1999). This literature clearly illustrates that identi- edominantly reproductive of prescriptive ideologies and discourses ass, gender, and sexuality wedged into larger societal contexts and then reflected in the school context (Fine, Weis, Powell, & Wong 1997; Lesko, 1988; MacLeod, 1987; McNeil, 1986; McRobbie, 1982). Much of this research explores how identities take shape among youth of color, focusing mostly on African American youth (Dimitriadis, 2001; Fordham, 1991, 1996; Helms, 1990; Hemmings, 1996; MacLeod, 1987; McCarthy, Critchlow, Dimitriadis, & Dolby, 2005; Peshkin, 1991; Shujaa, 1994; Thompson & Carter, 1997). Others add to the literature in exploring the experiences of first- and second-generation immigrants and white ethnic groups represented in U.S. schools (Phelen, Davidson, & Yu, 1998; Seller & Weis, 1997). These studies provide a penetrating look at the range of identities that students negotiate daily and a more textured composite of school experiences across differences (Proweller, 1999).

Many of these scholars offer an important alternative to research on youth that emphasizes the "storm and stress" of identity development (Griffin, 2001) by focusing, instead, on cultural production (particularly the cultural production of youth of color), positioning it within larger societal contexts (Dolby, 2002). Critical research and theory on racial identity development thus explores the complexity of notions of identity and difference and seeks to decenter whiteness (Fine et al., 1997; Giroux, 1997; Keating, 1995; McIntosh, 1990; McIntyre, 1997; McLaren, 1997; Proweller, 1999) by critiquing the various political, social, and economic forces that kept whiteness unexamined and ignored. Rebecca Powell (1996) asserts that whites fail to see their whiteness because their whiteness is "perceived as both neutral and normative" (p. 12). For, as Richard Dyer (1988) argues, being white "is not anything really, not an identity, not a particularizing quality because it is everything—white is no colour because it is all colours" (p. 45). As both nothing and everything, whiteness remains invisible as a social category and location of racial identity (Frankenberg, 1993).

Not content to let it retain its invisibility, researchers and theorists in recent years have begun to interrogate and expose whiteness (e.g., Frankenberg, 1993; Ladson-Billings, 1998; Swartz, 1993). A growing body of research shifted attention toward "studying up" in an effort to uncover the ways in which whiteness was represented and embodied as cultural meaning and lived experience (Fine et al., 1997; Giroux, 1997; Proweller, 1999; Thompson & Tyagi, 1996). Several of these scholars made a number of observations on the present level of white identity development, multicultural awareness, and understanding among whites, such as the denial of whiteness (R. Powell, 1996; Scheurich, 1993), color-blindness (Frankenberg, 1993; Helms, 1990), lack of understanding of systemic or institutional racism (Lawrence, 1997; Giroux, 1997), and the acceptance of unexamined white privilege (Kivel, 1996; McIntyre, 1997). As Sleeter (1996) points out, there is consistent unawareness among whites, and this unawareness manifests itself in their daily lives and work practices (e.g., teachers' attitudes and teaching practices).[6] Dolby (2002) adds to this point by claiming that "it is whiteness that specifically and deliberately detaches itself potential positive and liberatory spaces of identity that are open, ıd seeks refuge" (p. 24). Whiteness therefore becomes both nothing thing (Levin, 2003). In refuge, the privileging of whiteness remains ınd constant. As Wildman (1996) explains, "The invisibility of privigthens the power it creates and maintains. The invisible cannot be , and as a result privilege is allowed to perpetuate, re-generate and itself. Privilege is systemic, not an occasional occurrence" (p. 8). sible, whiteness is a powerful conception of identity and difference ins protected (McLaren, 1997).

research on the construction of racial identity thus points to the ce of understanding *how* identity is culturally produced and reprother than focusing simply on *what* identity is. As such, this schol- allenges the conventional understanding of identity as embodied ıaturalized categories (see Dolby, 2000) to one in which identity is , as Stuart Hall (1996) argues, "in specific historical and institutional in specific discursive formations and practices, by specific enuncia- gies" (p. 4).

s Ideologically Mediated Action

ıcknowledge the theoretical debates on identity (e.g., Dolby, 2000; 5), I employ as a means of constructing a framework of privilege as ın explicitly sociocultural approach to identity. Thus, identities are ıtally forms of *self-understanding*: "People tell others who they are, more important, they tell themselves and then try to act as though vho they say they are" (Holland, Lachicotte, Skinner, & Cain, 1998, se self-understandings are not, however, simply individual, internal, gical qualities or subjective understandings that emerge solely from tion (see Damon & Hart, 1988), or as a result of the resolution of ed intrapsychic conflicts or struggles (see Freud, 1923/1961). Rather, link the personal and the social—they are constituted relationally e & Weiss, 1983; Wexler, 1992); they entail action and interaction in a ıral context (Penuel & Wertsch, 1995; Tappan, 2000, 2005); they are ›ducts that live in and through activity and practice (Holland et al., d they are always performed and enacted (Butler, 1990, 1991; Tappan, llie, 2003).

and Wertsch (1995) view identity as a form of "mediated action." by the work of both Vygotsky (1978) and Bakhtin (1981), the con- ıediated action entails two central elements: an "agent," the person ing the acting, on the one hand, and "cultural tools" or "mediational he tools, means, or resources appropriated from the social world and he agent to accomplish a given action, on the other (Wertsch, 1995, also Tappan, 2005).

Methodologically, adopting a mediated action approach to identity formation ultimately means focusing less on what people say about their own "inner" psychological states or conflicts, and more on what they *do* with particular cultural tools or resources that shape and mediate their sense of self-understanding in specific situations and circumstances (see also Holland et al., 1998). Therefore, "when identity is seen in this framework as shaped by mediational means or cultural tools, questions arise as to the nature of cultural tools and why one, as opposed to another, is employed in carrying out a particular form of action" (Penuel & Wertsch, 1995, p. 91).

The cultural and historical tools, resources, or mediational means that are most critical for identity formation are the *ideologies* that are available in a particular social-cultural-historical context. This insight, of course, came first from Erikson (1968), who argues that, particularly during adolescence, ideologies give young lives meaning and purpose, ideologies give youth something to which to be loyal and true, and ideologies connect the past, present, and future:

> [C]ultural tools in the form of ideologies provide individuals with a coherent world view, something that, in [Erikson's] view, youth desperately need to fashion an identity. In that way, these ideologies are empowering, providing youth with a compass in a contradictory and complex world. At the same time, [however], these resources are, according to Erikson, constraining, in that individuals are limited in who they can become by the array of choices of ideology, career, and self-expression. (Penuel & Wertsch, 1995, p. 90)

Thus, for example, *moral* identity (to consider one important dimension of identity) consists, using this viewpoint, of an understanding of oneself as a moral person that comes not from oneself alone, gaining access to, or reflecting on, one's "true" or "essential" moral self (see Blasi, 1984). Rather, it comes from ongoing dialogue with others in one's social world—dialogue that is necessarily shaped and mediated by specific cultural tools and ideological resources. Chief among these tools and resources are what can be called *moral ideologies*—voices or orientations, religious or secular, that are carried and transmitted via others' words, language, and forms of discourse (Tappan, 1992, 1997; see also Gilligan, 1982). One finds one's moral identity, therefore, primarily in the ideologically mediated moral action in which one engages, not simply via a process of self-reflection. Moral identity is, as Tappan (2005) points out, "at its core, a function of the ongoing dialogical interchange between self and others" (p. 49). As such, identity development necessarily entails a process of "ideological becoming" (see Bakhtin, 1981), whereby one appropriates the words and language of others, and in so doing struggles to strike a balance between "authoritative" and "internally persuasive" forms of discourse (see Tappan, 2005).

the critical relationship between ideology and identity, it is impor- knowledge the critical role that ideology also plays in maintaining, ıg, and reproducing the dynamics of power, privilege, and oppres- le, 1995). To study and understand ideology, argues John Thompson ; to study the ways in which meaning serves to establish and sus- ions of domination" (p. 56). Starting with Marx's concept of ideol- ıpson expands Marx's analysis of relations of class domination and ıtion as the principle axes of inequality and exploitation in human to offer a more inclusive perspective on the ways in which ideology s and maintains various forms of dominant-subordinate power rela- so doing, he identifies five general modes through which ideology ıte to establish and sustain relations of domination: "legitimation, tion, unification, fragmentation, and reification" (Thompson, 1990, ese general modes of ideological operation, and some of their associ- egies, are further defined and elaborated in Table 2.1 (adapted from er, 2003, p. 37).

ɔson's analysis thus echoes Gramsci's (1971) theory of hegemony, ims that dominant groups use ideologies much more effectively than orce or violence to keep subordinate group members in their place, buff any attempts at resisting the status quo. Ideologies serve this ɔy convincing subordinate group members of the legitimacy of their n the social hierarchy, as Ellen Brantlinger's (2003) research on the 'hich middle-class parents negotiate and rationalize the advantages dren enjoy in school clearly illustrates. In particular, when she ana- ıarratives told by middle-class mothers about their children's school e for patterns of domination and subordination, Brantlinger finds ence of all five of Thompson's (1990) ideological operations, as well ɔf the associated "strategies of symbolic construction":

> le-class mothers'] depictions of their own and Other people's en provide the rationale and justification for the case they make ir children's need for distinctive and separated school circum- s. … [For example,] mothers readily relegate Other people's chil- o segregated settings and lesser conditions while claiming that rrangements are in the Other's best interest. (Brantlinger, 2003,

er clear example of the way in which ideological resources operate uce relations of domination—specifically, white supremacy—comes work of Eduardo Bonilla-Silva (2001, 2003). Bonilla-Silva describes ɔmenon of what he calls "color-blind racism"—whereby racism, racial n, and racial inequality are perpetuated in the United States in the f explicitly racist practices, policies, or laws, by specific ideological ions and discursive practices (i.e., forms of "mediated action"). He

Table 2.1 Modes of Ideological Operation

Legitimation	When relations of domination are represented as just and worthy of support **Strategies:** Rationalization: Defending particular relations or institutions Universalization: Representing arrangements that serve the interests of some as serving the interests of all
Dissimulation	When relations of domination are concealed, denied, obscured, or represented in ways that deflect attention **Strategy:** Euphemization: (Re)describing institutions, actions, or social relations in positive terms
Unification	Allows individuals to be embraced in a collective identity, irrespective of any difference or division **Strategy:** Standardization: Promoting a certain framework as the shared or acceptable basis of evaluation for all
Fragmentation	Dispersal of individuals and groups capable of mounting a challenge to a dominant group **Strategies:** Differentiation: Focusing on distinctions or characteristics that disunite individuals and groups Expurgation of the Other: Constructing an enemy so threatening that it must be resisted
Reification	Represents a transitory, historical state of affairs as if it were natural, permanent, and outside of time **Strategies:** Naturalization or Essentialization: Portraying a social creation as the inevitable outcome of innate characteristics Eternalization: Depriving phenomena of social-historical character by emphasizing their permanent, unchanging nature Nominalization: Focusing attention on certain themes at the expense of others that are marginalized or decentered

argues that "racism without racists" is produced and reproduced by a set of white-supremacist ideologies (i.e., particular discursive frames, rhetorical styles and strategies, and common storylines), all of which promote a racist identity and worldview and can be identified in the everyday racial talk of whites.

Bonilla-Silva (2003) does not explicitly employ Thompson's (1990) modes of ideological operation in his analysis of interviews conducted with white college students at three different universities and white residents of the Detroit metropolitan area. He does, however, begin his discussion of what he calls ıl frames of color-blind racism by invoking Thompson's (1984) claim ogies are about "meaning in the service of power" (p. 7):

> re expressions at the symbolic level of the fact of dominance. As he ideologies of the powerful are central in the production and cement of the status quo. They comfort rulers and charm the nuch like an Indian snake handler. Whereas rulers receive solace eving they are not involved in the terrible ordeal of creating and ıining inequality, the ruled are charmed by the almost magical es of a hegemonic ideology. (Bonilla-Silva, 2003, pp. 25–26)

blind racism, according to Bonilla-Silva (2003), entails four central ıl frames, which represent what he calls "set paths" (p. 26) for interformation about racial issues (see Table 2.2, adapted from pp. 28–29). isingly, these frames are remarkably similar to Thompson's ideologiions. Bonilla-Silva finds that whites, both young and old, use these l frames to talk about and explain a whole host of racial issues and —reinforcing their dominance, and expressing their "color-blind n the process. Their use of these frames, moreover, while very sinars ultimately to be largely unreflective.

ideological frames provide whites with a way to reinforce white y as a central component of the status quo, just as Thompson's l operations provide Brantlinger's middle-class parents with a way their socioeconomic power and privilege. Both Brantlinger and

deological Frames

iberalism	Involves using ideas associated with political liberalism (e.g., "equal opportunity") and economic liberalism (e.g., individual choice) in an abstract manner to explain racial matters. For example, whites have the "individual choice" to choose to live in segregated neighborhoods or to send their children to segregated schools.
ation	Allows whites to explain away racial phenomena by suggesting that they are natural occurrences. For example, whites claim that "segregation" is natural because people from all backgrounds gravitate toward people like themselves—that's just the way things are.
tereotypes	Relies on culturally based arguments and stereotypes to explain the standing of minorities in society. For example, "Mexicans do not put much emphasis on education" and "Blacks have too many babies."
tion	Suggests discrimination is no longer a central factor affecting minorities' life chances. For example, "It's better now than in the past" and "There's discrimination, but there are plenty of jobs out there."

Bonilla-Silva, however, confine their analyses primarily to what might be called the "cultural-social-institutional" plane—they do not, in other words, make an explicit move to the "personal" plane. But in making such a move, it can be argued that these ideological operations and frames also assist and enable dominant-group members to construct *privilege* as a central component of their own ideologically mediated *identities.*

This argument is supported by Butler's (1990, 1991) claim that identity is fundamentally *performed* or *enacted* (see also Goffman, 1959; Willie, 2003). Butler (1991) suggests, in particular, that identity is fragile, that the roles one plays are unstable, and hence actors must continually repeat their performances of identity in different contexts and for different audiences in order to provide some measure of stability and certainty:

> [I]f heterosexuality [for example] is compelled to *repeat itself* in order to establish the illusion of its own uniformity and identity, then this is an identity permanently at risk. ... If there is, as it were, always a compulsion to repeat, repetition never fully accomplishes identity. That there is a need for repetition at all is a sign that identity ... requires to be instituted again and again, which is to say that it runs the risk of being *de*-instituted at every interval. (p. 24)

So, if identity is a form of mediated action, and if it is performed or enacted (repeatedly, perhaps, in different contexts, for different audiences), then one's performance of one's identity must entail the use of specific cultural tools/mediational means—particularly ideologies, ideological operations, and ideological frames. Thus a fundamental question for researchers studying the manifestations and implications of ideologically mediated identity is to identify the ideological resources that are appropriated in a given social-cultural-historical context and to understand how these resources are used to mediate the enactment/performance of identity in that context—in both positive and negative ways (see Tappan, 2006).

It is important to note, however, that this view of identity as an ideologically mediated form of action/enactment/performance does not imply that persons are simply automatons, blindly following cultural and ideological dictates. Foley's (1990) ethnography of a small Mexican American town in South Texas is quite instructive in this regard. In this study, Foley shows how a school in this small town serves to construct a cultural ideology grounded in traditional American values. Members of this school community resist and change, as well as enact and maintain, expected roles. By performing different roles in various contexts, members constitute cultural meanings and practices that in turn shape their ways of being and behaving. By so doing, Foley argues, "Cultural traditions are constantly being homogenized and invented in modern capitalist cultures. This culture concept makes problematic the anthropological notion of an 'authentic,' stable cultural tradition that produces stable social

The idea of shifting 'lifestyles' tends to replace the idea of distinct, ng social identities" (p. 193). Foley further explains that students, in :, are not simply socialized through an "imposed cultural hegemony (p. 193), but instead, they enact and practice their identities.

al meanings, or ideologies, therefore, are neither imposed, hege- uctures nor stable. Individuals do not perform pre-scripted parts in ınd practicing their identities. These identities are being constantly ıd reshaped by the complex interactions of individuals' everyday nd lived experiences. As many have argued (see, for example, Apple, ;emonic ideologies are imposed on people in schooling and in larger ıt these meanings take on different values and forms as individuals ıese cultural meanings in constructing their identities.

ıore critical approach to understanding identity as ideologically action provides a framework useful in articulating an alterna- ·ptualization of privilege to that which has dominated much of the on privilege for the past 2 decades or so. This critical framework can ı shift the focus from identifying *what* privilege is to exploring *how* s produced and reproduced. By examining how privilege is actively and reproduced, we draw attention to the salience of privilege for ıding the workings of everyday life and for fashioning particular ıowing and doing.

gued in chapter 1, to think about privilege in this way is not to deny sh the importance of advantages that individuals and groups have 's; it is, in fact, to underline the relationship between advantages and ırmation, and thus to understand the ways individuals actively con- ⁊ilege. Privilege comprises more than the school and life advantages ls have; it is a crucial part of individuals and the self-understanding ɔoth inherit and re-create. This critical approach allows us to elab- extend our understanding of the available cultural processes and individuals use to construct a privileged identity. We can extend, 'ords, beyond commodified notions that divert attention from, and ıe concealed and sophisticated processes involved in the cultural n of privilege. By mapping out and exposing the contours of privi- ın begin to imagine the possibilities for interrupting the processes ɔrce and regenerate privilege. These possibilities are central to the nd focus of the studies of affluent schools included in this book.

3
In Pursuit of Excellence

ited States, access to an equal education has been regarded by most
) be the birthright of all students, regardless of their social, cultural, :onomic background (Nieto, 2005). As Brantlinger (2003) notes, re "thought to reward capacities rather than social standing" and 'to be meritocracies in which students have equal chances to suc- 1). Most Americans cherish this meritocratic ideal of schooling and)roblem with unequal outcomes between students as long as these :s in outcomes are those that they believe students deserve; that is, as ıcies, schools "are not based on an egalitarian principle of success for r they differentially reward high intelligence, athletic competence, c, and other types of student merit" (Brantlinger, 2003, p. 1).

ıcracies, therefore, create hierarchies that sort out the winners (high) from the losers (low achievers).[1] Even though in theory schools erate in fair and impartial ways in order for all students to have nces to be "winners" if they deserve to be, students' social class has a better indicator of whether they will be winners rather than their effort. Educational circumstances are not equal in the United States; 2005) points out, "A child's zip code is still almost a sure indication ıd of education he or she will receive" (p. 60). Nieto continues to t "rather than being a paragon of educational equality, U.S. schools ıistently ranked among the most unequal in the industrialized world of spending, curricular offerings, and teacher quality" (p. 61). Afflu- nts are advantaged by the character and quality of their schools (e.g., 980, 1981; Burton, 1999; Gamoran & Berends, 1987, Kohn, 1998) and fore more likely to be the "winners" in American schooling. There- ıite of the cherished ideal that the playing field in American schools is Brantlinger (2003) argues, "The actual American educational system : field to give the best chances to those who are already advantaged; e and winning are just as circular as the long-acknowledged cycle of nd failure" (p. 191).

:ocracy" becoming heredity was the fear of Michael Young, a Brit- logist and Labour Party expert who coined the term in a book of ence fiction called *The Rise of the Meritocracy*. In this book, he ana- iety from the vantage point of 2034 and, as Douthat (2005) describes, envisioned "a future of ever more perfect intelligence tests and educational segregation, in which a cognitive elite holds sway until the less intelligent masses rise to overthrow their brainy masters" (p. 123).[2] Most people ignore the fact that Young invented the word in order to condemn it and that he wrote the book to persuade individuals, specifically liberals, to abandon their commitment to the idea of universal, individual equal opportunity. Young argued that the more this goal is realized, the more deeply stratified society will become. He argued that equality rather than equal opportunity should be the overarching goal.

In the United States, however, as Lemann (1997) points out, "equal opportunity has almost always been the banner under which liberal progress has been achieved and by no stretch of the imagination represents a retreat from higher principles" (p. 32). Even though "many smaller skirmishes have been won" in the larger battle for equal opportunity in schooling, the outcome of the larger struggle remains uncertain and, in many ways, "is in greater jeopardy than ever" (Nieto, 2005, p. 60). The humiliating, segregating, and differentiating practices and policies supported and validated by meritocracies (Brantlinger, 1993) have become more prominent and accepted under the tremendous pressure to make schooling in this country more standardized. As many point out (e.g., Darling-Hammond, 2004; Howard, 2005b; McNeil, 2000; Meier, 2004; Pinar, 2004), the current reform efforts are widening the gap between the quality of education for poor and minority students and that for affluent, white students. By measuring student merit through standardized testing, schools are being designed to provide scientific evidence that inequalities in America are legitimate, justified, and natural (Shannon, 2006). The criteria used to measure individual merit in schooling do more to replicate than to reshuffle society's class system.

Many scholars have argued that meritocracies are not the best form of schooling for achieving democratic ideals (e.g., Brantlinger, 1993, 2003; Hinchey, 2001; Leistyna, 1999; Oakes & Lipton, 1999). However, regardless of evidence to the contrary, Americans still cling to the ideal that success in school (and life) follows from ability and aspirations. The meritocracy myth masks the reality that schooling favors children from dominant groups. Like most myths, as Oakes and Lipton explain,

> This one draws its strength from the grain of truth embedded in it. … Among those students who have the resources, opportunities, and connections that come with privilege, it may well be that the more ambitious and hardworking go further than those who simply do okay in schooling. (p. 16)[3]

However, when poor students demonstrate these meritorious qualities, they cannot parlay them into academic success to the same degree and frequency t students. Regardless of their merit, many poor students can never the disadvantages with which they began.

vith schooling disadvantages, research studies have demonstrated students continue to blame their failure in school on their own perk of ability or effort or failure to take advantage of opportunities (e.g., er, 1993; MacLeod, 1987). Merit permeates how both the advantaged isadvantaged make sense of American schooling—emphasizing the e individual while deemphasizing the role of the class advantages antages of that individual. This emphasis on actions and abilities luals is important in providing legitimacy to what might otherwise unfair or undemocratic (Oakes & Lipton, 1999).

mphasis on individual effort and merit rather than class advan- a powerful grip on the collective imagination of the community at the school described in this chapter. Although students undergo an ing education that many children in the United States cannot even most members of this community—including parents who wield uence to secure their children's advantages and success in school— at academic success depends primarily on ability, talent, effort, and ather than on wealth and personal connections. Within this culture, intages are rarely acknowledged, but individual merit and effort are y and openly celebrated. Because academic success is equated with ıerit, school is an arena in which students distinguish themselves and their sense of worth (Brantlinger, 2003). Students work very hard to above the rest at Bredvik, where success is the order of the day.

ıtablished Community

st is the largest incorporated suburban community in a midsize, rn city, with over 20 square miles slicing through the city's north- tip.[4] Three other suburban communities, whose residents are mostly ddle class, insulate the nearly 5,000 wealthier residents of Watercrest atmosphere of the city. These upper-middle-class residents identify their own communities than with their proximity to Watercrest, vhich they enjoy privileged status.

crest is the most exclusive and affluent community in the city, with ıousehold income in 2000 of approximately $210,000, which is sig- higher than the $40,000 median for the rest of the households in the value of the average house in Watercrest is approximately $1.7 million, well above the $400,000 average for houses in the three neighboring ities and the $125,000 average for residences elsewhere in the city.

crest's zoning is completely residential and agricultural. Only single- uses are allowed; the only exceptions are schools, churches, and vil- inistration buildings. About 60% of the land is zoned for lots of a n of 5 acres, about 30% for a minimum of 3 acres, and the rest for a minimum of 1 acre. As one village council member explained, "We think the zoning code preserves the value of people's investment and preserves the character of our community." The majority of residences are sprawling estates and mansions that are hidden from view on heavily wooded lots. Almost one quarter of the land in Watercrest is wooded area that is owned and preserved by the village. Over the years, a number of residents have donated this land to the village with the promise that it will never be developed.

Watercrest has no traffic lights, no supermarkets, no gas stations, no convenience stores, no barbershops, no billboards, no four-lane roads, no apartment buildings, and almost no crime. The closest business establishment is a members-only restaurant at the private country club in the community. Residents enjoy the benefits of a 19-officer police department, their own water department, six snowplows for the handful of days in winter that its 75 miles of hilly roadway needs plowing, backyard garbage pickup, and a 33-person, service-oriented maintenance department.

Watercrest is largely a white, Protestant village of old, established wealth. "If you're old money in the city, then you live here," a resident proudly explained to me. Less than 6% of the community is nonwhite, with the largest minority group being Asian American (4%) and the next largest being African American (less than 1%). Several Jewish families live in Watercrest, but they feel mostly excluded from the influential social circles of the community. For example, it is widely believed that the village's private country club, which is perceived as the main social gathering place for the community, offers membership to only white Christians. Some point to the fact that the wealthiest family in Watercrest is Jewish but not members of the country club as evidence of the club's tradition of discrimination. The very small number of African American families are even more excluded within the community. Several African American residents reported to me during conversations that they felt ignored by and cut off from the other residents and often found their social circles outside the community. Some of the families have reported being harassed by the village's police department and feel that they do not receive the same type of service from the village's offices as do white residents. The "special quality of life" that so many residents claim comes from living in Watercrest is enjoyed more often by white, Christian residents than others.

There are two school systems in Watercrest—one public and one private. The village's public school district often attracts attention at the local, state, and national levels for portraying privileged schooling. As one reporter wrote, outsiders visiting Watercrest's four public schools "see how brightly fortune smiles" on their students. The district's expenditure per pupil is 63% higher than the state's average, and additional funding for extracurricular activities and instructional supplies is raised by an active parent's group.

The district's four schools are on two campuses and enroll approximately 2,000 students. The primary and elementary schools are located less than a ı the campus of the middle and high schools. All four schools are superbly maintained brick buildings with state-of-the-art equipment ology surrounded by extensive playing fields. Sixty-nine percent of y have master's degrees or beyond, and 53% have at least 10 years of experience. The average class size in the district is 16 students. The students consistently perform well on state and national tests, with ge test score ranking in the top fifth of the nation and at the highest he state's proficiency tests. The high school offers three counselors to st all of the 150 seniors to college. Of the last graduating class as of ng, 94% went on to attend 4-year colleges, 85% of which are ranked selective.

k School, a private, nonsectarian, coeducational school, is located in of Watercrest, about 2 miles from the campus of the public high and hools. Even though Watercrest's public schools offer a de facto pri- ol education, attending Bredvik has more to do with status than edu- uperiority. A group of businessmen founded Bredvik in the 1920s as preparatory school, preprimary through twelfth grade, for boys of wealthy families. The original founding principle of Bredvik's mis- to produce young men of character, intellect, and athletic prowess. 50s, girls were admitted through sixth grade, and in the 1970s the came coeducational. Today, there are 850 students, and the faculty nearly 125.

pper School enrolls approximately 260 students, of whom 23% are of color (i.e., 13% African American, 4% Asian American, less than /a, and 5% unidentified) and 44% are female. Over 85% of the stu- in suburban communities, with approximately 30% living in Water- school offers partial financial aid (that is, no more than 50% of the) 22% of the students. Of those on financial aid, 45% are African . Of the 34 faculty members at the Upper School, one is a person 2% are female, and 72% have master's degrees or higher. Although more females on the faculty, all the department heads and other positions in the school are held by males. As one female teacher , "The school hasn't been an all-boys school for years, but it still has nd atmosphere of a male-dominated institution. We carry that his- us."

ts are encouraged to explore a broad range of experiences by par- in the numerous extracurricular activities offered at the school s, publications, travel, creative/performing arts) and are required mesters of the school year to participate in a sport (football, cross occer, hockey, wrestling, gymnastics, horse riding, basketball, base- sse, tennis). The school promotes its strong commitment to athlet- of its effort to educate the "whole student." Its athletic program is to "not only aid in our students' physical development, but … also [provide] another venue to help students develop responsibility and build self confidence and self esteem, and gives them the tools to succeed in life."

One hundred percent of Bredvik graduates attend 4-year colleges. During the year of my research, nearly one fourth of them went on to attend Ivy League colleges, and the others attended some of the highest-tier private and public universities and colleges in the United States. The National Merit/National Achievement Programs recognized 22% of Bredvik graduates that year, which was the largest percentage from any single public/independent school in the state. For the most part, Bredvik remains committed to the mission established by its founders, which is to have each student leave the school "with superior academic preparation, having grown personally in areas of social interaction and self awareness" and to have each student "exhibit high moral character, integrity, and respect for others, participating responsibly in the immediate and worldwide communities of which the school is a part."

Getting It Right

The two-lane road directly leading to Bredvik is lined with gated driveways marked by nameless mailboxes. Since most of the mansions are hidden away on heavily wooded estates, no clues are offered as to what lies at the end of the driveways. A police car with an off-duty officer is parked just inside the closed gates of the estate closest to Bredvik. It is the residence of the wealthiest and most well-known family in Watercrest. "They receive threats all the time," one of the teachers told me. "Not because they have so much money, but it has to do more with how they've gotten so rich." A few years ago the city's main newspaper published a front-page story exposing the alleged corrupt dealings of one of the family's companies. The reporter who wrote the story was fired, and charges were filed against him the next day for obtaining his information illegally. The newspaper retracted the story. The family remained protected.

The lush playing fields that stretch in front of the main structure of Bredvik gradually appear behind the thicket of trees bordering the road. In the midst of hidden estates, the school campus seems open and inviting. Elegantly designed, the main three-level structure of the Upper School provides a modern and sophisticated character to the school's 62-acre campus. The new $20 million structure replaced a one-story wood building 2 years ago. Architects from two firms in different parts of the United States spent a year talking with parents, students, teachers, and community members in the process of designing the school. The building was conceived to be adaptive to the fundraising, cultural, and social needs of the school while meeting the functional needs of its educational program. The Upper School houses a 530-seat state-of-the-art theater that measures up to the city's downtown legitimate stage, where touring Broadway shows are performed; a library and technology center; a commons area and art gallery; a 400-seat dining hall; a science center with atories; and high-tech classrooms with access to a wireless computer

teacher is provided a laptop computer by the school and attends hroughout the year on using technology in the classroom. In the s, Bredvik made the commitment to emphasize technology through- ıcational program. Since then, the school has become a place where ınd teachers "breathe technology," as one teacher described. The new vas part of Bredvik's technology initiative. "We needed a building to r educational program," the headmaster explained. He added, "We n't accomplish all we wanted in terms of fully integrating technol- ghout the curriculum with our old buildings. We needed new facili- uilt them with technology in mind."

ned single-level buildings of the Lower and Middle Schools sit next hind the Upper School. Next to the modern angular structure, these ings seem more ordinary than they actually are. They give some hint astically the campus changed with the new building. The headmas- ence, a cottage for the preschool, and an athletic center that houses enter, swimming pool, gymnastic training center, and basketball arther back from the main building. The eclectic architecture, the vell-equipped playgrounds and open spaces, and the acres of woods r form a handsome campus.

day I arrive in late March, the bright sun, the temperate air, the bud- , and the variety of flowers scattered across the campus grounds give ı that spring has arrived.[5] It is lunchtime and several girls are gath- outside the school's main entrance. Some boys are playing football d in front of the school and taking liberty from the dress code that tudents to wear collared shirts tucked in their pants. In the parking ıl groups of students have just returned from lunch and continue ıt by their expensive cars and SUVs. The school allows juniors and go off campus during their breaks and lunch. Most of them hang out town just outside the limits of Watercrest crowded with indepen- stores, pristine retail shops, upscale restaurants, chic coffeehouses, ılized grocery stores. With no teachers or adults in sight, the scat- ıps of students are enjoying a break from the school day while soak- sun.

the building on my way to Mr. Perkins' classroom 10 minutes before s. A few students are sitting along the hallway leading to the central area playing on their computers. Eavesdropping on their conversa- cover that they're playing a video game on the Internet with each some cyberfriends. There are a few other students in empty class- rking quietly on their schoolwork. I find Mr. Perkins in the teach- oom crouching over a copier machine shuffling papers as he talks other teachers. The four live on the same street in a middle-class neighborhood just south of Watercrest. They are having an animated conversation about an ordinance just passed in their community. The tone of their conversation reveals that they find enjoyment in disagreeing with each other. When I enter the room, Mr. Perkins gives me a quick nod but continues talking and preparing for his afternoon classes. Mr. Perkins is the type of person who always seems busy—always doing something important. He never seems scatterbrained or distracted, though. Even when he is doing three other things while talking, he seems engaged in the conversation.

Mr. Perkins spent most of his childhood in upstate New York and his adolescence in Boston. After graduating from a large public school in the Boston area, he followed his father's footsteps and attended Harvard. After his first year, he left college for the next 5 years to pursue his dream of becoming a professional musician. "During those years, I worked mostly as a produce clerk and insurance salesman than a musician," he explained. "But I did get married during those years and decided to finish my degree." He returned to Harvard and finished his bachelor's degree in English. After college, he received a Fulbright Fellowship to teach in France at a public high school for 1 year. He then returned to the United States to begin teaching English and French at a boarding school in North Carolina. While there, he earned his master's in English education at the University of North Carolina–Chapel Hill. After earning his master's, he moved to Georgia to teach English at a private school for 4 years. He then moved back to the Northeast and accepted the position of assistant headmaster at a boarding school. He left this administrative position after 1 year to begin his work at Bredvik.

Mr. Perkins has been at Bredvik for 5 years as an English teacher and chair of the English department. At Bredvik, he teaches the advanced placement and freshman English classes. He also teaches electives on Asian literature and creative writing that seniors take for a quarter of the year. As chair, he facilitates the evaluation and development of the English program and holds one of the leadership positions of the faculty that directly reports to the head of the Upper School. Mr. Perkins is considered by colleagues, administrators, and families as the most influential faculty member at the school.

With a motion to follow him, Mr. Perkins and I begin to head toward his classroom. With no customary greetings, he immediately begins to explain what he has prepared for today's class. He tells me, "I think I need to explain a little about the beginning so you're up to speed with what I'm trying to do. I'm going to divide the class for the first few minutes so that I can work with those who did poorly on the grammar test they took the other day. Some of the students just can't proceed without some more work." He continues to describe the rest of his lesson plan until we reach his classroom. As he does with his students, he checks whether I understand him and asks if I have questions. I understand and have none.

rkins makes it a point to explain his lessons before I observe him. His
ons are more to assure me that he has put thought into his lessons
epare me for what I am about to observe. During our first meeting,
ed that he was skeptical of those of us in the field of Education (with a
"I think we focus too much on pedagogy instead of what really mat-
old me. "I care little about a teacher's opinion of cooperative learning
er of his theories on learning. I think it's more important for English
o be intelligent people who are widely read and who can carry on a
ion about literature." He returned to this point in a later conversa-
ying, "I may teach only one Dickens novel, but I've read eight of
enefits my students tremendously that I've read as much literature as
re so than what new approach I could use in the classroom." When
these comments, he wanted me to respond. I didn't. However, he
hat I did not share his views, since I am one of those who focus "too
edagogy than what really matters." Most of the time, he began with,
you don't agree but … " and ended with, "I know your textbooks
gy will say something different." Our unspoken disagreement was
sent in our conversations about teaching and learning.

f the students are seated at their desks, have their laptops open, and
o begin class when we enter. The desks are arranged in a semicircle so
re facing toward the front of the room at different angles. Two large
es overflowing with books, piles of paper, and supplies run along the
of the back wall, and large windows looking out over the campus
ake up the upper half. A few posters, mostly relating to Shakespeare
ins' favorite writer), and a couple of original pieces of art decorate
walls. When the bell rings, one of the students, Melissa, asks, "Mr.
an we go outside today? It hasn't been warm for a long time."

e don't ever do that." Several students ask him why, and he responds
tempt at a famous quote, " 'Ours not to do and die; ours not to rea-
Where's Will when I need him?"

a student who frequently talks during class discussions, informs Mr.
You're misquoting."

rkins replies, "Ours not to reason why, theirs is not to reason why,
to reason why," and then begins to laugh. While Mr. Perkins walks
loor to take his position in front of the class, he asks, "Shall we …?"
quietly with his hands folded until he has the attention of all his
He gives one of those severe teacher's looks to a couple of students
ill chatting while he waits. With all eyes on him now, he continues,
got a third of the class not passing an assignment, I don't want to
d. We need to get everyone up to speed."

f the students are ready to begin their usual 10 minutes of free writ-
ir journals at the beginning of class. A student asks Mr. Perkins if
oing to free-write and he tells them not today. He goes on to explain

that he is dividing the class into two groups—a grammar group and a poetry group. After this announcement, some of the students close their laptops and grab their books, ready to get into groups. "Hold on!" Perkins exclaims. "I haven't even finished telling you what we're going to do."

He continues, "There was no middle ground in the range of grades on the test you took the other day. Two thirds of you did very well and one third did poorly. I'm grouping you so I can spend more time with those who did poorly. We're going to spend the first 15 minutes of class for the next three classes in our groups. Those of you who did not pass the test will come over here." He points to the left side of the room. He adds, "This group will work on a grammar exercise with me." He then names the six students who are in the grammar group. He tells the rest of the students to gather in a circle on the other side of the room for a "fireside chat" about poetry.

As the students begin to get in their groups, Janora, one of the students I interviewed and a member of the grammar group, grumbles, "This sucks!"

Mr. Perkins has heard her and responds, "I will not tolerate that, Janora. I'm doing this to help you." He then addresses the entire class, "Stop for a minute. I'm doing this to help, not to punish those who did poorly. Let's get a better attitude about this."

His comments do not seem to change Janora's opinion that the grouping sucks. She rolls her eyes and sways her body in a way that clearly shows that she is still upset while she joins the five other students in the group. Janora expresses her opinion more openly in front of Mr. Perkins than do the other students. "I'm not going to be fake in front of him like everybody else," she later told me in an interview. "Everybody kisses his ass, afraid he'll take it out on them with their grades." Most of the students do act differently in front of Mr. Perkins and their other teachers than they do when they are not around adults. Even Janora has a different demeanor in Mr. Perkins' class than when I have seen her hanging out with friends without teachers being around, despite her claim of being her true self.

Bredvik students are very good at being good in the presence of adults. It is not clear whether staying in good graces with teachers wins them higher grades, but most students believe that it does, since the grading process in most of their classes is quite subjective. As Janora further explains, "They set things up to give you what they want. You never know exactly why you're getting the grade you're getting until you get it. It's just not that clear." Several other students agree with Janora that most teachers, especially English teachers, are not clear about their process for determining grades. This fuzziness of how grades are determined causes most students to connect favorable standing with good grades. Since students will do just about anything for higher grades, they seem to put forth a lot of effort to make sure their teachers like them.

Janora is one of the four African American students in the class. She entered Bredvik in the sixth grade after spending her elementary years in a Catholic school in the city. She came to Bredvik through a foundation that African American students scholarships to attend one of the seven hools in the city. The foundation awards scholarships to high-achiev-nts of color whose families can't afford the high tuition of a private ucation. The scholarships cover the entire amount of the school's which is different from the scholarships and financial aid awards the private schools in the city. The maximum amount of finan-fered to students at Bredvik covers at most only 50% of the school's he school's policy is not to exceed 50% "to ensure that families are financial commitment to the school," as the headmaster explained. 's family may not be financially comfortable enough to afford the xpensive tuition, but they are solidly middle class. Both of her par-ublic school teachers and have advanced degrees in education. Her es about 30 miles from Bredvik in another, primarily African Amer-urban community. Since both of her parents work full time, they l the time to volunteer for the school. "Most everybody's parents are y at the school doing stuff for them, but my parents have real jobs have the time to be here all the time," Janora informed me. Her par-ever, keep informed about Janora's progress at school by contacting ers on a regular basis.

earns mostly C's in her classes. Before entering Bredvik, she rarely low an A, but at Bredvik she has struggled to maintain the minimum her classes to keep her scholarship. Mr. Perkins believes that most merican students at Bredvik struggle because "they just don't have ration like the other students who have been at Bredvik since they chool."[6] Janora offers a different explanation, though. She explains, es are harder at this school, but black students aren't treated the same hite people. It's hard to do good when people don't think you can ou're black." Some teachers talk openly about the racism at the school, eadmaster publicly speaks of the need for the school "to create an ent where all students feel welcomed." However, as an African Amer-nt explained, "Nothing is done to address problems blacks face in this here's a lot of talk, but nothing is really done about those problems."

of the four African American students in the class are in the gram-p. Mr. Perkins seems indifferent to the fact that almost all of his merican students failed the test. His general attitude that African students have a "tough time" at Bredvik gives some indication as is racial segregation of his class may seem normal and unavoidable e frames the failure of African Americans, or lack of academic suc-pared with white students in his class, as the absence of ability (Gay-. Entrenched in the traditional cultural-deficit stance, Mr. Perkins at African American students at Bredvik are less advanced academi-"most other students" (his euphemism for white students). He adds,

"They come to Bredvik unprepared for the rigor of our academic program. They haven't developed the skills that most other students developed earlier."

Even though one of the African American students in the grammar group has been at Bredvik since preschool, he uses the arguments that "they're latecomers" and "haven't adjusted to Bredvik's academic program" to rationalize and justify the "academic struggles of black students." In his rationalization and justification, he constructs a binary between the academic success of white students and the academic failure of African American students. As Brantlinger (2003) points out, "The creation of binaries is not neutral or benign" (p. 38). His explanations establish clear distinctions that place African Americans at the disadvantaged side of the binary. The disproportionality of African American students in the grammar group, therefore, could be more plausibly explained as an artifact of Mr. Perkins' beliefs and actions (O'Connor, 2002). However, Mr. Perkins' grouping of African American students in his class (and all that this grouping represents, such as low ability, struggle, and failure) not only reflects his own beliefs and actions, but also represents enactment of the dominant Bredvik culture as defined by a racial hierarchy (Horvat & Antonio, 1999). This particular episode is consistent with the various and frequent ways African Americans are marginalized within Bredvik's larger school culture.

Janora is aware of her peripheral status at Bredvik, and she is "not afraid to let teachers know that I don't like being treated that way," she claims. She openly resists actions that relegate her to this status, but eventually, as she explains, "I calm down and just go with the flow." As usual, after letting Mr. Perkins know that she disagrees with being placed in the grammar group, she joins the other students in the group without further resistance. They all sit quietly waiting for Mr. Perkins while he gives instructions to the poetry group.

Mr. Perkins gives the poetry group two poems to read and discuss. "At first these poems will seem to be addressing different subjects, but they aren't," he tells the group. "Your task is to discover the connection between the two." He asks for one of them to facilitate the discussion, and Keegan, the other student I interviewed, volunteers. As soon as Mr. Perkins leaves them to join the grammar group, Keegan jumps right into his role.

Keegan, who is white, has been at Bredvik since preschool, except for a semester at a boarding school in the Northeast at the beginning of his ninth-grade year. "I went to boarding school for a change of scenery but really didn't find what I was hoping for," he initially told me. Over the course of our conversations, I learned more about his short stay at boarding school. While living at the school, he was harassed frequently by a group of his classmates. He explained, "They made me do all this shit. I mean, I wasn't the only one they picked on, but it seemed like I was their favorite target." During winter break, when he let his parents know how he was being treated, they decided it would be best for him to return to Bredvik. He thinks that returning to Bredvik was lecision for me not only socially but also academically." He furns, "I was too worried and stressed out about everything there. I ›ncentrate on any of my classes." He and his family worried that, as wouldn't keep the grades up there enough to get into college." Even parents were mostly concerned about his safety at the school, the t the harassment had on his grade point average was "a major facır deciding that he needed to return to Bredvik.

vik, Keegan earns mostly A's in his classes. Mr. Perkins describes e of the smartest students in the sophomore class," and most of his ıers describe him similarly. He is involved in several school-sponrities and loves to play sports. He is a member of the school's footling, and lacrosse teams. His main interest, though, is found outside plays guitar for a band that regularly finds gigs at parties and funcıearby area. His dream is to become a professional musician, but he ursuing a degree in business after high school. His love for music, ts out, "isn't enough that I can be sure that I won't need a day job to od living." Even though his family is independently wealthy and he at he "doesn't have to worry about money when I grow up," Keegan ned "to make a good living on my own and not just rely on my e rest of my life." Keegan wants a "secure day job" while he pursues of becoming a professional musician. He is going into business to his father's footsteps. His father is a successful businessman even eir wealth has been passed down for several generations.

Keegan leads the discussion in the poetry group, Mr. Perkins joins nar group. He begins by telling them, "I'm eager to get you up to a rade. Work with me and I'll work with you." It's not difficult to see udents are upset by failing the test and being singled out in front of s. Mr. Perkins continues by asking, "Can we get past being upset so ın get in the right mindset to work on this?" The students nod yes, ›ody language reveals that they are not ready to move on. This is not me that Mr. Perkins has announced to the class who failed and who Vhen he returns graded assignments, he makes it a point to let the v who received the highest marks and to praise them for their sucfrequently, he lets the class know who failed, like he did today. Mr. ıys he does this "to encourage students to do better." His approach eem to be very effective, since the list of achievers and nonachievers ıanged over the course of the semester.

, this approach seems to undermine chances for students to improve. plains that these public comparisons make her feel "stupid" and "not ugh" and cause her to be less motivated in Mr. Perkins' class. She "I feel so stupid that I can't do any better than I'm doing." Janora hat no amount of effort will lead to the success that most others in the class enjoy. These public comparisons seem to undermine the confidence, effort, and persistence needed to improve by reminding students (especially pedagogically fragile students like Janora) who is smart and who is not. Oakes and Lipton (1999) argue that these public comparisons trigger easy social comparisons, make shortcomings seem worse, and decrease students' sense of self worth. They point out that these public comparisons further refine "the distinction between those students who the classroom culture expects to meet the class's highest standards and those from whom that culture expects little" (p. 199). These effects of public comparisons not only discourage students from improving (the opposite of what Mr. Perkins claims), but also stand in the way of students becoming "fully engaged in their own learning or care about others' success" (p. 199). In a climate of comparison, attention to differences pits students against each other and makes their own status the primary focus of their attention and effort. Such conditions further reinforce and reflect values of individualism and competition.

Janora and the other students in the grammar group respond to these conditions by letting Mr. Perkins know through their body language and facial expressions that they are unhappy with their placement in the grammar group. Mr. Perkins is frustrated with their response but continues with his planned activity. He spends the rest of their group time working with the students on a grammar exercise in their textbook. Unlike his assigning of an analytical activity to the poetry group, Mr. Perkins tells the grammar group exactly what to do step by step. Students in the grammar group are doing largely mechanical, rote work and do not work cooperatively, as do the students in the poetry group. Following the traditional method of guided practice, he goes over the grammar problems of the exercise one by one and then asks students to complete the problems. After they do so, Mr. Perkins checks to see if they have done them correctly. When they make mistakes, he provides corrective feedback. By the end, the students seem less upset about being singled out as failures and ready to do what it takes to get a better grade.

After 15 minutes of group work, the students come back together as a whole class. Mr. Perkins gets their attention and begins to explain their next paper assignment. He begins, "As you know, we're beginning our poetry unit this week and I asked you to bring me your favorite song. I looked at what you brought and the songs aren't ones I necessarily know. It's probably no surprise that I do not have an extensive collection of contemporary CDs, especially hip-hop and West Coast rap. Why would I give such an assignment?" Several students raise their hands, and he calls on Jenni, a student who rarely participates in class.

"You want us to use the song as poetry," she answers.

"Yes, go on," Perkins urges.

"I don't know ..." she pauses and then continues: "The lyrics of the song are poetry, and can be considered poetry."

Keegan adds, "We're going to look at our songs and analyze them like we would one of the poems in the book."

Mr. Perkins responds, "That's exactly what we're going to do. What about the song do you think I'm going to ask you to focus on?"

Keegan answers, "We're going to look at the meaning."

"Give me the fancy word for that," Mr. Perkins responds and then tells the class that he is "looking for the fancy word for meaning."

After a brief pause, Keegan says, as if he's surprised that he has thought of it, "Theme."

"You found the fancy word," Perkins affirms. "Is it logical that I write a poem about a theme that somebody else addresses in a song? That somebody else might address in a paper? That somebody else might address in a building?" The class responds by nodding their heads yes. He continues, "Why would this be true? Why would someone express a theme in a building and not a poem? Or express a theme in a song and not a poem?"

Chris, who usually competes with Keegan to answer Mr. Perkins' questions during class, responds, "People want to express a subject in different ways. They may find a way to express what something means by writing a poem about it instead of singing about it."

Mr. Perkins again affirms, "I agree. We work within the medium we work in, don't we?" The students nod and answer yes. "Yet, the artistic temperament has a certain—and I don't say this to put it down—*commonness* that allows people to work in these different modes. So we actually should have some fun with this assignment, because here is something that you picked because presumably you like it. I will select a poem that matches the theme of the song you've chosen and has something to say to your song. You will have the chance then to build yourself a little essay that shows these comparisons."

Chris asks, "When is this essay due?"

"I will get to that in a moment. Actually, I will give you a handout at the end of class that will have all the specifics about this assignment on it. Now, you have two ways that I know of, that are relatively simple, of organizing your thoughts. Let me give you this choice and then you can individually see what you think will work for you. I know that no matter what you do, your essays will have similar beginnings and endings in terms of their structure." He writes beginning and ending on the board. Although Mr. Perkins' classroom is well equipped for use of technology, he rarely uses what he calls "the gadgets" in his teaching, prefering the blackboard instead.

The older faculty at Bredvik hasn't entirely embraced the school's emphasis on technology. They call the younger faculty's willingness to integrate technology into their teaching a "generational thing" and the school's focus on technology "trendy." Mr. Perkins explains, "The faculty my age and older are accustomed to ways of teaching that don't include a computer screen. I use the stuff when I think it will provide something for the students that I can't with the old-fashioned chalkboard and class discussion."

While Mr. Perkins writes on the board, he asks the students, "I know that an effective essay has to begin with what?"

Chris answers without delay, "Essays need to start with an introduction."

"Yes, thank you. See, it is so simple that some of you thought I was looking for something more complicated. And the paper needs to end with what?" Several students say "conclusion." He adds introduction and conclusion to the list on the blackboard. "I know that your introduction must accomplish three things," he continues. "Do you know what those are? I bet you do—some of you, at least." Several students give suggestions, but not what Mr. Perkins wants. He interrupts their flow of suggestions to tell them, "An introduction must create interest, provide necessary background, and state a thesis. What is a thesis?"

Chris answers, "It's a sentence that tells the main idea of your paper." The question-and-answer session has been an exchange mainly between Chris and Mr. Perkins. The other students are paying attention, but no one tries to join in their discussion.

Mr. Perkins replies, "Exactly. If you do this for the next 8 years of your life, you will have a successful high school and college careers in English, history, psychology, and all the other disciplines you have to write for. If you leave these things out, there will be moments when you will not have success, because it is very hard to write something that is clear if, for example, we don't know the thesis. It is logical. It is not just a structure someone just invented for no reason at all."

"You're making it sound too easy," Chris comments.

Mr. Perkins grins. "It's more about being logical than easy."

Nancy, a student who rarely speaks, interrupts the exchange between Chris and Mr. Perkins to ask, "Are you talking about the introduction? We'll do it right if we have those three parts in our introduction?"

Perkins answers yes and then draws eight squares on the board. He continues, "Then you go to these 'body paragraphs,' as we call them."

Keegan interrupts to ask, "Is that how many we need to have in a paper?"

Mr. Perkins erases two of the boxes and responds, "There we go. It may be any number. Maybe it's two. Maybe it's seven. It depends on what you have to say. And longer is not always better, in that you may write forever for no purpose at all. We have people in here that can write beautiful, relatively short, nice, and concise paragraphs. We have others in here who write wordy paragraphs that need to be cut into little pieces or something."

Most of the students are attentive and taking notes on their laptops. Perkins continues: "OK, model one is to write a paragraph about your song and follow it with paragraphs about the poem. You might take them one at a time." He writes on the board the structure of the paper—song, song, poem, poem.

He adds, "Then you might write in your conclusion about how they are similar and different. That would work—but there is another way of doing it, though, and that takes us back to this." He points to the squares on the blackboard that represent the body paragraphs. "What could we plug into these paragraphs, since we are comparing themes?"

Ramon, whom Mr. Perkins calls the "troublemaker" of the class, because he socializes too much during it, answers, "You could define the similarities and differences. Or your conclusion can do that."

"Good, Ramon. Song–poem–similarities–differences would be another way of organizing your paper." Mr. Perkins writes this pattern on the board. As he's writing, Nancy asks, "What about the conclusion? Doesn't it change when you change the structure?"

"Ah, that is actually a little trickier and a little more open-ended than the introduction. So don't be worried about that, yet. You can worry about the conclusion after you find a logical structure for the paper. You incorporate your logic in your conclusion. You bring it home for the reader, so to speak." He continues to write on the board and then asks, "Is there another possibility?"

Chris replies, "Well, there could be endless possibilities, right?"

Mr. Perkins asks him, "Do you mind sharing your genius and submitting one of the possibilities?"

Chris complies. "Maybe you could do the song and then the poem, like a paragraph each. Then you could write a paragraph about their similarities and then a paragraph about their differences. Then your conclusion would be determining whether they are more alike or different."

"But that's not really different in a significant way," Perkins responds. "Let's make sure everybody is thinking about this. Are we thinking about this?" Several students respond to let him know that they're trying to think of another way of structuring the paper. He then says, "Your suggestion, Chris, gets stuck into this rhetoric," as he points to the structures on the board and then continues, "There is another way to think about this."

Ramon joins in, "You would need a completely different format."

"Yes, that is exactly what I'm thinking. For example, you could write about more than one theme. I have a lot of boxes here. I don't know if there are seven different themes that these things have in common," he tells the class.

Janora interrupts, "Are those boxes paragraphs?"

"Yes, where have you been? Stay with us. Let's take a poem that I'm not going to assign to anyone, 'The Raven.' What is this poem essentially about?"

Keegan answers, "A mental imbalance from loss."

"A mental imbalance from loss," Perkins echoes, looking around. "That sounds good. Who said that?" Keegan tells him that he gave the answer. Mr. Perkins continues, "Of course you did, Keegan." He laughs and then asks the students, "Give me a song in which a person seems to be mentally imbalanced. I don't have to know the song."

" 'You Ought to Know,' " answers Katie, who Mr. Perkins considers one the best students in the class. When Keegan and Chris aren't dominating the class discussions, Katie usually participates more. ("I'm not interested in getting in the middle of their contest to see which one of them has Mr. Perkins' attention the most," she told me at an earlier point.)

Ramon reacts with disdain. "I hate that song." And most of the male students agree with him.

Mr. Perkins replies, "Wait a minute, you don't have to like it. Why is he imbalanced? Katie, you're our expert. Why is the narrator mentally imbalanced?"

"Well, actually a woman sings the song," she replies.

"I don't know the song. Tell me about it," he urges her.

"Alanis Morisette sings it, and she is talking about her boyfriend," she explains.

Mr. Perkins asks, "Is the boyfriend dead?"

"No, but she is haunted by her ex-boyfriend. She thinks of him and is crazy about it. She's just crazy," Katie explains.

"OK, you've provided me enough to go on. There is a theme that deals with loss. In Katie's song, loss comes from somebody ditching another person. In Poe, it is an actual death. So, in your paper you would talk about the different losses and effectively make that contrast. Agree?" Katie and several students do. He goes on, "Mental imbalance is another theme. Can you prove this imbalance by referring to the words of the song?" The students say they can. "Good, this is the key. Every paragraph I will read in your papers should contain something that proves your argument. Are there any final questions about the assignment?"

Keegan asks, "Can we do it different from what is on the board?"

Mr. Perkins replies, "Well, that worries me, but the answer is always yes. If you do something different, then you ought to ask me to see the specifics. We have spent more time on this than I had planned. We still have another activity to do before class ends. If you have more questions, then you can e-mail me or use the old-fashioned way, which is to ask me in person. This is how we communicated in my day—you actually *saw* the person you were communicating with."

He goes over to his desk to retrieve a handout for the students. "We're shifting gears now. I've got a little item for you. This test …." Several students interrupt him with some alarm to ask why he is giving them a test. He corrects them. "Calm down. Did I say test? I meant quiz."

Chris interjects, "It really depends on how well we do. It can be a test if we do well on it or a quiz if we don't."

"Always a funny man, Chris. I need you to fill this out by yourself. I'm only going to give you 5 minutes to rank these according to that little instruction at the top, during which time I'm going to my office to get the paper assignment. This quiz is highly subjective. Just fill it out based on your own opinion."

Mr. Perkins comes over to let me know personally that he is leaving to go to his office and hands me the quiz he just gave the students.

On the quiz are 12 statements, such as:

A boy who can play Beethoven sonatas well at age 8 grows up to become an insurance agent.
A mother of three children dies in a car accident at the age of 30.
A valuable racehorse is struck by lightning and dies instantly.

The students are asked to rank the statements from the most to the least tragic. As Mr. Perkins pointed out before leaving, they are to rank the items according to their own opinion. From their reactions to the assignment when he leaves, though, they are still stuck on thinking that the handout is a test. They are also skeptical of the subjective nature of the assignment. Students have doubts about Mr. Perkins' claim that there is no "right" way of ranking the statements.

Even though Mr. Perkins frequently encourages students to share their opinions when he introduces a new topic (such as "tragedy"), students have a more difficult time with these types of assignments than with more objective ones. Consistent with what Anyon (1981) found in her study of a school like Bredvik (i.e., the "executive elite school"), there is a perceived pressure in Mr. Perkins' class to get the *right* answer. Anyon explains that the nature of knowledge is less about "creativity or thinking independently or making 'sense.' … Rather, these children spoke to the need to know *existing* knowledge and to do well, to understand, explain, and answer correctly (and quickly)" (p. 29). Even though students complete the quiz as instructed, they are constantly aware of Mr. Perkins' attention to their displays of knowledge. Students are not willing to risk making mistakes. When they are given subjective assignments they typically ask numerous questions for clarification and spend more time than usual in completing their work. Keegan explains that he feels "like teachers are trying to trick us [with these assignments]. They're trying to prove how wrong we are about something before we learn it. You don't know what teachers are really up to." Feeling like they are not fully aware of Mr. Perkins' intentions, they are reluctant to share their responses publicly when they have completed the assignments.

When Mr. Perkins is in the room they rarely complain when he asks for their opinion on a particular topic, but within a few moments after he has left, the students' dispositions shift from quiet and well mannered to noisy and frenzied. With Mr. Perkins out of the room, they no longer feel the need to keep up their refined classroom behavior.

Janora asks her classmates, "Does anyone know which one is the most tragic on this sheet?"

"I don't know," replies Theresa, who sits on the other side of the classroom. "I think it's the girl starving to death, because she's so young. Everybody else dying is older than she is."

Chris joins in, "I think it's the violin getting stolen. That's $600,000 gone."

"You're crazy," says Eric, who always sits next to Chris. "Money isn't more tragic than somebody dying. That would be the *last* thing I'd check off on this sheet."

"That's a shitload of money, though," Janora empathizes with Chris. "You got a point."

Chris can't stand it anymore. "You know there has to be a right answer to this! He *has* to have a point to this! I *hate* these fuckin' assignments!" He looks over at me, apologetic that he has just used profanity. "My bad," he says. Shrugging my shoulders and shaking my head, I let him know that I'm not offended.

Keegan, who knows me better from our earlier discussions, assures Chris that he doesn't have to worry about me. The students usually do not pay much attention to me. I am known as the person who sits quietly in the back of the room and talks with Keegan and Janora outside of class time every once in a while. They do not feel a need to impress me.[7]

They continue to complain and be stressed out about the assignment until Mr. Perkins returns. Not one student has completed any part of the assignment in the nearly 10 minutes Mr. Perkins has been out of the room. They are too focused on getting the right answers to move forward. Students are trying to come up with what Mr. Perkins wants. When he enters the room he asks, "How are we doing? Have you completed the quiz?" Several students tell him that they are having difficulty with it. Mr. Perkins glances at a few students' papers and discovers that they haven't even started the assignment. He asks, "What's the problem here?"

"We're not sure what the right answers are for these situations," Ramon tells him.

"I assumed you knew what 'subjective' means," Mr. Perkins replies.

Ramon continues, "I know what it means but I'm not sure what you're looking for."

"I'm looking for your opinion. Let's take 2 minutes more on this to make your final decisions." He seems frustrated that the students did not work on the assignment while he was out of the room. He looks up at the clock and notices that there is less than 1 minute left before class ends. "You don't have time to finish this assignment today. Finish it at home, and we'll discuss it tomorrow after we meet in groups." He gives the students the instructions for the paper assignment almost as the bell is ringing. After the students leave, Mr. Perkins tells me, "They are so frustrating sometimes. They try to make everything bigger than it needs to be."

Playing the Game

According to Bourdieu (1993; Bourdieu & Wacquant, 1992), the social world is structured through "fields" that encompass the social relationships through which various forms of capital are acquired and exchanged. As Holland and associates (1998) explain, fields are "lived worlds ... organized around positions of status and influence ... and the cultural narratives that posit particular sorts of characters and their dealings with one another" (p. 59). Similarly, Grenfell and James (1998) argue that field is "a structured space of forces and struggles into which individuals along with their habitus-specific dispositions enter" (p. 161). Fields include all social spaces (i.e., institutions, family, community) that individuals encounter throughout their lives (Carrington & Luke, 1997). The relation between habitus and field is dialectic, whereby individuals both shape and are shaped by their interactions in the world (Grenfell & James, 1998). Furthermore, it is within and through the dialectic between habitus and field that hierarchies of power are played out.

Bourdieu uses the concept of field to capture the "rules of the game" (Bourdieu & Wacquant, 1992). As Grenfell and James (1998) point out, each field has "its own orthodoxy, its own way of doing things, rules, assumptions and beliefs; in sum, its own legitimate means" (p. 20). Fields are fields of forces that are constantly at play (Harker, Mahar, & Wilkes, 1990). Bourdieu (1993) explains, "Fields present themselves systematically as structured spaces of positions (or posts) whose properties depend on their position within these spaces and which can be analyzed independently of the characteristics of their occupants" (p. 72). While there are general laws of fields—i.e., commonly understood stakes of the game and players willing to play—each field has its own system of judgment and practice.

Much conflict and competition in society is aimed at gathering the power to name and construct the rules of interaction within fields. Bourdieu and Wacquant (1992) write, "A field is simultaneously a space of conflict and competition ... in which participants vie to establish monopoly over the species of effective capital in it" (p. 17). Over time, when subordinate groups acculturate the codes of distinction, the codes valued in a specific field then change, or new codes are introduced, to perpetuate the dominant order. Therefore, the concept of field is the embodiment of the rules of the game as well as the struggle to control these rules. For, as Bourdieu (1994) points out, "Symbolic power is a power of constructing reality" (p. 166).

As Bredvik students use different strategies and take different paths in their pursuits of excellence, this concept of field is important in their understanding of how they gain greater symbolic capital and power within Bredvik. They determine what they are willing and able to do in achieving academic success. They decide how much they are going to "play the game," as both Keegan and Janora call what students must do to be successful at Bredvik. Attempting to win the favor of their teachers; being well mannered; participating in the right amount of service, academic, and athletic activities; and playing to win are all rules of the game. Most students have learned to be really good at being excellent. As Keegan points out, "We have spent our lives learning what we need to do and how we need to act to be successful in school so that we'll be successful in life. We're all good at being good." He goes on to say, "If you do what you need to do and work hard, then you'll be successful." He gives an analogy to illustrate his point:

> It's like being at a track meet. You decide how much you want to put into it. You've practiced so you can run your first three laps without having much problems. When you get to the fourth lap, you have to really put everything you have into it to succeed. You can decide whether to just get by or run extra hard in the final lap. To do well, you have to run extra hard and not just jog along.

Keegan believes it's up to the student to decide "how bad you want to reach your goals" and to put forth the hard work it takes to achieve those goals.

However, some students believe that what it takes to be successful is not this clear-cut. Consistent with what Fairbanks and Ariail (2006) point out, not all students are willing or able to be molded in ways to follow the rules of the game in order to gain academic success. In fact, as Grenfell and James (1998) further explain, some students create their own "orthodoxies" in relation to the "official fields" that surround them (p. 20). They resist the social constraints of the orthodoxies that control their school lives. Janora explains these social constraints by offering a different analogy than Keegan's:

> It's maybe a plant in a whole bunch of weeds. The plant is in a weed garden and the weeds are trying to choke you each minute. But you got to keep growing like a plant.

She feels that the rules of the game are not as fair for African American students as for white students. From what I witnessed during my observations and heard in my conversations with teachers and other students, I agree with Janora. African American students at Bredvik do not experience academic success as often or at the same level as the majority of their white peers.

Within the white culture of Bredvik, African American students are defined as different, lesser, and Other. As Janora further explains, "We're not treated the same. People at this school just don't think we can do as good as white kids. We're just looked down on at this school, like we shouldn't be here. It sure is a game all right, but we're the underdogs. We're on the losing team. [The whites] are on the team that wins all the time." Janora goes on to explain that most African American students, including herself, just "deal with the unfairness" in their pursuits of excellence. She explains, "We all want to go to good colleges and learn what we have to put up with, what we have to become to get good grades and do all the stuff you have to do to get to good places. It really comes down to us having to be white. We can't be black at this school and get good grades and be successful." Consistent with what other studies have found (e.g., Ogbu, 2003), she says that several African American students have to "act white" in order to be academically successful at Bredvik. Although she resists conforming to Bredvik's white culture, she admits that she must "act white every once in a while to survive this place." Janora believes that academic success is more easily gained for African American students when they assimilate into the school culture.

Even though Keegan recognizes that African American students "have a tough time" at Bredvik, he still thinks the rules of the game are fair. He believes that Bredvik prepares all students for success and that to take advantage of what the school offers, all students must obey the rules. He explains, "It's no doubt that a lot of black students have a tough time here, but no matter who you are, you have to do certain things a certain way to get what you want out of life. I don't think it's a racial thing. I think it's the way life works." Keegan believes that all students, not only African Americans, have to assimilate (or follow the "orthodoxies of the field") in order to achieve academic success. Students must follow the rules of the game.

However, consistent with Delpit's (1988) claim about those who have power, Keegan seems unaware of or unwilling to acknowledge his unearned advantages in the game as a white, affluent male. He also is unaware that some of these rules clash with common African American cultural ways of knowing and doing, such as the focus on individual gain rather than an emphasis on communal efforts (see hooks, 1994). Several scholars (e.g., Brantlinger, 2003; Watt, 1994) claim that this lack of awareness of advantage is convenient. Keegan rationalizes the inconvenient truth that African Americans are at a disadvantage at Bredvik by claiming that students who work hard and conform according to the rules thrive at Bredvik. This reasoning positions African American students as lazy and unruly, because they experience difficulties at Bredvik. Consistent with Thompson's (1990) ideological modes of legitimation (representing relations of domination as legitimate) and dissimulation (obscuring relations of domination), Keegan attributes the difficulties of African Americans at Bredvik to their decisions, attitudes, and actions. In so doing, he diverts attention away from his own advantages. He keeps his privilege unrecognized, denied, distanced, and diminished in importance. His privilege remains protected; he secures his powerful position within the field of Bredvik.

A Competitive Game

Bredvik students both shape and are shaped by their competitive interactions with others in Bredvik's community. The push at Bredvik toward high grades, awards and honors, top scores, and college entrance spurs an ideology of achievement that is rooted in competition. Even though students' (and their families') competitive pursuits of excellence play a part in shaping this ideology, the culture of Bredvik reinforces and facilitates it. Even though Bredvik stresses the importance of community and cooperation, the competitiveness that is reinforced in and outside the classroom at the school negates these values (hooks, 2003). Similar to what Pope (2001) found in her study of adolescents "doing school," Bredvik students are caught in a system where achievement depends on not only hard work and a willingness to go through the correct motions, but also outdoing others. Students participate in a seemingly endless succession of contests to affirm their own worth by proving that they are better than others. They learn to become competitive players in the game of pursuing excellence.

Outside the classroom, Bredvik requires all students to participate in sports in order "to teach them the skills necessary to have a competitive edge in life," the headmaster explains. Students spend a great amount of time on playing fields honing their competitive attitudes and skills. According to the headmaster and others at Bredvik, participation in sports is a form of apprenticeship for a successful life, or as Riesman put it, "The road to the board room leads through the locker room" (as cited in Kohn, 1992, p. 85). Similarly, in the classroom context, students are playing to win and often will do anything to achieve success. They have the same attitude that they have on the field that success (winning) is the primary focus of their attention and effort. In Mr. Perkins' class, I observed some of the costs of this hyper focus on winning. At times, students were not able to move forward with their schoolwork for fear that they were not getting the right answer—that is, the answer they thought Mr. Perkins wanted. Their anxiety at these moments paralyzed their learning process. Playing the game in the classroom context regularly stifled independent and critical thinking that the school claims to encourage. Such conditions prevented students from becoming fully engaged in their own learning or finding an importance in their learning other than winning the game.

Although I witnessed only one student cheating on a pop quiz over the course of my research, both Keegan and Janora maintain that cheating is a common practice at Bredvik. Janora explains, "You're under so much pressure from your parents and teachers. Everybody's nagging you to do good and you want to be good also. Even if you do semi-good in classes, everybody is nagging you to do more and be better. It's a lot of stress. It's never enough. You always need to do better. It's like you're on a treadmill and you do all this walking but never get anywhere. A lot of people will cheat or do whatever they can to survive." Keegan offers a similar view by saying, "The intense stress here makes a lot of students risk it all for their goals. They will do things like cheat to get ahead or keep their heads above water, knowing that if they're caught, then they'll be kicked out of Bredvik." Faced with unrelenting pressures to excel, Keegan and Janora claim that students engage in behaviors such as cheating to cope with the stress associated with these pressures (see Gilbert, 1999; Luthar & Becker, 2002).

Neither Keegan nor Janora admit that they have cheated in their classes (an act that I assume not too many students would confess, even to an outsider such as a researcher), but they both understand why students cheat at Bredvik. Janora claims that cheating is about "survival." Keegan similarly explains, "It's a competitive environment here, and we'll do whatever it takes [to be successful]. I can see why some students cheat here, because there's so much pressure that's put on us. Too much pressure at times." Similar to Pope's (2001) observations, both Janora and Keegan believe that this pressure to be successful in school causes students "to compromise who they truly are and how they've been raised," Keegan explains. They feel that to survive at Bredvik, students are forced to cheat even if "they normally wouldn't do stuff like that," Janora adds. They are in a constant tug-of-war (Yair, 2000) between what they are "supposed to do" and "what you have to do," Janora explains. She admits, "I sometimes catch myself when I get so caught up in [being successful in school] not acting right and going against what I think is right. This place makes you act crazy sometimes. You do stuff here that you wouldn't do in other places. You just have to work the system."

They both claim that parents and teachers "have no idea what goes on here," Keegan explains.[8] He adds, "They are clueless about what kids do [at Bredvik] to get good grades and do everything they have to do [to be successful]. I don't think they want to know, really. They just want us to do well. Period. I bet they just want to overlook what it takes for us [to be successful]." Janora claims that "teachers set [students] up" in ways to force them to cheat. She explains, "They give you so much work that it's not possible to do everything without taking shortcuts. Some people believe that the only shortcut is to cheat. There are other shortcuts, but that's the most common one." Since Janora believes that teachers "set students up," they are "probably" aware that students cheat. Keegan similarly believes that "teachers must know that there's a lot going on that they don't want to know about."

Both Keegan and Janora claim that parents are more concerned than teachers about how students behave in their pursuits of academic success. Even though Janora's parents put a lot of pressure on her to be successful, she says that "they don't want me to act like other people here. They want me to keep it real. They want me to be a good person." For Keegan, his parents similarly want him not to compromise values such as honesty in his pursuit of excellence, but he claims that they place a lot of pressure on him "to do the best that I can." Both Janora and Keegan claim that their parents put a lot of stress on them out of love and caring. As Janora explains, "[My parents] just want me to be a success in whatever I do. They love me and want to make sure that I have a good life."

Both at home and at school, students are taught important lessons about what it means to be successful and how they should go about gaining this success. Their lives are situated in a competitive race to be better than others and to win at all costs. Students learn to use strategies in the game of being best and winning that compromise values that their families and Bredvik claim to promote. Competition overshadows more positive, productive lessons on how students should live and relate to others, and what is important in life. In their pursuits of excellence, students are caught in a system in which values such as honesty, cooperation, and respect come second to what it takes to stand out above the rest. In an environment where competition is the order of the day, there is little room for arousing collective concern for anything other than self-interest.

4
College-Oriented Desires and Expectations

The social class–based cultures of schools enable or constrain students' educational mobility. Groups collectively generate or appropriate distinctive mannerisms and practices in order to control educational, social, and economic resources (McDonough, 1998; Weber, 1978). The competition for this control of resources depends upon the structure of the distribution of the means. This competition generates scarcity, and those who possess more will appropriate more. Affluent groups appropriate educational credentials for the intergenerational transmission of social status, advantage, and power (Bernstein, 1977). Through this appropriation, other groups, especially the poor, are at a decided disadvantage in obtaining the credentials necessary for educational mobility. These groups have a tenuous connection to forms of highly valued cultural capital that affluent groups possess (Giroux, 1983a).

Bourdieu (1977) defines cultural capital as the general cultural background, knowledge, disposition, and skills that are passed from one generation to the next. From a Bourdieuian perspective, cultural capital can be classified into three states: embodied, objectified, and institutionalized. Embodied cultural capital takes the form of long-lasting dispositions of the mind and body (Bourdieu, 1987). The objectified state takes the form of cultural goods such as books and machines, and the institutionalized state most often takes the form of academic qualifications or credentials. As Swartz (1997) points out, these various forms of cultural capital "suggest that culture (in the broadest sense of the term) can become a power resource" (p. 75). Although all groups have their own distinctive forms of cultural capital, the most socially and economically valued forms are possessed by affluent classes. These valuable forms are transmitted to younger generations to supplement their economic capital in order to maintain class privilege across generations (Bourdieu, 1977). Affluent families highly value a college education as a means to secure and maintain this privilege. They understand the central importance of education in preserving their competitive advantage in society.

McDonough (1998) argues, "Cultural capital is precisely the knowledge which elites value yet schools do not formally teach. With the complexity of college choices in the U.S. system, a college education is a status resource and symbolic good, and high school students' college-choice processes are influenced by their social, cultural, and organizational contexts" (p. 183). With valuable forms of cultural capital, affluent students have been provided useful strategies for how much and what kind of schooling they need to make decisions about college that will secure their economic privilege. Their parents have transmitted cultural capital by informing them of the value and the process for acquiring a college education. Students have been provided knowledge of what a college education means in terms of occupational attainment, why attainment of a college education is important for future economic security, the admissions process, and the diversity of institutions. Affluent students' families have transmitted the forms of cultural capital to influence their college-oriented desires and expectations.

The Bourdieuian concept of habitus is also useful in understanding the deeply internalized, permanent system of outlooks and beliefs about the social world that individuals gain from their immediate contexts. Habitus is a common set of subjective perceptions held by individuals of the same group or class that influences an individual's expectations and aspirations. As McDonough (1998) explains, "Those aspirations are both subjective assessments of the chances for mobility and objective probabilities" (p. 184). Individuals use this common set of subjective perceptions of their class or group to make reasonable and realistic choices for their own aspirations (Brantlinger, 1993; MacLeod, 1987). For aspirations relating to college attendance and choice, as McDonough (1998) continues to explain, "Habitus exerts an influence on individual decision-making in organizational contexts by creating a common set of expectations of appropriate college choices that limits the universe of possible colleges into a smaller range of manageable considerations" (p. 184). Schools mediate groups' collective consciousness in regard to the processes and outcomes of college choice. Schools are in a mutually influencing process with families that affects individual student outcomes (McDonough, 1998).

Research studies have documented the ways that affluent schools transmit power and privilege and how affluent families use their children's schools to maintain their social class (e.g., Cookson & Persell, 1985; Peshkin, 2001). Attendance at elite schools, for example, is associated with higher income in later life, and most research on this association has investigated the mechanisms generating this advantage. As a rule, graduates of elite schools are more likely than graduates of other high schools to gain entrance into high-status, highly selective colleges. This then often leads to entry into high-status graduate programs and/or into careers providing wealth and power (Falsey & Heyns, 1984). Affluent families choose elite schools for these promising prospects for their children.

Elite schools offer the organizational structures for their students to have advantage in the college admissions process.[1] As Berliner and Biddle (1995) point out, students who attend elite schools "are exposed to programs that stress leadership and encourage them to apply to such colleges; ... they are required to take a focused curriculum suitable for college entry; … the high-status colleges discriminate in their admissions decisions in favor of graduates from those elite schools; … elite schools actively negotiate with high-status colleges for the admission of their graduates" (p. 125). Although most affluent public schools do not have the same network power with high-status colleges as do elite private schools, as McDonough (1998) found, affluent public schools provide "networking and insider information for guiding students who may be interested in following their predecessors' footsteps at particular colleges" (p. 190). Affluent schools, both private and public, provide the institutional culture, the college counseling, and the college preparatory programs necessary for students to gain entrance into high-status colleges.

Like other affluent schools, Parker Day School, the school described in this chapter, prepares its students for selective colleges through strong guidance programs, curricular options, an array of extracurricular activities, and strong relationships with high-status colleges. Everything about Parker conveys that all students will continue on to college, and most likely "good" colleges. The interaction of family and institutional influences places Parker students on the ambitious track toward gaining admission to high-status colleges and acquiring the educational credentials necessary to secure and maintain their privilege.

A Separate Place[2]

North Avenue ends where three roads meet, and each road leads to a different community representative of the racial and social class divisions within the city. One road leads to a mostly white, affluent neighborhood with an average home value reaching nearly $2 million. About a mile down this road, dense woods conceal and isolate that neighborhood from the surrounding areas. The second road runs through the southern part of Somersville, a poor, predominantly African American neighborhood, and then into a white middle-class residential community. Traveling down this road, the scenery changes dramatically—from a rundown urban area to a quiet, livable community. The third road leads to a poor, predominantly urban Appalachian neighborhood. Brick, four-unit apartment buildings, fast-food restaurants, and gas stations line the road leading to this community. The frontal boundaries of Parker Day School, a private, nonsectarian, coeducational school, run along North Avenue and connect with this intersection. The midsize, Midwestern city where Parker is located consists of neighborhoods that divide people according to race, culture, and social class. Each community is separate from the larger population of the city and has its own character and tone.

Parker Day School is one of the two schools in Somersville. The community is infested with gang-related activities, which are thought to be the primary causes of the high crime rate. The center of Somersville looks gray and shabby. Along the main street, the boarded-up buildings are marked by graffiti, drug dealers hang out beside benches and phone booths, and groups of young men stand on the corners day and night. At the midway point of this street, a side street leads to the community's other school, a public elementary school. There are over seven hundred children (of whom 90% are African American and 10% are urban Appalachian) crowded in a single-level, medium-sized brick building. Over 20% of the students are enrolled in the school's special education program. For children who begin their education at this elementary school, the high school dropout rate is approximately 65%, with a significant number dropping out before they even make it to high school. The school is considered a "low-performance" school by the state, with over 80% of the students failing the state's proficiency tests. Behind the school one can see the section of the community where most of the students' families live. Poorly maintained two-level, brick apartment buildings form this section. In front of the school one can see Parker Day School on top of a hill overlooking Somersville.

The students at Parker do not live in the surrounding communities, but instead live mostly in white, affluent suburban communities. The texture and atmosphere of the landscaped grounds of Parker's 25-acre campus are a far cry from the surrounding community. The school's modern, sophisticated-looking buildings, numerous and spacious fields, swimming pools, tennis courts, and football stadium sit on top of the hill detached from Somersville. As the headmistress explained to me during our initial meeting, "We are truly in our own little world here. The school was here before Somersville became such an absolutely horrible place. Besides our address, you wouldn't even know you were near that type of community when you're on our campus."

Parker's roots date back to the beginning of the 1900, when a community leader founded a college preparatory school in her mansion located in a wealthy community of the city. About 20 years later, the school opened a second campus in Somersville, which has since become the main campus of the school. The high, middle, and one of the elementary schools of Parker are located on the main campus. Another elementary school for prekindergarten through fifth-grade students is located at the original location in the heart of an historic neighborhood of ivy-covered mansions and tree-lined streets. Over the years, the founder's large mansion was renovated to include a spacious library, computer center, and large classrooms. Two other buildings that reflect the traditional and graceful architectural style of the original home were constructed in the early 1970s. One building contains a well-equipped science center, an art studio, and classrooms for music and drama, and the other structure houses several classrooms for the preschool and the school's extended day program. Outdoor spaces of the campus include a soccer field, two new playgrounds, and a children's "secret garden" (adults may enter only with a child who is 12 or under) that is located close to a large brick courtyard surrounded by beautiful plants.

The other elementary school, named for a former headmaster, is located on the east side of the main campus. The large, single-level main building, a fine arts building, a science center, a cottage that houses the early childhood center, and a red barn for drama make up the elementary school. A flower garden and playground are located near the main building. The middle school is an L-shaped building located in a wooded area of the campus. First-floor classrooms of the building open to the outdoors with easy access to tennis courts and playing fields. Upper level rooms are bright and spacious with high ceilings, skylights, and many windows.

Parker Upper School's buildings are centrally located on the campus. The main classroom building is at the school's entrance and includes 24 wired and wireless classrooms, six state-of-the-art science labs, five language classrooms, an art gallery, and a technology center. The library and media center in the main building is fully equipped with computers, fiber-optic and wireless data connections, and three technology classrooms. Directly behind the main building are the high school's three other buildings. The athletic center houses the gymnasium, a weight training area, a climbing wall, and a well-equipped gymnastics facility. Next to this building is a small structure that houses the cafeteria and commons area, which is an open space for students throughout the day. The arts center building contains a theater, a drama studio, two large art studios and a kiln room, a choral studio with individual rehearsal areas and choral performance space, and a large reception area and art gallery.

The 35 faculty members at the high school are all white, 57% are female, and 66% have master's degrees or higher. The school enrolls approximately 240 students, of whom 22% are students of color, which is representative of the local private schools, and 44% are female. There is limited financial aid available for tuition. Grants are based on need, merit (academic ability, potential for leadership, and contribution to the total school community), and funds available. Approximately 20% of students receive need-based assistance, and nearly 60% of these students are African American.

Over 70% of all Parker students live in one of the string of affluent suburban communities just north of the school campus, whose residents are considered "nouveau riche" and liberal by the wealthier and more established communities of the city. Parker School's families generally accept this external perception of their status and beliefs. As one parent described, "Of all the private schools in the city, Parker is the place for kids who come from families with new money and who have more progressive beliefs." The families see themselves as separate from "the uptight, snobbish, conservative community of old money," another parent informed me. Although the public schools in the communities where most Parker students live are well funded and offer strong college preparatory programs, families choose Parker for its smallness (e.g., the average class size is 14 students) and its record of success in helping students gain admission to highly selective colleges. One hundred percent of

Parker graduates attend college. During the year of my research, 18 graduates went on to attend Ivy League colleges and the vast majority of the other graduates attended some of the highest-tier private and public universities and colleges in the United States.

A Busy Environment

When classes are in session, the mood on Parker's campus is more active than one would expect. Students are running around on playgrounds and sports fields, and hanging out around campus and in the hallways. "Why are there so many students roaming campus grounds instead of in classrooms studying?" I asked myself on my first visit. I later found out that students have at least one free period during the day to relax, socialize, or study. Students have the freedom to decide how they use that time. When the weather permits, a lot of them spend their free period outdoors. "We get out of that building that we're stuck in all day," a student explained. Throughout the day, cars are pulling in and out of the parking lot. Parents visit the school frequently to volunteer, and juniors and seniors are allowed to go off campus during their free period and lunch—most of them take advantage of this freedom. Physical education and some academic classes are held outside as much as possible, and teachers regularly hold meetings with colleagues and students in one of the several courtyards on the campus. Parker's campus is a busy place during the school day.

I arrive in late April on a magnificent spring day. The school's landscape is lush green, and the coordinated varieties of flowers spread throughout the campus grounds are in full bloom. It is lunchtime, and several students are gathered in small groups on the lawn in front of the main building. There are a few students sitting on the lawn working on their assignments and reading. Others are playing basketball on the outside court, and a large group of boys and girls are running around playing some sort of a game—kind of like football, but not exactly. I was told that students come up with games to distinguish their activities from those at other schools. "It's a Parker thing." Juniors and seniors have not returned from lunch yet, which makes finding a parking space a lot easier than at other times during the day. They usually arrive just in time to make it to their next class on time.

As I walk through the parking lot, I notice the college decals on the back windshield of cars. Almost every car has the family's credentials displayed for all to see. Several prestigious colleges are represented in the lot (including Harvard, Yale, and Bryn Mawr), but not one car displays a decal of the city's public university. Only "brand-name" colleges have real cachet. This practice has more to do with status and success than school spirit. Parents want others to know of their children's success, which is often measured by admission to top-flight colleges, to represent their own success as parents. "Every parent wants to be able to tell others that their child goes to Harvard or Yale or colleges like those," a mother confessed. She continued, "If your child goes to a top-notch college, then they know you're a good parent. You've done your job as a parent." Back windshields are their message boards.

I enter the main building on my way to visit Ms. Perry's tenth-grade English class. Beyond the inner doors, there is a central lobby with an electronic message board mounted on one wall announcing athletic and academic achievements and events. The other walls of the lobby display wooden plaques with students' names engraved on brass plates identifying the students who have received school awards, and a glass case with pictures of the previous year's graduating class identifying the college that each student attends. A group of mothers are in the lobby gathered around a table stuffing envelopes. They are planning a social event to raise money for the school. Parents organize most of Parker's fund-raising activities and plan them to be opportunities to socialize with one another while they're conducting business for the school. Another table holds all the cookies and snacks they've brought to eat as they work.

Two hallways lead from the lobby to opposite ends of the building. Along the corridor leading to the west side of the building, what's known as "senior row," the seniors have decorated their lockers with colors and symbols of the colleges they plan to attend next year. Seniors spend days during their free time and after school painting their lockers after they've gained admission to college. This practice is a tradition at Parker to let the school community know that seniors "have accomplished what they've been working toward for years," a senior explains. She adds, "It also lets people see visually what our class has achieved." Another student describes this tradition as "therapeutic, in a sense, because you're so excited that you feel like screaming, and it gives you an outlet for that energy." Painting their lockers also sends the message that the pressure is off. With only a month until graduation, all of them know where they're going and do not feel the same pressure to keep up their grades or keep their schedules jam-packed with enrichment activities as when they were doing whatever it took to brighten up a college application. They are ready to move on to college.

The other hallway leads to Ms. Perry's classroom, which is the last room on the east side of the building. Ms. Perry started her teaching career in 1972 at Parker. She taught at the school until 1978 and then quit teaching to run legislative programs for a company. In 1988, the company's department she worked for was eliminated, so she then devoted all of her time to completing a book that she had been working on for several years. That same year, Parker lost a high school English teacher in the middle of the year, and the department head called Ms. Perry on a Friday evening to ask her if she could be in the classroom Monday morning as a long-term substitute. She agreed and then was hired full time the next year. Collectively, Ms. Perry has taught at Parker for 20 years.

Ms. Perry has always lived in the city where Parker is located. She graduated from a high school only 20 minutes away from Parker and received her bachelor's degree in English education from one of the city's universities. Unlike the majority of the teachers at the school, she holds a state teaching certificate. As with most private schools, Parker does not require teachers to be certified; they have to hold only a degree, preferably a graduate degree, in the discipline they teach. Ms. Perry teaches five classes, including one journalism class and an honors English course. In addition to her teaching responsibilities, she supervises the student publications for the school, serves on several faculty committees, and chairs the English department.

In Ms. Perry's classroom, the students' desks are circularly arranged around a large table that sits in the middle of the room. During class, students sit either at the desks or around the table, and a few students sit on the floor. Ms. Perry's desk and bookshelves are located in the adjacent publications room. With piles of papers scattered all over, the room looks disorganized, but Ms. Perry claims, "Students and I have our own system for the room—we know where things are and how to get what we need when we need it." When Ms. Perry is not teaching or in faculty meetings, she spends most of her time working alongside students in the publications room. "I work best when students are around me working," she explains. An entrance with doors that are always open separates this room from her classroom. Two narrow windows extending to the ceiling provide a scenic view of the east side of campus and natural light for the room—the overhead lights are never turned on during the day. Next to one of the windows another doorway leads to the outside. Beside the other window, a mounted chalkboard takes up half the space of one wall. There are two small, student-produced posters about Shakespeare, and three small paintings of the Elizabethan period on the other two walls.

I arrive at her classroom before Ms. Perry has returned from a lunch meeting with her department. Brian and Aaron, students of Ms. Perry's seventh-period class, are sitting quietly at their desks reading science fiction novels and eating their lunch. They briefly look up when I enter the room and then return to their reading. Though I usually talk with students before class begins, I don't disturb them and just take my usual seat in the back of the room. Three other students are working on the school newspaper in the adjacent room while eating their sandwiches in between conversations and typing on the computer. They have a deadline to meet in a few hours for this week's paper. A few minutes before the bell rings, the other students begin to arrive in class and spend the last few moments of lunchtime socializing with each other.

Social Hierarchies and Ambition

After lunch, Ms. Perry teaches sophomore English, which covers a chronological survey of British literature from the Middle Ages to the present. The class exposes students to a wide variety of British literature that they will focus on more in depth during their junior and senior years. In addition to the study of literature, "This class is a turning point for students as writers. They are no longer writing simply to report what they've learned, but writing to form solid arguments based on their analysis," Ms. Perry explains. One of the most extensive activities for the students during this semester is completing a research paper. Sophomore English introduces students to what Ms. Perry describes as "academic, scholarly writing and research that they will need for their remaining years of high school and on into their collegiate careers." During the semester, students are required to meet with Ms. Perry frequently outside of class time to work on their research papers. She explains that she uses a "tutorial model" in these meetings in order to have "more in-depth conversations about what they need to do to improve their writing and research skills." Ms. Perry feels that she becomes very familiar with each student's strengths and weaknesses and can "guide each student individually to completion of their research papers" in these tutorial sessions. During class time, she focuses on other aspects of the course, including other forms of writing.

A bell rings to warn students that they have 4 minutes to get to their classes. The students who were working on the school newspaper during lunch grab their backpacks and head out of the room. They write a note letting Ms. Perry know that they'll be back after school to finish the paper, and tape the note to the chalkboard. Shannon, a student who is known for, and admits to, being unable to be silent for an extended period of time, enters the room in mid-sentence interrupting the individual conversations of the six students in the classroom. She is telling the group some gossip she heard during lunch about another student. Eric, who is identified by Ms. Perry and the other students as the "smartest student" in the class, says, "Shannon, can't you shut up? I bet you can't be quiet for more than 2 minutes."

Shannon responds, "Yes I can. I just choose not to."

Josh, another student, enters their exchange, "I bet you a dollar you can't stop talking for an entire bell." Three other students also offer a bet of a dollar to Shannon.

Shannon agrees to the bet with the four students and then asks, "When do you want to do this?"

Eric responds, "How about this bell?" She asks them to be more specific and three of the boys tell her now. She agrees and puts her hand over her mouth to give a gesture that she has stop talking.

This is not the first time that Shannon has challenged the male students (especially Eric) to a "contest of willpower." Eric and Shannon have an ongoing feud. Shannon gets on Eric's nerves for talking too much, as he frequently tells her, and Shannon thinks Eric is a know-it-all. Most students (especially the boys in the class) share Eric's opinion of Shannon and often join him in teasing her. She usually ignores them and does not respond when they make fun of her. She believes that Eric and the others who tease her "are immature and wanting to get attention." She claims that they tease her as a way "to shut down everybody else in class and specially girls." She adds, "Eric and [the boys in class] try to intimidate us all the time. They want to always be the ones talking and letting everybody know they know it all. They're control freaks." In some ways, the rest of the students who are not a part of "Eric's group" agree with what Shannon points out, but, unlike Shannon, they do not challenge this group.

In my first observation of Ms. Perry's class, I discovered that girls and boys have different roles in her classroom. Boys control the conversations and girls rarely speak up in class. Shannon challenges this pattern by participating in discussions nearly as much as the boys. In a class where the boys' voices dominate discussions, where the boys seem more confident and more aggressive than their female peers, Shannon is viewed as not knowing her place as a female—too confident, too aggressive, too talkative. The expectations placed on Shannon and the other girls in Ms. Perry's classroom are consistent with the ample evidence that suggests that girls are expected to follow different roles in schooling than boys (e.g., Fairbanks & Ariail, 2006). They often need to make sure they are seen as nice, kind, and helpful in order to position themselves in ways to be successful in schooling (Walkerdine, 1990). Edward and Hamilton (2004) explain, "Whereas boys are socialized to express dominance and independence (power and status) in social interaction, [traditional gender expectations] hold the feminine role within communal qualities that include inclusion, support, and solidarity" (p. 1).

These expectation barriers are constructed powerfully through the different ways that teachers respond to boys and girls. Ms. Perry seems unaware of not only the differential status of boys and girls in her classroom, but also of the ways that she facilitates a classroom environment where boys dominate classroom activities, interactions, and discussions. In fact, Ms. Perry describes herself as someone who believes that "women and men should be treated equally and you should hold women and men to the same standard." She claims that her beliefs "come from years of working in a male-dominated field" before she returned to teaching. She believes that this work experience "had a profound impact on how I view my students. I hold high expectations for all of them, no matter who they are—girl, boy, black, white, and so on." Ms. Perry's sentiments about gender equality, however, do not reflect her practices. Ms. Perry's actions, like those of others found in research (e.g., Sadkar & Sadkar, 1994), communicate different expectations for boys and girls in various (and often subtle) ways, such as asking boys more questions during class discussions, calling on them more to answer her questions, allowing them to dominate class activities and interactions, and giving them more attention and praise. Such actions place pressure on girls to conform to traditional gender expectations.

When girls (like Shannon) do not conform to these expectations they "pay a price" (Fairbanks & Ariail, 2006). For example, Reay (2001) found in her study on the socialization of girls in schooling that assertive behavior from girls is often seen as disruptive and may be viewed negatively by adults. In Reay's study, when girls asserted themselves in ways contrary to traditional femininity they were labeled by teachers in derogatory ways. In one of my first discussions with Ms. Perry about students in her class, she apologized for Shannon's behavior. She said, "I don't know what's wrong with her. She's insistent on being disruptive and talking all the time and manages to irritate her peers. She's really an outsider and does very little to help change that status." Ms. Perry's apology and explanation for Shannon's behavior reinforce the notion that girls' assertiveness is a character flaw, while boys' assertiveness is praised. Even though Scott and Eric, for example, behave more assertively than Shannon by calling out answers, correcting other students, and even calling attention to the occasional mistakes that Ms. Perry makes, she regards them as "the best students in the class." Scott's and Eric's behaviors are praised, while Shannon's assertive actions are discouraged and criticized by Ms. Perry. This double standard positions Shannon and the other girls in the class in ways that follow a particular "storyline" for how they are to act (Enciso, 1998).[3]

Even though girls are often required to be silent in performing this particular storyline, Shannon is performing an alternative storyline for girls by positioning herself against Eric and the other boys in his group. She is challenging their dominant position. With hand over her mouth, she seems very determined to win the bet and prove that she can beat them at this game. As the other students arrive, the four boys who made the bet with Shannon take turns explaining what occurred. The bell rings, and the students begin to find their usual spots in the classroom. Josh and Eric lie on the floor propping their heads on their backpacks at the side of the center table closest to the adjacent room. Even though Ms. Perry allows students to lie down on the floor during class, most of the students decide to sit in chairs. Nicole, one of the two students I interviewed during my research, takes a chair from the table to share a desk with one of the male students, even though there are four empty desks.

Nicole came to Parker at the beginning of her freshman year from a magnet public school that emphasizes a performing and creative arts curriculum. Throughout the day, she can be frequently found in the art studio working on her latest painting. She continues to make creative arts an important part of her education, even though Parker does not emphasize the arts. Nicole earns almost all A's in her classes, even though she's "not overly focused on keeping a perfect GPA." She plans to attend "a good college" but is not working toward gaining admission to one of the highly selective places. "Students who want to go to Ivy colleges dream about it and will do whatever it takes to get into them. I just don't want it bad enough," she admits.

Nicole describes herself as very athletic. She is a member of the school's soccer team during the fall, plays basketball during the winter, and participates in track during the spring. She also participates in her church's athletic program. Her favorite sport during the summer while her family is vacationing on their island off the coast of Maine is sailing. Although she keeps active with other water sports (sea kayaking is her second favorite sport), she goes sailing several times a week during the summer. She describes her family as a "traditional American family with strong religious values." She uses the word "traditional" to describe their conservative views. She often complains about Parker being too "liberal," but she criticizes the more conservative private schools in the city, like Bredvik, for "being too stuck up and too pretentious." Nicole's comments reveal her own family's status as nouveau riche.

Nicole and Melissa, another member of the class, are trying to force Shannon to talk by asking her questions about last night's reading. Josh interrupts them by saying, "Leave her alone. We want this to be fair."

David, one of the students who placed a bet with Shannon, announces to the entire class, "No one talk to Shannon during this class. Let's see if she can be quiet for an entire period." They agree to leave Shannon alone.

Shannon is sitting at the center table by herself with her hand still over her mouth. Nicole and Josh begin to talk about the previous night's basketball game while the rest of the students listen. Joe, who is sitting next to them, is the leading scorer for the team, and the other students are congratulating him for his good game. Joe seems a little embarrassed that they are praising him so much and starts talking about the other players.

Scott, the other student I interviewed, arrives a few moments after the bell rings and sits next to Joe. Scott is one of the several "lifers" at Parker, which means he has attended there since preschool. He actually began attending the school's program for 1- to 3-year-olds, what Scott calls, "preschool preschool." Scott's parents divorced when he was seven. He lives with his mother and stepfather but frequently sees his dad. His father is an urologist. His stepfather is also in the medical field, a cardiac surgeon, and his mother does not work, so that she is able to devote full attention to Scott and his three siblings. His mother also actively volunteers for the school in various capacities and participates in community service events.

Scott maintains a grade point average just barely below 4.0, which he is very proud of, since he is not "one of those students who takes easy classes to get good grades." Since his goal is to become a physician, he takes mostly honor math and science classes, and selects electives that prepare him for a premedical program in college. He did take one art class last year, but then decided that all of his elective classes needed to focus on his career objective. In addition to his academics, Scott is involved in several activities. He holds a leadership position in the student senate, is a class officer, and volunteers in community service activities. He also participates in athletic programs in and out of school. He plays for the school's soccer and basketball teams. He also plays for a regional select soccer team that travels internationally to compete against other select teams throughout the world. This select team is composed of high school males throughout the Midwest who have both athletic ability and the financial means to afford the fees and travel expenses. The parents are responsible for paying all expenses accrued by team participation, which Scott calls "a very expensive activity." In addition to his soccer travels, Scott's family has traveled extensively throughout the world.

Shortly after arriving in class, Scott relays a message from the basketball coach to Joe. The coach wants to meet with Joe before practice to ask him about what Scott calls "the smack" going on during last night's game. Players on the other team were verbally harassing Joe during most of the game. Joe complains to Scott, "I don't know why he wants to see me. I didn't really say anything back to them. I just told them to shut up and play and ignored what they were saying." Joe seems worried that he may be in trouble with the coach.

Scott tries to comfort Joe by explaining, "He just wants to find out what they were saying to you. He overheard some of it and is going to talk with their coach." Some of the other students join in their conversation to offer their ideas about the coach's reasons for meeting with Joe later this afternoon. Most of them reassure Joe that he has nothing to worry about.

Five minutes after the bell, Ms. Perry enters the adjacent room and gathers her books and papers from her desk while saying to the students, "I'm so sorry about being late. We were in a department meeting and we ran over. I apologize. So, John Donne today, right? Let's turn to page 237." The students get out their textbooks and notebooks.

Josh informs Ms. Perry while she is preparing, "Shannon can't talk today, so don't call on her. We made a bet that she couldn't be quiet for an entire period."

Ms. Perry responds, "You all are an enigmatic bunch." Ms. Perry sits at a desk in the circle closest to the chalkboard. While some of the students are still finding the right page in their textbook, she begins class by telling them, "Let's use our empirical skills today. Let's take a look at Donne, an empirical look. What do I mean by empirical?" She rises from her desk and writes empirical on the board.

Scott answers, "Scientific."

Ms. Perry replies, "OK. What else?" She writes scientific on the board underneath empirical.

Josh asks, "Does it mean you're gathering information about something to understand it more?"

Eric adds, "You gather that information through a particular process. Like Scott said, a scientific process."

Ms. Perry adds what Eric and Josh said to the list on the chalkboard and continues, "Exactly. We're going to gather information about Donne through the poems we've read and information that I'll provide you about Donne's personal life to understand what he's writing about. The four poems that we've read provide sufficient information for our search and analysis."

She pauses for a moment to allow a couple of students to find the right place in the textbook and to open their notebooks. She notices that I do not have a textbook, and she asks Scott to get me one from the publications room. I usually borrow one of the extra books before class begins, but I forgot to get one for today's class. As Scott goes to get me a book, he teases me about not being "prepared for class." I smile and promise him that I'll try to do better. The other students and Ms. Perry chuckle. Ms. Perry rarely lets me just sit and observe the class, but instead she regularly invites me to join their discussions and to offer my opinion about the topics they're discussing. She and her students find it difficult to think of me as just a researcher. They identify me as an English teacher at a private school that they all know, and they relate to me not as an outsider studying their school, but instead as one of them. At Parker, teachers observe each other frequently to give feedback and to encourage "the faculty to engage in conversation about teaching and learning and be reflective about their practice." When teachers observe classes, they participate in class discussions and activities. "We invite our colleagues into our classes as teachers who can contribute to what we're doing. It's just the way we work together as a faculty," Ms. Perry explained in our first meeting. Because I'm regarded more as a teacher than a researcher, there is an expectation that I follow this custom.

When Scott returns with a book for me, Ms. Perry continues class by asking, "What is the one way that these poems are alike?" Seven students provide various incorrect answers, and eventually Ms. Perry interrupts them by saying, "Let's not play games. You can do better than this. What is the date of each poem?"

Cindy, a student who doesn't usually participate in class discussions, replies, "They're all 1633."

Ms. Perry answers back, "Yes. One would be led to believe that 1633 is the date these poems were written, right?" Almost the entire class responds to agree with her. Ms. Perry continues, "The brief biographical sketch we gathered from last night's reading suggests something different. Sixteen thirty-three is a publication date and not the date the poems were actually written."

Melissa interrupts to ask, "Why do they put the publication date? Do they not know when he wrote the poems?"

Four boys raise their hands to answer her question. Ms. Perry calls on Eric and he explains, "Isn't that for all publications? When we were writing our bibliographies for our research papers, we put the copyright date of our sources. That's not necessarily the date that they were written."

Josh responds to Eric's comment by saying, "But when we looked at Shakespeare, underneath his poems were the dates he wrote the poems. The older writings always have the dates they were written."

Ms. Perry further explains, "You both are correct. We use the date of publication for Donne because we do not know the exact dates that he actually wrote these poems." She explains why there is a publication date for Donne instead of the date when he wrote the poems and then continues, "But we can look at the historical evidence and can locate what sequence they were written by knowing about Donne's life."

Scott interjects, "By looking at the topics of the poems and correlating them with who he was at different times?"

Ms. Perry responds, "Exactly." She tells the class that she is going to give a mini-lecture about Donne's life for the next few minutes. She begins by saying, "Donne's poetry is the best-loved poetry next to Shakespeare's."

Josh responds, "I like it a lot more than Shakespeare." Five other students agree with him and provide various reasons why they like Donne more than Shakespeare. The students recently finished reading *Hamlet* and had a test on it last week. They are not big fans of Shakespeare right now.

After the students respond to her initial statement, Ms. Perry continues, "We can best understand Donne if we divide his life into three parts. He had an interesting life, with three distinctly different lives in one lifetime." She tells the students that Donne was known as Blackjack during his youth because of his uninhibited lifestyle. After he married, he became a romantic, and during the last part of his life he was consumed with his mortality. Throughout her lecture, she relates Donne's writings to Chaucer's *Canterbury Tales*, the works of Marlowe, Shakespeare's poetry, and other classical works. Ms. Perry recalls passages from different works with ease. The students ask questions during the lecture and also relate Donne's writings and life to other classical works. Imitating Ms. Perry's style, Eric even quotes a Shakespeare passage when he raises a point in the discussion.

After her lecture, she asks me if I want to share any information about Donne with the class. I tell them that I can't think of anything else to add. Ms. Perry continues, "OK, let's begin with 'Song.' This is truly one of my favorite poems. May I have a volunteer to read?" Five students ask Isabelle to read because, as one student expresses, "I love the way Isabelle reads." Ms. Perry says, "Let's not pressure Isabelle. She always reads. Isabelle, do you mind reading?" Isabelle agrees and reads the poem.

When she finishes, Ms. Perry asks, "At what point in Donne's life do you think he wrote this poem?"

Eric answers, "During his Blackjack stage."

Ms. Perry responds, "Yes, how do we know that?"

Scott interjects, "Because of what the poem is talking about."

Ms. Perry asks, "What is this poem talking about? What is the theme of the poem?"

Scott responds, "That beautiful women can't be faithful."

Eric adds, "Only ugly girls are faithful because nobody wants them. Beautiful girls know that they can get anybody they want. They have too many men going after them to be faithful. I think Donne knows what he's talking about."

Josh adds to the discussion, "It's almost better to be with an ugly girl because you never have to worry about her going anywhere." The entire class laughs, and all of the male students agree that "beautiful women can't be faithful."

After a few minutes of male and female students expressing their conflicting opinions regarding the faithfulness of beautiful women, Ms. Perry interrupts in a loud tone of voice, "OK, class. Let's move on. I'm being drowned by testosterone here."

Nicole makes a final response to the male students by saying, "You guys are so sexist."

Ms. Perry quotes the first stanza of the poem without reading it while she is standing, and then asks, "What is Donne saying here?"

Shannon says, "That he wants her to teach him things that only women know." Shannon's comment generates an immediate response from most of the students.

Josh says, "You see? I told you she couldn't be quiet for a whole period! Where's my dollar?"

Shannon responds, "I'll give you your dollar." The other three students who made a bet with her remind her that she owes them also. Shannon gets money out of her pocket and gives each of them a dollar.

Eric sarcastically tells her, "You could have waited to give us the money. You're interrupting class. We know where to find you." Ms. Perry and the other students laugh at his comment. But Shannon seems annoyed, and as usual when Eric discovers he has "struck a nerve" with Shannon, he adds one more verbal punch: "Don't be such a—"

Ms. Perry interrupts him before he comes up with something to call Shannon and tells them to stop bickering. She tells Shannon, "I'm glad you're liberated." A couple of boys continue to talk about Shannon losing the bet until Ms. Perry tells the class that they need to return to the poem. The students eventually stop talking about the bet, and Ms. Perry quotes the second stanza of the poem. She then asks the students, "What's this stanza saying?"

Eric responds, "It's talking about a perfect woman. The first stanza is also talking about a perfect woman."

Scott adds, "He's asking this perfect woman to teach him things. She's so perfect that she can tell him about things he couldn't get anywhere else."

Josh adds, "But it's not just focusing on her intellect. He's saying she's beautiful and that no one compares to her."

Nicole says, "I agree with you guys, but I also see Donne as being jealous because she's so beautiful and perfect. When he says, 'to keep off envy's stinging,' to me this is saying that he's jealous and doesn't want her to go with other men."

Shannon responds to revisit the earlier discussion. "Guys are so jealous and insecure. They feel like they need to be protective of beautiful women or they'll leave them. They think that some other guy will come around and take her or something."

Eric responds, "Because most of the time it's true. Guys are smart enough to know that beautiful women can't be trusted." Most of the other boys agree with Eric.

Shannon replies, "I'm not even going to respond to that. You guys need to go back in your caves."

Always wanting to get the last word, Eric tells her, "Good. You finally know when you need to shut up." Ms. Perry immediately jumps in and tells them that she's not going to continue "being their referee." She attempts "to cool them down" so that the class can move forward. She continues with the lesson and quotes the third stanza of the poem. She asks, "How does this last stanza sum up things for us?"

Shannon answers, "There's not a woman like he describes in the rest of the poem."

Ms. Perry responds, "OK, that's part of it. What else?"

Scott says, "On one hand he's saying that there's not such a woman, but on the other hand he's saying that if you find such a woman like he describes, then let him know."

Shannon adds, "He wants to know so he can hook up with her."

Eric interjects, "But at the end, he says even though he wants a woman like that, he knows that she'll be untrue to him."

Josh adds, "Like I said before, she won't be faithful to him."

Ms. Perry asks the class, "Do you see how the theme of this poem lets us know when Donne wrote it?"

Scott responds, "Yeah, he was a player during his Blackjack stage, and he's talking like a player in this poem."

Ms. Perry responds, "I'm not sure what a 'player' means, but if it means he flits from girl to girl without getting truly attached to them, then you're right." She talks to the students for a couple of minutes about the theme of the poem and then directs them to another one.

Ms. Perry looks at her watch and realizes that class is about to end. She gives them a homework assignment for tonight and tells them that they'll focus more on the next poem during tomorrow's class. While most of the students are writing the homework assignment in their planbooks, she continues, "We have a couple minutes left. Let's continue our empirical look at Donne. What point in Donne's life do you think 'A Valedication: Forbidding Mourning' was written?"

Melissa answers, "During the middle years."

Ms. Perry responds, "Yes, and how do we know that?"

Josh explains, "Because he's saying good-bye to his wife."

Eric adds, "And the way he says good-bye. You can just tell that he was ultimately lovestruck."

Ms. Perry responds, "I agree with you that we can begin to understand the depth of his love for his wife. To better understand what this poem is talking about, we need to understand that the way we travel today is not the same as in Donne's day. He is about to travel to France and is going to leave his wife for an extended period of time."

Shannon interrupts, "Oh, is that why he's saying good-bye?"

Josh responds, "It tells you that in the summary."

Ms. Perry asks Scott, "If you were leaving for Paris this weekend, what would you have to do to prepare for the trip?"

Scott replies, "I would have to pack and get my airplane tickets. I would need to have money and plans for my stay there."

Ms. Perry asks, "Would you have to worry about the real possibility that you'll not return and never see your family again?" Scott shrugs his shoulders and does not offer a verbal response to her question. Ms. Perry then answers her own question, "No. You don't have to worry about that. But in Donne's day, travelers needed to be deeply concerned with the realization that they might never return. They didn't have airplanes to whisk them away to another country."

The bell rings and the students start gathering their books. Ms. Perry says, "Please just give me a minute more." The students stop moving around to listen to Ms. Perry's final instructions. She continues, "When you take a closer look at Donne's poem tonight, I want you to take on a perspective which considers both his personal life and the period in which this poem was written. Extend yourself beyond your own perspective." She dismisses class and the students leave. As I'm walking out with them, Ms. Perry tells me that she is frustrated that she ran out of time. "I never find the time to accomplish all I need to accomplish in class," she tells me and then asks if I experience the same "dilemma" as a teacher. I tell her that I often feel the same as she does.

The Real Fudge

As is typical with private schools, Parker has demanding graduation requirements (e.g., Alt & Peter, 2002; Cookson & Persell, 1985) and a wide variety of classes (Lawrence-Lightfoot, 1983; Peshkin, 2001). Parker's graduation requirements include 4 years of English, 3 years of math, 3 years of science, 3 years of history, 2 years of a foreign language, and 2 years of courses in fine and performing arts. Students also are required to take a physical education and health course each year, to successfully complete a series of English composition competency examinations, and to demonstrate competency in computer skills, either by successful completion of a computer course or by successful performance on a computer competency examination. The belief that a solid education includes some "hands-on" experience and travel runs deep in the Parker view of learning. The school offers their students opportunities to study and be involved in activities off campus, mainly community service ones. Students must complete 30 hours of voluntary service to a needy community outside the school. The school also strongly urges students to participate in exchange programs that allow them to study abroad or to take part in domestic exchange programs.

Parker's overall curriculum provides students a variety of opportunities to read deeply and widely and to develop their writing, speaking, and creative and critical thinking skills. The programs in music, theater, and visual arts, for example, are designed to develop students' creative skills and facilitate their artistic vision. Courses in these programs emphasize the process of creation, as well as the created product. The program in mathematics encourages students to develop "the habit of puzzling over mathematical relationships, because it is this questioning that leads to true understanding, rather than mere remembering," as stated in the school's handbook. The program in history provides a perspective that enables students to see themselves in "time and place," a body of knowledge that helps them better appreciate their Western heritage as well as to understand cultures different from their own, and an awareness of the pleasure to be found in the study of history and the social sciences. At all levels, the history department works to help students develop the ability to read critically, to reason logically, to discriminate carefully, to draw conclusions objectively, to write and speak in a clear, well-organized manner, and to use sound methods of historical research. The English curriculum places equal emphasis on literature and composition. Students read widely and write frequently, learning to understand and enjoy a range of styles and content. The sequence of courses is designed to provide students with a working knowledge of grammar, forms of literature, and writing competence.

Similar to what Cookson and Persell (1985) found in their study of elite boarding schools, Parker's curriculum offers "students an abundant buffet of regular course work, electives, volunteer opportunities, travel, and independent study from which to choose a course of study" and encourages "students to treat academic work as an exciting challenge rather than just a job to be done" (pp. 77–78). The school's curriculum not only passes on culture (that is, cultural capital) but also increases students' competitive edge in gaining admission to highly selective colleges. Although teachers enjoy a fair amount of freedom in developing Parker's curriculum,[4] their curricular decisions are powerfully influenced by the pressure to get students into good colleges.

In my second interview with Ms. Perry, she directly discusses how the "college factor" (Peshkin, 2001) influences her pedagogical and curricular decisions. We meet during lunch for this interview, which is the only period she finds time to have meetings. Always in motion, she acknowledges me with a nod when I arrive but continues working with a group of students in the publications room who are completing various assignments. After a few moments of carrying on five different conversations simultaneously, she turns to me and says, "We're going to have to go somewhere else or we're never going to get a chance to talk." She makes a final point to each student before we head toward another classroom.

On our way to the other room, Ms. Perry asks me, "As a teacher, not as a researcher—you can share your thoughts as a researcher later—what do you think about some of the ways I approach the class?" I remark on her close relationships with students, her ability to facilitate an interesting class discussion, and her extensive knowledge of literature. I tell her that I plan to use some of what I observed her doing in my own teaching. We continue our teacher-to-teacher discussion about various teaching strategies, writing assignments, evaluation methods, and literature until she points out, "We only have about 25 minutes left. We better get to some of your questions."

I take a moment to look over the questions that I've prepared for our interview and begin by asking her to tell me about her overall approach to teaching. She takes a moment to think and then tells me, "As a teacher, I try to make the readings and assignments real. My colleagues and I do our very best not to teach by rote but to teach students to think and to challenge them. I try to find the things about literature that will enable them to connect with it, and I think you help students connect by making what they read and do real. For example, Donne is heavy literature. But Donne is what my son calls "real fudge," his works are part of a tradition. If students are going to be fully prepared for college, then they need to have read some of his work. When I first started teaching, I thought students would never cotton to Donne, but the truth is he's a great poet and they do."

I ask, "Do students always connect with 'real fudge' material? Do you only select literature that students will connect to and find interesting?"

She replies, "I feel a strong responsibility to get these kids out of here as educated human beings. For instance, I don't really like Milton. I don't like Milton at all, and I'm frank about it. I think Milton is tedious, but Milton is magnificent in certain ways, and to be educated you really ought to know about him and you certainly shouldn't come through British literature without ever having encountered him. And there are bits of iconography that are already in their heads and they ought to know where it came from. I hate Milton. I just don't like to read it, but I want the kids to know him. That's content and they need that. I want to get them out of here not only knowing how to look up John Milton if they need to find something about him, but knowing about him. It seems to me their lives will be richer. And it seems to me that they will be educated."

I ask, "To be educated well enough to do well in college?"

She responds, "Yes. If you would ask us what kind of school this is, the first thing anybody on this faculty would say to you is that we are a college preparatory school. My primary responsibility is to prepare students for college. I have a responsibility to make sure they have knowledge of literature such as John Milton's to be prepared for college coursework."

"Learning certain content prepares students for college?"

"Yes. There is an established body of work that students should know to be educated enough for college, and for that matter to be an educated human being."

"Besides covering a particular body of content, what are the other ways you fulfill this responsibility of preparing students for college?"

"In the English department, we make sure that our students are culturally literate, that they have read certain works of literature that will prepare them to be college students, that they have some background in literature, that they understand how to read and approach literature critically, how to write a persuasive essay discussing their analytical findings, and how to do other kinds of writing. We give them underpinnings, both cultural and literary underpinnings that will enable them to be successful in college."

"Do you feel that you and other teachers accomplish all of this?"

"I really think we do. We are committed to providing a solid education that prepares students for college. Teachers here fulfill that responsibility in diverse ways, but that's our mission here. I know it's the same at your school."

I respond, "Absolutely. Preparing students for college is what we're expected to do."

"And not just any college, but we're talking about only top colleges," she adds. She continues to explain, "Families pay a lot of money for their children to attend private schools, and they expect them to be fully prepared for college. They expect us to get them into those highly selective schools and do what it takes to prepare them to be successful once they get there. They want a return for their money; they want their children to be accepted to good schools." We talk for a few moments about the similarities between Parker and the private school where I teach.

She looks at her watch and lets me know the lunch hour ends in 2 minutes. I ask my final question. "In preparing students for college, you've said that they need particular skills and knowledge of certain material. What do you feel are some of your other responsibilities as a teacher?"

She answers, "I wouldn't be here teaching English if I didn't think it had a really important purpose. I think it is how we teach each other about, and how we pass on, the values of our culture. I think it's important to give dignity to what students do because I think it's all too easy to have them do mindless activities that do not prepare students fully for the world. There is enough real work to be done in school that we shouldn't create unreal busywork for students. There's enough real fudge for us to deal with."

The bell rings to let us know that lunch has ended. I end the interview and walk with Ms. Perry to her classroom. By the time we get there, most of the students are positioned in their usual places either sitting at their desks or lying on the floor. Brian and Aaron stop reading their science fiction novels when they notice Ms. Perry and dig in their backpacks for their textbooks and notebooks. The second bell rings to signal the beginning of seventh period. I sit at my usual desk in the back of the room and get ready to observe class.

Ms. Perry grabs some books and a pile of papers from her desk while asking the students, "So, John Milton today, right?"

Twists and Turns

Like most students at Parker, Nicole and Scott lead busy lives. Both of them compete in different sports all year long, perform community service, travel, and participate in numerous other extracurricular activities while maintaining a nearly perfect grade point average. They are motivated and find the energy to manage their hectic schedules by their college-oriented desires and expectations. Nicole and Scott, like their classmates, spend their lives, and educational careers, striving for acceptance to selective colleges. As the guidance counselor at Parker explains,

> Thinking about college starts before students enter school and doesn't let up until students receive that admissions letter. … Parents fret about what nursery school will set them on the right path to a good college. Then they worry about the choices they have to make about which school has the best reputation with colleges, what types of activities their children should be involved in to make them well rounded enough for college applications, what summer camps they need to attend, what classes they need to take, what foreign language they need to learn, and so on.

To make these right decisions, some students at Parker spend thousands of dollars for private college-admissions counseling.[5] Scott's family hired a counselor when he was in the seventh grade to help him select the proper enrichment activities, "balance" those activities, choose the right classes, and provide information about colleges. A counselor will also help arrange visits to colleges when he begins what he calls the "college circuit" this summer. This counseling is in addition to the extensive college counseling offered at Parker that begins when students enter high school. Besides counseling, most Parker students, including Nicole and Scott, attend workshops and have private tutors to help them get high scores on the SATs. They take practice tests until they "know it like the back of our hands," as a student explains.

"We have to do more than get good grades and test scores, we have to be well rounded," Scott explains. Parker students participate in a variety of activities (e.g., sports, clubs, community service) to build their resumés for the college-admission process. Scott continues, "You have to be involved in a variety of activities, though. You can't be too involved in one thing because you won't be well rounded enough. For example, I like playing sports, but I can't do sports too much or I'll seem like a jock. I want to get into a pre-med program, and being a jock won't help me get into a good one. You have to find the right balance." Scott hopes to attend an Ivy League college and believes that he has "more pressure to get this balance right." Even Nicole, who doesn't want to attend a highly selective school, admits that she keeps a jam-packed schedule to build her resumé for college applications and participates in a variety of activities to balance her credentials.

Not all of what students do is entirely motivated by what has been referred to as "transcript packing" (Peshkin, 2001), that is, students getting involved in activities that will impress college admissions officers. Parker offers an abundant array of school-sponsored activities, and students normally participate in the ones that they find most interesting. As Scott points out, "This isn't to say that the *only* reason we play sports and get involved in other things is to get into a good college. There's a lot for us to choose from and we get involved in what we find most interesting. But we all know that we have to get involved in a lot and have different types of experiences under our belts if we want to get into the school of our choice." Even though students are involved in activities that interest them, the pressure to acquire the credentials necessary for successful college admission remains the overriding reality in students' lives. As Nicole explains, "We always feel the pressure to keep busy in a lot of things at once. When we decide to be involved in something, we're thinking about how this will benefit us in getting into college." Scott adds, "The reality is that you're always asking yourself how this will help you, even when there can be other reasons for what you're doing. It's so natural in our thinking that it takes over. I may like something for a lot of reasons, but none of it seems more important than helping me reach my future goals." Students rarely find anything in what they do more important than how it will help them get into selective colleges.

Scott and Nicole believe that their involvement in extracurricular activities is important, but the crux of college preparation takes place in the classroom. Nicole says, "Nothing we do is more important than what we do in our classes. We have to make the grades to get to college, and teachers have to get us ready for college work. We have to learn certain content that makes us ready for college and will help us get good scores on tests." Scott adds, "We would be involved in sports and other activities wherever we went to school. But we're here because we know that this school provides the education we need to get in good colleges."

Similar to Ms. Perry, both of them believe that the salient purpose for what happens in the classroom is to prepare students academically for college. They believe that Parker prepares them for the academic demands of college by providing a rigorous and broad educational program, making what they do and learn in the classroom reflect college-level coursework, and allowing students to make choices about their education. As Scott explains, "This school is really academic. There's a lot of work to do. The teachers treat us as if we're already in college. The classes pretty much have a college format. Teachers give you long-term projects, semester core tests, and a lot of research papers. In our classes, we get a broad education. We establish a strong basis in different subjects. This helps us to figure out what we like. I just experiment with all the different classes, seeing what I want to do later. I know that I want to become a doctor, but I may change my mind. This broad education also helps us learn skills that help us to adapt to different situations. It helps us be able to take more twists and turns."

Echoing Scott, Nicole explains some of the ways that the education at Parker prepares students academically for college: "The teachers treat us like we're mature and give us work that is college-like. Teachers give us a certain amount of freedom, which is significant in college, and this gives us the support we need to make smart decisions about our lives. We also gain the essential knowledge for building the foundation we need for college. We've read the right books, know enough math and science, and have learned how to write papers that we'll have to write in college." Nicole and Scott believe that what they do in their classes teaches them the content and help them acquire the skills that they need to enter, and to be successful at, a selective college.

Students enter Parker knowing that the school will provide them with the opportunities to acquire the credentials necessary for successful college admission. But they don't attend Parker to just be prepared for college. As Nicole told me, "All of us would go to college if we went to another school. We pay the hefty tuition here to get into a *good* college." Her sentiments reverberated throughout my conversations with teachers, administrators, students, and parents. Parker promises not only to prepare students for college, but also to place students at an advantage in gaining admission to prestigious colleges. With unfailing college-oriented desires and expectations, students and their families pay the "hefty" yearly tuition to attend Parker for this advantage. Families buy the top-notch college preparatory education at Bredvik fully aware that it will advantage their children in reaching the elite strata of the next educational level (Horvat & Antonio, 1999). Just as if they were shopping for a state-of-the-art home entertainment center or a luxury car, they pick Parker for their advantaging features (e.g., good reputation with selective colleges, college counseling, college preparation curriculum, enrichment activities). The advantaging education at Parker is considered a commodity that will help them win "the college prize."

Getting In

Two years later, I visit Parker just before Nicole, Scott, and the other students who participated in my study graduate. I arrive at lunchtime to find most students running around campus enjoying the magnificent spring day. As I approach the entrance of the main building, I see Scott standing with a group of his friends. He's grown about 3 inches taller and looks a little older since I saw him last. We make eye contact and he acknowledges me with a wave and a big smile. I walk toward him and when I get within earshot, he says, "I'm about to graduate."

"I know, just about 3 weeks away," I reply.

He tells his friends how he knows me and then introduces me. "We've finished our classes. Seniors finish before everyone else," he informs me.

"What are you all doing at school then?" I ask them jokingly.

One of his friends responds, "It's habit. We're pathetic and can't find anything else to do with our free time." We laugh and then Scott tells me that they are "doing some shit" for the school. He isn't specific and I don't ask for more information.

I ask the boys where they're going to college next year. Scott's friends take turns telling me which colleges they will attend and then Scott tells me that he's "off to Dartmouth." Even though all the boys will attend highly selective schools, Scott is the only one in the group who has achieved the ultimate goal at Parker by gaining admission to an Ivy League college. He goes on to tell me, "My dad's really happy, because that's where he went. I got into some other places but decided that it was the best match for me. I can't wait. I'm ready to move on and do something different."

His friends listen patiently while Scott and I talk for a few moments about what has been going on in his life over the past two years. He describes his junior and senior years as "nonstop" and "jam-packed." He tells me, "I need a rest before I start college. I know that I'm going to keep the same pace as I did here." To get this rest, he informs me that he's planning to spend the summer traveling in Europe. I discover from the group of boys that traveling to Europe the summer before going to college is the current "in thing" at Parker. Scott plans to spend the summer without specific plans and go "where I want to go without worrying about anything." He is looking forward to a stress-free summer and a break from his "normal life."

5
Trust

In April of 2006, the number-one talk show in America, *The Oprah Winfrey Show*, devoted a two-day special report on the crisis in American schooling (Winfrey, 2006). During the first episode, Oprah had several well-known guests who provided a depressing picture of public schools. Bill and Melinda Gates told Oprah that they were terrified about the disastrous consequences of the nation's failing high school education system. CNN's Anderson Cooper exposed viewers to the appalling conditions of a Washington, DC, school just a few minutes from the White House. Lisa Ling, an investigative journalist, revealed the silent epidemic in suburban America of the high dropout rate.[1] During the episode, Oprah and her staff also conducted their own experiment of swapping inner-city Chicago public high school students with those from a suburban school to demonstrate the poor conditions of inner-city schools.

In talking about the reason for these two shows, Oprah said, "Most Americans have no idea how bad things really are. We are in a state of emergency. I'm blown away that this isn't what is on every parent's mind when it comes to elections. That people are not in the streets fighting for their kids." According to a poll that was part of this two-part programming and conducted with *Time* magazine, most Americans, however, do believe that schooling in their country is in crisis.[2] The poll revealed that 61% of Americans thought that the public school system was in crisis, and 52% of those polled believed that public schools had gotten worse in the last 20 years. In fact, most Americans have become accustomed to hearing about just "how bad things really are" in their country's public schools.

Headlines, news articles, and television news reports, like this two-part special of *The Oprah Winfrey Show*, portray the grim picture of American schooling, a picture stunning and consistent enough to frighten most Americans into concern for the future of their nation. On a frequent basis, American media seem to supply citizens with frightening story after story about the dreadful state and failures of education in this country. These stories provide a gloomy overview of the problems in American public schools. Some of the major themes in these stories are that student achievement in schools has recently declined, schools are not staffed by qualified teachers, and American schools come up short when compared with schools in other countries (Berliner & Biddle, 1995). These messages have been repeated to the point that most citizens have come to believe that the nation's public schools are in a crisis state.

These criticisms of American education have been steady and strong since at least 1983, with the publication of *A Nation at Risk*. In that study, the National Commission of Excellence in Education made several claims about the failures of American education, such as declining test scores, the weak performance of American students in comparison with those of other industrialized nations, and the number of illiterate adults. According to the report, American education needed to be made more rigorous and have higher expectations for students, as well as better-qualified teachers. Meier (2000) points out that the "battle cry" called out in this report to improve American schooling "launched an attack on dumb teachers, uncaring mothers, social promotion, and general academic permissiveness. Teachers … were declared the main enemy" (p. 9).

Associating school performance with the future economic strength of the country, this report galvanized Americans and moved the topic of education to center stage. Within two years after *A Nation at Risk* was published, hundreds of local and state panels were formed, more than 40 states increased requirements for graduation, 33 states instituted testing for student promotion and graduation, most states increased the length of the school day and/or school year, and most states required teachers and students to demonstrate computer literacy (Hill, 1989). Despite being grounded on two unexamined and misleading assumptions—that testing is an accurate measure of education quality and school is responsible for the nation's economy—the report was successful in convincing citizens that American schools had truly gone wrong and something needed to be done. This marked the beginning of the current standards-based reform movement, which eventually led to the federal No Child Left Behind legislation in 2001.

This also marked the beginning of an era of distrust in American schooling that continues to reflect American attitudes toward schooling today. As Meier (2002) explains:

> The dominant American attitude toward schooling these days … is a fundamentally new level of distrust. We don't trust teachers' judgment, so we constrain their choices. Nor do we trust principals, parents, or local school boards. We don't trust the public school system as a whole, so we allow those furthest removed from the schoolhouse to dictate policy that fundamentally changes the daily interactions that take place within schools. Nor do we trust in the extraordinary human penchant for learning itself. (p. 2)

One of the greatest shortcomings of the current efforts to address the "crisis" in American schooling through standardization is that they "fuel the very distrust they are aimed to cure" (Meier, 2002, p. 2). Pinar (2004) argues that the effects of standardization "not only make a nightmare of education in the present," quoting Linda McNeil (2000), but "*over the long term, standardization creates inequities, widening the gap between the quality of education for poor and minority youth and that of more privileged students*" (as quoted in Pinar, 2004, pp. 229–230; italics in original). Whether the crisis in American schooling is real or not, the current efforts undermine the possibilities for Americans to gain trust in their nation's public schools.

The four schools described in this book, however, are largely unaffected by these realities that govern most schools in this country today and the far-reaching distrust of schooling. Since the criticisms are directed toward the nation's public schools, this distrust in schooling has little to do with the three private schools. As Berliner and Biddle (1995) point out, "For years many Americans have thought that private schools are generally superior to public schools and that this superiority is confirmed by studies showing the higher achievement of students who attend the former" (p. 115). One of the most well known studies was conducted by Coleman, Hoffer, and Kilgore (1981). Coleman and colleagues found that private schools were doing a better job at educating students than were public schools. According to the Coleman Report, not only were students attending private schools better behaved, but they also scored higher on tests. Without critical examination of much of the evidence offered by Coleman and his associates,[3] the study's findings were released with great fanfare and provided more evidence of what many Americans already believed about the superior nature of private schools.

Although the popular criticisms have been directed toward public education, this distrust also has had little to do with public schools with affluent student populations. National concern and educational reform efforts have been directed toward solving the well-documented achievement gap that parallels race and class distinctions (Darling-Hammond, 2004). The focus of public concern has been on raising the achievement levels of traditionally "underperforming" groups; that is, mostly those who are from low-income families or racial minorities. Schools that serve these groups, therefore, are the focus of the public's concern for education. Schools like Oakley High, the public school described in this chapter, with students who are more likely to be found at the higher end of the achievement spectrum (Noguera & Akom, 2000), are far removed from this national concern and distrust.

A Special Place to Live

It is the second week of September but the hot weather gives no indication that summer is coming to an end. After an hour and a half of driving during late afternoon rush-hour traffic, I exit the highway to take the two-lane road leading to Oakley, a small, rural village located in the Midwest. About a mile from the exit, the landscape abruptly shifts from the overdeveloped residential and commercial areas just off the congested three-lane highway to vast and open farmland with scattered houses along the rural route. Hand-lettered signs advertising eggs, vegetables, and hay for sale are alongside the road with "Save Our Farm" painted on paper and wood signs of various sizes.

Just before I reach the village's limits the sunflower fields lining both sides of the road come as a beautiful surprise. I pull off the side of the road to take a longer look. On the other side of the road at the corner of the field, I notice a woman painting. When I get out of my car, she looks over at me and offers a warm greeting. I wave but do not want to disturb her. I stand for a few minutes looking out over the field trying to visually capture the landscape surrounding me. Acres and acres of sunflowers provide a beautiful entryway to the village.

I get back in my car and head toward a coffeehouse on Main Street where I am to meet Jackie, a resident who agreed to take me on a tour of the village. On the right side of the road, the village's only high school slowly appears behind the sunflower fields. Large playing fields surround the school's buildings. Boys are playing soccer on the field closest to the road. Another group of boys are playing football directly behind the school. A group of adults, who I assume are mostly parents, are standing on the sidelines of the football field watching the boys practice.

The residential streets that lead to the central part of the village are quiet and tree lined. No two houses look the same, each house reflecting an idiosyncratic style and structure. Older brick and stone structures, perfectly restored and cared for, are nestled comfortably next to homes reflecting contemporary architectural designs. Most homes have manicured lawns with diverse selections and arrangements of flowers, trees, and shrubbery. I pass several people walking their dogs and others who are jogging. I drive down the streets sharing the road mostly with people riding their bikes; I pass only a couple of moving cars. The tone of the residential area is quiet and unpretentious, reflecting the village residents' diverse tastes and styles.

Just before turning down Main Street, I go by the public elementary school, which is located at the center of the village. It is difficult to discern the boundaries of the school's campus because it blends so naturally into the landscape of the village. The school is a single-level, brick structure that sits at the center of the campus. Large trees surround and hide the building. The playground at the side of the school building is full of activity, with children running around, laughing, and just having a good time. Several women are sitting on benches beside the playground supervising them.

Lining Main Street are bookstores, restaurants, banks, two small grocery stores (one of them stocking only organic food), the public library, a hardware store, a drugstore, clothing shops (one specializing in hemp clothing), arts and crafts shops, and two gas stations that sell gas about 10 cents higher than the stations just outside the village. The village's one-screen movie theater is located at the midway point of the street and shows only artsy, independent films and, on occasion, films and videos made by students at the local college and high school. The sidewalks are crowded with people walking, sitting at tables outside coffeehouses, window-shopping, and gathered in front of stores talking. For such a small village, there are a good number of people out and about.

Oakley has a population of approximately 3,750, of whom about 81% are white and 15% are African American. The residents are mostly professionals (approximately 73% of the residents over the age of 16 who work) and artists who are socially concerned and liberal. Tourists come from far and near, mostly on the weekends, for the eclectic assortment of arts and crafts shops, and the frequent art and music shows and fairs. The alternative, liberal arts college (with about 700 students) located in the village heavily influences the tone and atmosphere of Oakley. Although typical town-gown frictions exist, the college and village cling to a similar character.

I find Jackie talking with another woman in front of the coffeehouse. Jackie has been living in Oakley since she started teaching at the college 5 years ago. "It's a sophisticated, artsy-fartsy, open-minded, liberal, atypical small town separated from its conservative neighbors," she told me in one of our first conversations. She introduces me to her friend, another professor at the college, and then we head on our walk around the village. She takes me to different stores and galleries to look at artwork made by locals, the park dedicated to women, the museum and outdoor education center of the 1,000-acre nature preserve, and the campuses of the college and the public elementary school. Jackie and I spend most of our time talking with people we meet along the way. Once they find out that I am taking a tour, nearly every person tells me a story and shares bits of information about the village. As the residents share the history and their appreciation of the small-town qualities of Oakley with me, they express a great deal of pride in their community and its distinctive identity.

It's almost dark by the time we finish our walk and return to the coffeehouse. Before heading home, Jackie takes me to one of the most well-known landmarks of Oakley—a working dairy farm that makes homemade ice cream. The dairy farm is the village's most popular recreational center. Playing miniature golf, watching farmers milk cows, petting the goats and other farm animals, practicing golf swings on the driving range, hitting balls in the batting cage, and taking hayrides around the farm are some of the activities people do during their visits. But the main attraction is the ice cream.

When we arrive, the line of people ordering ice cream extends outside the restaurant. "It's always like this. No matter what time you come here, there's always a line," Jackie informs me. As we're walking from her car to get in line, Jackie points in the direction of the golf driving range and asks, "Do you see that mound over there?" I look over in that direction and she continues, "That's the only conservative spot in Oakley. When Bob Dole was running for president, he gave a campaign speech there. The word is that he came here for the ice cream. We don't have too many Republicans campaigning in Oakley because they know it's a waste of their time. His presence will forever loom over that spot."

After a long wait, we finally make our order and then head outside to sit at one of the tables in front of the restaurant where it's a lot quieter than inside. Jackie and I talk more about the village for a while. I ask her about the "Save Our Farm" signs that I noticed earlier. She explains, "A 940-acre farm went up for sale a couple years ago when the owner died and left the land to her children. Her children didn't want to keep it even though it had been in their family since the late 1800s. They put it up for auction and developers were foaming at the mouth. Oakley residents formed a task force and dug deep in their pockets to raise a little over a million dollars to save the farm from developers. It turned out that a family bought it for over three million dollars and then filed an environmental easement with the county to ensure that the property is never sold for development."

She continues to tell me about the community's recent efforts to preserve the small-town character of Oakley. She tells me, "It's been real hard for us to keep Oakley small in order to keep this a special place to live."

Keeping Oakley "a special place to live" has come at a price. On the average, houses that sold for $100,000 in 1990 sold for at least twice that amount a decade later. As Oakley has become a more expensive place to live, the population has become more white and affluent. Although the population of the village has remained relatively stable over the last decade (with a 5.2% drop, from 3,973 to 3,761), the number of African Americans has decreased 37%. Also during this time, family median income in Oakley rose 62%, whereas family median income on the national level rose 39%. Less than 7% of the families in the village live on an income at or below the national poverty level.

Many residents have expressed concern about Oakley becoming more homogeneous. A couple years ago, a group of residents proposed a plan for developing affordable housing on farmland owned by the village, and their proposal passed through Village Council, but Oakley voters rejected it. "We know it's a problem and something has to be done. We just haven't found the right solution that all of us can agree on," Jackie tells me. She continues, "Oakley is becoming less diverse, which goes against the character of the village and the values of the people who live here. For the most part, residents are politically and socially progressive. The village becoming an exclusive community doesn't match with who we are or what we believe in." Residents of Oakley struggle between holding on to their progressive ideals and protecting their class interests. Consistent with what others (e.g., Brantlinger, 2003) have observed, Oakley residents choose to protect their class interests over keeping committed to their progressive ideals.

After talking for over an hour, Jackie tells me that she has to get home to prepare for her classes tomorrow. We say our good-byes, and I begin my drive home. I drive through Oakley and pass only a couple of people. One of the gas stations is the only business open. Most people have gone inside for the evening. The streets are dark and quiet.

Shared Vision and Commitment

At the edge of the village's limits, right off the main road leading to the highway, sits Oakley High School. The main building of the school is medium-sized and L-shaped, with a dome structure at one end that houses the practice space for the band and orchestra, and a three-story block that houses most of the school's classrooms at the other end. The central part of the building has a few classrooms and offices in the front and a gymnasium in the rear. A small, box-shaped building sits at the left side of the main building, where the seventh- and eighth-grade classrooms are located. The school is surrounded by playing fields that stretch to the adjacent farmland.

Oakley High School has a little over 300 students in grades 7 through 12, with a ratio of one teacher for every 14 students. Reflecting the demographics of the village, 16% of the students are African American and almost all of the other students are white. Of the 23 faculty members, 2 are African American and the others are white. On the average, 80% of Oakley graduates continue on to college immediately after high school. School officials, however, estimate that well over 90% of students eventually attend college. According to a school official, "Most of the students who don't enter college immediately after high school wait a year to attend college and use that year to travel and/or work." The list of colleges attended by graduates is full of selective schools, the majority located in the Midwest.

Most students follow the school's college preparatory program, with graduation requirements including: 4 years of English, 3 years of mathematics, 3 years of science, 3 years of social studies, 2 years of a foreign language, and 1 year of art. As part of the college preparatory program, advanced placement courses are offered in English, mathematics, music, physics, biology, chemistry, art, and American history. The school also offers a general program, which does not require foreign language or art classes. Through the school's inclusion program, special needs students (approximately 10% of student body) are enrolled in regular classrooms. In addition to the classes required for graduation, students in grades 9 through 11 are required to perform 15 hours of community service each year, and seniors are required to do a final project (e.g., video/film, artwork, community service) and present their projects to the school community.

In 1997, the U.S. Department of Education selected Oakley High School as a National Blue Ribbon School of Excellence. Although criteria for selection goes beyond test score data, the local community believes that the school demonstrates educational excellence primarily by its impressive track record of students scoring significantly higher than state averages on proficiency testing for all basic academic skills. Because the best predicator of how well a student will do on these tests is family income (Sacks, 2001), the affluence of Oakley's student body makes the outcome quite predictable.[4] In 2002, for example, Oakley students far exceeded the state standard (90% of students passing) on the ninth-grade proficiency test, which students must pass to graduate high school. Every student passed the reading and writing sections, 98% passed the citizenship section, 96% passed the science section, and 90% passed the mathematics section.

In addition to high test scores, Oakley High shares similar characteristics with other "blue ribbon" high schools in the state and even in the nation, most of which (like Oakley) are located in well-funded districts. For example, George Wood (2004) found in his study of blue ribbon high schools in Ohio that when compared with the average high school, the blue ribbon high schools in the state:

- Spent 17% more per student than state average per-pupil spending
- Had a low teacher/student ratio
- Were not culturally diverse and had virtually no poor students
- Had few special education students
- Paid teachers in excess of $10,000 more than the state average
- Had a low student mobility rate (pp. 46–47)

Given the funding of public schools by local property taxes, it can be expected that schools in well-funded districts offer a better education to their students than do poorly funded schools in low-income districts (e.g., Kozol, 1991). As Brantlinger (2003) explains, "Local control of school finance means that along with better life conditions, students from wealthier families receive a better education" (p. 13). As with other affluent schools, most of the characteristics that make Oakley an excellence school reveal their class advantage.

This class advantage, however, is rarely addressed by those in the school community. They judge Oakley to be better than other public schools in the area, most of which are in low-income areas, even though members of the community (i.e., student, parents, and educators) typically have little first-hand knowledge about the poor communities surrounding Oakley. Most parents and educators describe these surrounding communities as "conservative" but never talk about class distinctions. Only one teacher during my research discussed this aspect: "It's hard for this community to acknowledge we have [class] advantages over others. It seems in direct contradiction with our political ideals and who we say, think, and believe we are."

Even though the adults in the community seem to have only fuzzy awareness of their class advantages, consistent with other studies (e.g., Brantlinger, 2003; Wildman, 1996), Oakley parents insist on the resources it takes to ensure the highest quality of education for their own children's school. One teacher explains that "parents are very persistent here in making sure their kids get a top-notch education. They don't settle for second best. They are very present in their children's education." Similarly, a mother of an Oakley student admits, "I know the school must think I'm pushy but I'm no different than the rest of the parents in this community. We want the best possible education for our children, and it takes a good quality school with good teachers, a good principal, and resources to provide that quality." Although the parents are "pushy," they feel comfortable that "the school is providing a solid education for our children," this mother adds. She further explains, "Our pushiness isn't because we're worried about whether the school is doing their job; we know they are. We have excellent schools in the village; but to keep them excellent, it takes all of us being concerned about education. Parents have to be involved in what goes on at the school."

To make sure the village's schools stay "top-notch," an Oakley mother explains, "We make sure they have the resources they need to provide a quality education to our children." Her husband adds, "We're proud of our schools and they've consistently shown us that they know what they're doing over there. It's easy for us to give them the support they need." One important way the community has demonstrated support to the school is through successful passage of every property tax levy for nearly the past 50 years. He further explains, "If the school says they need money, then we give them money. They have shown us that they know what they're doing." Consistent with what others have documented about school disparities (Darling-Hammond, 2004; Kozol, 1991), the average expenditure per student at Oakley High is significantly more than the state's average and the amount that is allocated for each student at other public schools surrounding Oakley. These class distinctions remain ignored and not talked about within the community.

Beyond the financial support the school receives from the community, the parents provide support to the school through their involvement. Similar to what Horvat, Lareau, and Weininger (2002) note about affluent parents' level of involvement, parents are knowledgeable about what goes on at Oakley High and are integrated into school functions and information networks. The relationships among school officials and families are close and trusting; there is a genuine collaboration. Meier (2002) suggests that schools build trust with parents when schools:

- are clear about their agenda and how decisions are made,
- provide opportunities for parents to feel comfortable that the school's and teachers' intentions are good,
- allow parents to make informed judgments about the professional competence of the school,
- provide time for building relationships with parents, and
- are clear about what to do when parents and educators disagree. (pp. 51–56)

Oakley is committed to and follows many of these "good" practices for building trusting relationships with parents. As the principal explains, "We do more than just talk about parental involvement. We devote the time it takes to build positive working relationships with parents. Building these relationships take time and effort. We make sure we give that effort and time."

One of the most important ways that Oakley builds relationships with parents is by providing opportunities for parents to have meaningful decision-making roles. For example, a few years ago, teachers, administrators, students, families, and other community members worked together to establish the following mission for the school: "Oakley High School provides dynamic educational experiences, skills, passion, and knowledge needed for students to reach their fullest potential as individuals and as responsible members of the world community." Through this collaboration, three main objectives of the school also were developed:

1. To build a safe school environment that promotes learning and is flexible to individual needs;
2. To build an environment free of verbal, physical, and emotional abuse;
3. To develop a school community where members are:
   a. knowledgeable and interested in the subjects;
   b. interested and respectful of others' interest;
   c. interested in the progress of students, and the school community in general, as evidenced by active involvement;
   d. promoting positive achievements through role modeling;
   e. good communicators and recognize individual differences, which are valued;
   f. responsible, active, and respectful citizens;
   g. interactive in creating a healthy partnership for a positive school environment.

The school's mission statement and objectives are not just words on paper, but instead inspire and direct the thought and efforts of all those associated with Oakley High. As a member of Oakley's Board of Education explained, "These statements guide our ideas and make what we do at the school a shared enterprise. They allow all of us—teachers, students, parents, and others—to share a common purpose and vision for the school." It is through these objectives that one begins to gain a sense of their strong emphasis on community.

A Trusting Environment

It is a cold Tuesday morning in early February on one of my visits to Oakley High School. Snow covers the ground, creating a smooth, white landscape around the school. When I pull into the parking lot, I notice a man—probably one of the custodial crew—bundled up in snowsuit tossing salt on the sidewalks in front of the school. He is the only person I see outside; the streets near the school and the campus grounds are very quiet, devoid of people out or about.

I arrive at the school just before second period. I check in at the main office just across from the school's entryway and then head toward Mr. Linn's physics class. Mr. Linn's classroom is tucked away in the far left corner of the gymnasium across a narrow hallway from the boys' and girls' locker rooms. It was once a space for industrial arts classes, most commonly referred to as "shop" classes. The classroom holds three rectangular tables with chairs around them and a station for conducting experiments at the front of the classroom. The walls are covered with student-generated work and informative posters about topics such as the winners of the Nobel Prize in physics and the periodic chemistry table. At the back of the classroom, a door leads to another room where students have space to work on long-term projects and experiments.

Mr. Linn grew up in a little town just north of Baltimore. Right after high school, he entered Johns Hopkins with the intent of becoming a physician. His career plans changed when, as he explained to me, "I had a pretty tough third year at Hopkins, so I didn't do very well, and that made me a marginal candidate for medical school. I only got wait-listed at one school." During college, his life also changed directions when he got married, and "she was the solution to my third-year problems," he explained.

Not accepted to medical school, he and his wife joined the Peace Corps and worked in Nicaragua to promote water systems built by the government to generate income for the country to pay back the World Bank. After returning to the United States, he entered graduate school in Rhode Island to study zoology, which "was the medical school redirection," he told me. While in graduate school, he worked as a teaching assistant and discovered his interest in teaching. He enrolled in education courses and earned his certification to teach science at the middle and secondary levels.

Mr. Linn began teaching at Oakley High in 1981. He was initially hired to teach industrial arts. When he started, it was understood that he would also eventually teach seventh- and eighth-grade science, which happened about four years later. Until 1990, the school offered shop classes because, as Mr. Linn explains, "students just didn't feel comfortable going to the county's career center. It's not an Oakley kind of place. Largely because we're a pretty academic community and the career center is less so. So the school ran the shop program for a long time to allow everybody in the high school to get some experience if they wanted to." The county's career center and vocational school seem a "strange place" for Oakley students, because, as Mr. Linn adds, they "get used to this culture, which I think is influenced by the focus on college preparation and the makeup of our student body, and feel out of place in other educational environments." The school eliminated the industrial arts program so that Mr. Linn could teach science full time. This decision also reflects Oakley's increased focus on college preparation in recent years.

"We've been a college prep school for years, but there has been more pressure from the community to get students into good colleges," another teacher explains. "Our curriculum has gradually changed as the community's priorities have changed."

When I enter Mr. Linn's classroom, he looks up from his paperwork and offers a warm greeting. Mr. Linn has a calm and affable demeanor and a gift for making others feel comfortable in his presence. We talk briefly about his plans for this class and then I take my usual place at a desk in the back of the room. While Mr. Linn takes attendance, the students are milling around, talking, and getting ready for class. After taking attendance, he returns to what he was doing before I arrived. There are 13 students in his second-period physics class—a little over half are juniors and the others are seniors. Only three of the thirteen students are female. Earlier in the semester, I asked one of the girls why there were mostly boys in the class, and she replied, "I think it's because it's physics, and more guys are interested in the subject than girls. There are some girls, like me, who like science classes more than other classes, but most people who are into science are guys." I asked the same question later to one of the boys and he offered a similar explanation.

The bell rings and the students take their seats, but most of them continue to talk. Mr. Linn is looking over papers; he never begins class when the bell rings. He gives students a few moments "to settle in and to give them time to make a transition from what they were doing last class to physics," he explains. Two students sitting closest to me, Andrew and Michael, are working together on last night's homework. Michael is struggling with one of the problems. "I understand what you're saying, but it still doesn't make sense to me," Michael tells Andrew.

"You're not getting it because you're getting frustrated. Just calm down," Andrew replies. With thoughtfulness and patience, Andrew then starts over and shows Michael how to figure out the problem again.

I overhear one group of boys talking about their plans for this weekend. They are planning to go out to eat and then just hang out afterward to play a computer game that one of them recently purchased. One of the boys suggests going to a restaurant in a nearby town so that they can charge their meals to his father's account. "My dad has an account there and he lets me charge anything I want," he informs the group. The other boys eagerly accept his offer.

A few minutes after the bell, Mr. Linn looks up from his paperwork, looks over at Andrew, and asks, "Has Michael figured it out yet?"

"We're still working on it," Andrew answers.

"We'll have time in class to work on the problems that I assigned," Mr. Linn informs the two boys. He then turns to Kevin, one of the two students I interviewed during my research, and asks, "Since you were not here yesterday, are you going to make up the lab that we did in class during lunch?"

"I wasn't planning on doing it during lunch. That's when I have to eat and socialize," Kevin responds. Mr. Linn smiles at his response. Kevin then asks, "Can I do it during class or at another time during the day?"

"When we start working on homework, then you can," Mr. Linn tells him.

Kevin is well liked both by his peers and by his teachers for his easygoing and lighthearted personality. He is a junior and has always lived in Oakley. His father is an owner of a small business, and his mother is an interior designer. He is the only child of his parents living at home; his older brother and sister attend college. Before entering kindergarten at Oakley Elementary, he attended a private preschool ran by "a local woman who pretty much set up a preschool in her basement, and a good amount of kids around the town went to it," Kevin explains. He adds, "The school provided a home environment to help make our transition from home to school easier. The woman who ran it became like a second mom and even became my babysitter after I entered kindergarten for several years." He has attended Oakley's public schools since he entered kindergarten.

Kevin rarely earns below an A in his classes and has earned a few honors credits, which are grades awarded to students who achieve a grade average above 100 percent. Influenced by his relationship with a mentor who is a lawyer and youth counselor at his church, Kevin intends to be either a lawyer or a psychologist—he hasn't quite made up his mind. In addition to his academics, he is involved in several activities. He plays for the school's soccer and baseball teams and participates in his church's youth group and several school-sponsored clubs. He also works one day a week as a dishwasher at a local restaurant. "My parents think it's a good idea for me to work. They want me to work to make me more responsible and to make me value things more," he explains. Kevin appreciates his parents' efforts to have him "not be a spoiled brat and take everything for granted." He adds, "Don't get me wrong. I'm not excited about my job, but I know what my parents are trying to teach me and I respect that. They made my brother and sister work when they were my age and they turned out to be level-headed people." He further explains, "I'm young and I know that I don't know everything. I usually see what I can learn from my parents."

Mr. Linn walks to the center of the room and without saying a word waits for the students to direct their attention toward him. Except for two boys who continue to talk, he has the full attention of the class. Breaking his silence, Mr. Linn tells the two students talking, "Listen up. We need to get started." They immediately stop talking.

"We're going to review some of the principles we've covered in the two chapters that we've been working on," Mr. Linn explains to the class. "What we're doing here is following the rules and doing what they tell us to do. There is a way of working out these problems, and we have to follow the rules of the principles to find that way." He discusses three principles with the class and asks students several questions during his discussion. Andrew and another student, Trevor, are the only two students answering. Although Andrew and Trevor talk more in class discussions than the other students, they usually are not the only students talking. The rest of the class usually participates and at least attempts to answer Mr. Linn's questions.

"You seem to be awful quiet out there," Mr. Linn tells the class. He then asks them, "Do you not understand these principles? Am I making sense?" Most of the students respond to let Mr. Linn know that they don't understand. "What we need to do is work on some problems. It's sometimes hard to understand these principles without doing some problems. We need to do some problems and see what you don't understand," he concludes.

Michael asks, "Can you do problem number 53 on the board?"

Mr. Linn asks, "Is that the one that you and Andrew were working on?"

"No, Andrew helped me figure that one out. This is a different one," Michael replies.

Mr. Linn asks Michael to read him the problem, and he writes the formula needed to solve the problem on the board. He works the problem out on the board and explains each step to the students. Andrew and Trevor are the only two not watching Mr. Linn; they are working on the problem on their own. After Mr. Linn finishes the problem, he checks the answer at the end of the book and discovers that he has made a mistake. "My answer doesn't match the one at the end of the book. I'm not sure what went wrong," Mr. Linn admits to the class. Andrew and Trevor finish the problem and have the right answer.

"You made a mistake there," Trevor tells Mr. Linn and points to the board.

"I'm not sure where you're pointing. Come up here and show me," Mr. Linn replies. Trevor shows Mr. Linn where he made a mistake in the problem and Mr. Linn thanks Trevor for his assistance.

"Sorry about that. It seems like I made a mistake on my calculator," he updates the rest of the class. I have observed similar moments in class when Mr. Linn did not get things right, and his students joined him in figuring out the correct solution. He feels at ease to make mistakes in front of his students. "I'm only human and I'm not perfect, and as a teacher I shouldn't put a lot of effort into not being myself," he told me at an earlier point. He added, "I think students appreciate this about me. It shows them that it's okay to make mistakes, and when we work together, we'll figure out what went wrong and fix it." From my observations, I agree with his evaluation. Students seem comfortable with his and their own mistakes—it is a part of their teaching and learning process. In a nonjudgmental and accepting environment, mistakes are identified and worked on without embarrassment.

After correcting the problem, Mr. Linn asks the students, "Is it okay to erase the board?" Several students respond by telling him that they've written down the problem. After erasing the blackboard, he writes the names of three principles on it. Before he has the chance to talk about them, Kevin says, "Mr. Linn, I'm not sure if I completely understand the last one."

Mr. Linn asks, "Spherical aberration?"

"Yeah, that one," Kevin replies.

"Let me show you." Mr. Linn goes over to the metal cabinet next to his desk and gathers equipment to demonstrate the principle—a candle, a book of matches, a sheet of clear glass, and a 16-ounce drinking glass. While gathering the equipment, he asks the students sitting at the table closest to his desk to stand over on the other side of the room. He then places the glass sheet upright in a holder on the table. He goes to the sink in the room, fills the drinking glass with water, and then places it behind the glass sheet. He asks one of the students to turn out the lights and then places a lit candle in front of the glass sheet. With everything in place, he asks the students, "Do you see that the candlelight appears to be inside the glass of water?" The students nod their heads yes. He then asks them to go behind the table to see if the candlelight is inside the glass of water. Each of them takes a turn going behind the table to discover that there is no reflection of the candlelight behind the glass sheet. Kevin invites me to come with him to look behind the table. I get up and take my turn with the students.

As we're returning to our seats, Mr. Linn asks a student to turn on the lights and then asks the class, "Who can explain this?"

Trevor volunteers, "Virtual reflection produces image."

Mr. Linn adds, "Virtual means your brain plays tricks on you, right?" He then provides more information about why we could see the candle only through the water in the drinking glass.

At the end of his explanation, Diane, the other student I interviewed, tells Mr. Linn, "This makes so much more sense. Every time you do those experiments with us and show us what you're talking about, everything seems to make more sense." Mr. Linn tells her that she has offered him good feedback and that he will do more "showing instead of telling" in the future. Diane and the other students often provide Mr. Linn feedback about what "works for them" as learners, and he makes concerted efforts to use their feedback to teach in a way that meets their needs. In an earlier conversation, Diane explained, "We know that we can tell Mr. Linn what works for us as learners and he not only listens to us, but also will take our advice. He really takes us seriously and that makes us more comfortable to tell him how we can understand what we're studying better."

Mr. Linn describes Diane as a "serious and focused student and a caring and gentle person." Physics is not one of her favorite subjects, but she has "grown to love it because of Mr. Linn." She is a junior and has always lived in Oakley. In fact, she has never really traveled to other places. "I like being at home and don't like to travel much," she explains. Her family has lived in the same house in one of the most affluent sections in Oakley her entire life. Her dad is a computer programmer and her mother is a librarian. Diane says that her mother doesn't work for financial reasons because her dad "makes plenty of money," but rather she works "because she loves what she does." Except for two years, she has attended Oakley's public schools. Because her older brother did not have a positive experience during his seventh- and eighth-grade years, her parents decided to send Diane to a nearby alternative private school after elementary school until she entered ninth grade. She describes the school as "a kind of hippy place where students learn what they want to learn, and you get to do more than just sit in a classroom and listen to the teacher. Students have opportunities to learn the way that they learn best."

During her ninth-grade year, she had some academic and social difficulties. She explains, "It was a tough transition from a really progressive school to a more traditional school, even though you can't really call Oakley a traditional school." Since adjusting to Oakley's traditional program, she has earned straight A's in her classes. Diane keeps a busy schedule by participating in several activities, most of which relate to her strong interest in sports. "I'm really a sports nut," she confesses. She prefers tennis, volleyball, softball, and golf, but she will "play almost any sport to at least give it a try." In addition to sports, she regularly participates in service activities sponsored by Oakley and her church. Service is an important part of her life, and she is committed "to stay involved in our community in important ways." She also participates in several clubs and is on student committees at Oakley. Diane has no idea what she wants to do after high school other than attend one of the small liberal arts colleges close to home. "I think it would be too big of a change for me to go to a big school or a place in another state," she explains. She doesn't worry about future plans much because, as she explains, "I still have a lot of time to figure out what I really want to spend my life doing."

After the experiment, Mr. Linn explains the other two principles listed on the board by working out problems next to them. After finishing the problems, he informs the class, "This takes a couple of minutes to get used to, and I'm going to give you that time to get used to it." He then hands out tonight's homework assignment while telling the class, "You can work on your homework that I'm handing out. I'll be walking around the room. If you need me or have a question, then I'm available to help."

Mark, a student who frequently doesn't bring his book to class, asks Mr. Linn for permission to get his book from his locker. Mr. Linn makes a joke about Mark's regular forgetfulness and gives him permission.

Michael asks the class, "Have you all heard about the new detention policy?"

Kevin replies, "That you get a prize if you don't get any detentions for a semester."

Andrew asks Mr. Linn, "Is that true?"

"Yeah, it's supposed to be an incentive for students not to get detentions," Mr. Linn responds.

Andrew tells Mr. Linn, "It sounds like you don't completely believe that it'll work."

"I don't really have an opinion about the policy," Mr. Linn replies.

Trevor interjects, "It's going to be a shitty-ass prize."

Kevin replies to his cynicism, "If it is, then it won't do what it's supposed to do."

"Let's be fair and just see how it all works out," Mr. Linn responds to the class and then says, "Let's get back to our work."

Kyle continues to make another point about detentions, "Ms. Matthews in first period gave me a detention. I wasn't even doing anything."

"Like now. If you don't think she was fair, then tell *her,* not us," Mr. Linn says to Kyle. "Open your book and use this time to do your work." Kyle opens his book but continues to complain about Ms. Matthews. Mr. Linn then announces to the class, "If you have your homework all done, then I can take it. Not the work I just gave you, but what you did last night." After collecting homework from the students, he asks Kevin to join him in the back of the classroom to set up Kevin's lab. Meanwhile, the class continues to talk about the detention policy.

"Are you working yet?" he asks a group of boys after he has finished helping Kevin get started with his experiment.

One of them replies, "We're thinking."

Mr. Linn looks at him with one of those do-you-think-I-was-born-yesterday expressions and responds, "Let's get to work. Take advantage of the time you have in class to work on your problems and to ask me questions."

Mark returns to class with his book and then asks Andrew in a whisper, "Can I see your lab report?"

Andrew asks, "Why?"

"I didn't finish it all. I didn't write it all down when I was doing the lab," Mark explains.

"Can I borrow your eraser? Can I steal your pencil?" Andrew sarcastically responds and doesn't let Mark "borrow" his lab report. "You should have done your work. Nobody's going to let you copy their report," Andrew adds before letting the subject drop. Mark doesn't respond and attempts to finish writing his report.

Mark is the only student who I have observed attempting to cheat in Mr. Linn's class. He rarely finishes his homework before class, but instead tries to copy another student's work during class time. But no one ever lets him. Kevin calls him "shady" and lazy for trying to cheat off other students. "He's the only kid in class that wants to cheat in Mr. Linn's class," Kevin explained at an earlier point. "That's pretty sketchy for this class. Mr. Linn is so flexible and will bend over backwards to help you. There's not this pressure to get it right or you're going to fail. He's just acting shady because he's too lazy to do his work. Nobody is going to let you cheat if the only reason for cheating is that you're lazy." I asked him what he would consider a good reason for cheating. He answered, "When teachers put too much or unfair amount of pressure on you, then it becomes a survival thing. You gotta do what you gotta do." Kevin maintains that in Mr. Linn's class, "there's not that pressure to make you switch into survival mode. He is like most teachers at Oakley and is too supportive of you to justify cheating." But Kevin argues that even when a teacher puts too much pressure on them, cheating "really doesn't help the situation." He adds, "If you don't do the work, then it just comes back to bite you on the ass later on. You don't learn what you need to learn when you cheat."

What I find most interesting about Kevin's comments and Andrew's response to Mark is that students seem to regulate each other's behavior in the absence of adults. Students have a particular code for acceptable behavior that they follow for the most part. The few students who challenge this standard receive disapproval from their peers. Diane explains that "cheating is unacceptable not because teachers and parents tell us that it is, but because it's part of how things work with students. Of course, we've learned those values from parents, teachers, and other adults, but they don't stand over us and control us." In fact, Kevin argues that "[their] giving us freedom shows that they respect us, and we don't take advantage of that respect. We want to keep their respect and trust."

Mr. Linn is walking around the room checking to see whether students have questions about the assignment. Diane asks Mr. Linn for help, and he goes over to work with her. Two other students who are sitting next to Diane join their conversation. After working with her for a few minutes, Mr. Linn tells Diane, "You weren't kidding. You're really having a tough time with these problems."

The rest of the class proceeds, with Mr. Linn working with students individually when they have questions about the assignment. He does not simply answer their questions, but instead offers a series of clues to help them figure it out on their own. He gives reinforcing praise when they work through a problem and discover the correct answer. As he goes from student to student, they call out for his assistance. With gentle ease, he helps students understand the work they're doing.

A Trusting Community

"Mr. Linn is just so trusting. He trusts his students and we trust him," Diane responded when I asked her what characterizes Mr. Linn's teaching. She provided an example of Mr. Linn's trust of students by explaining, "One time I didn't have time to take a test in class and Mr. Linn said that I could take it home to finish it. He trusted that I wouldn't cheat on it. That really meant a lot to me." Echoing Diane's sentiments, Kevin said, "Mr. Linn is such a nice guy. He really respects and trusts students. Most students treat him the way he treats us."

Diane went on to describe the other teachers at Oakley by explaining, "Oakley High is a really nice school to go to. If I have problems, then I know that I can go to the teachers and they'll help me. Teachers really care about their students here." Similar to Diane, Kevin explained, "For most of the teachers, there is a very informal relationship between the students and teachers. And you can talk to them almost like a friend—kind of like a friend but with your guard up. We know we can't completely talk to them like we do people our own age. But still, we think of our teachers more like friends. They give us a lot of freedom, and trust we'll not abuse that freedom."

Mr. Linn emphasized the importance of having trustful relationships with his students when he explained his philosophy of teaching:

> My philosophy is wrapped up in being mostly a good role model, and that includes behavior, of course, that includes community activity, that includes understanding and trusting students, and that includes enthusiasm for physics. Just being a reasonable person, which I think is really important. I think it's important to give students a lot of freedom and have them face the consequences of their actions—good and bad. I also take some pride in the feeling that I'm teaching good physics. I want students to be successful. My courses are easy to succeed in, but I don't think they're easy courses.

His philosophy reflects the overall faculty's understandings of teaching and learning. He explained, "We have a whole lot of different role models among the teachers. I think by and large we're pretty good role models but we're different types of role models. We offer different approaches and examples. But we're all committed to similar goals and values for our school community. I think trust and freedom are our trademarks." He further explained different expressions of Oakley's "trademarks" through a metaphor: "I compare our school community to an atom where you've got a nucleus and then you have all sorts of things zinging around close to the center. So it may look very disorganized but it hangs together as an entity. I think if you look at the staff, that's true. I think if you look at the students with the spread of personalities, that's true. I think that's true in a lot of ways throughout our community."

The trustful relationships between students and teachers, between families and the school, and teachers trusting each other define the "nucleus" of Oakley High School. The school facilitates a trusting community through its routines and practices. The school's structures, policies, and goals express four main community standards that build trust: familiarity, respect for differences, honesty, and responsibility.

Familiarity

The small size of Oakley High makes it easier than at larger schools for members of the school community (i.e., parents, students, teachers, and other school officials) to know each other.[5] As Mr. Linn explained, "Being a small school significantly helps us to know each other well. Teachers have a level of familiarity with students that allows us to treat students as individuals.

Students and their families also know who we are because we make efforts to show them who we are." The small size of Oakley plays an important role in establishing the level of familiarity essential to developing trustful relationships. Diane added, "It's hard not to know everybody because of our size. I think by being a small school, we get to know each other, and this lets us trust each other easier. I couldn't trust a person if I didn't know them."

Teachers make concerted efforts to know their students as individuals in order to meet students' needs and engage them in the learning process. "I really feel that there's a high priority for students here. The teachers respect us and spend a lot of time and effort getting to know us," Kevin explained. Similarly, Diane claimed, "Teachers treat us as individuals and not just a number. I think our size plays a big part in this, but it's also how teachers relate to us. Teachers get to know us because they think it's important for our education." Knowing students and establishing social and personal bonds with them is one of Oakley teachers' most important pedagogical goals.

Teachers and other school officials also make efforts to invite parents into the life of the school. The parents have a close relationship with the school and contribute to the school's agenda. Mr. Linn explained, "We have a high level of parental involvement because of the types of parents we have. They are mostly educated and very concerned about the education we're offering. Parents are really a cause of the way we treat the students here." He further described family/school relationships by saying: "We have a very vocal set of parents. So we hear a lot from them. But by and large, they are satisfied customers. I think they think we're trying hard. I'd say that they are reasonably pleased. Parents are really interested in their kids getting a good education, and so there's a lot of home supervision. Parents in Oakley are just extremely vocal, and so one way to perhaps placate the parents is to consider things in a larger context than just here. I think that's part of the way it is. The parents don't let the school get away with anything with their kid."

Although the school feels pressured by parents to include them in the life of the school, family/school relationships are respectful and collaborative. As Mr. Linn explained, "There is a good and respectful relationship between parents and the school. We work together to provide their kids a good education."

Respect for Differences

With the mostly white and affluent student body and the very few teachers of color, Oakley High School's community seems homogeneous to the outsider. But the internal rather than the external perceptions of the school emphasize the diversity of its community. According to community members, the diversity of the school is reflected in the qualities of the teachers and students, who express a broad range of skills, styles, and characteristics. The school community respects the diverse qualities of its members.[6] As Mr. Linn explained, "We value the differences of people in our community. We're not just tolerant of diversity, but instead it truly makes up who we are. We're proud that we're so diverse."

Both students spoke of the various groups that form student culture, of the friendships that they have with others different from themselves. As Kevin explained, "Everyone is not running around in sync, a lot of people are open to a lot of different things. There might be cliques at our school, but everyone will hang out with each other. We let people be who they are." Diane similarly described the acceptance of differences in student culture by saying, "There aren't really cliques here. People here really don't care about what you look like or how you dress. This releases the tension that could be there if people weren't so accepting of differences. Everyone is comfortable with who they are because they can be who they are without people pressuring them to be something else." Diane and Kevin agreed that the community's acceptance of and respect for differences are essential for building trustful relationships. Diane said, "We get to know people for who they are and not for what we think they should be. We get to know people better. I can trust that people will accept me for who I am, and they can trust that I'll accept them also."

Diane and Kevin similarly explained why students respect differences and individuality. Diane said, "Oakley is a progressive town and we've been raised to get to know people for who they are and not to judge people right off. We see a lot of different kinds of people in our community and we've been taught not to judge them and let people be themselves." Kevin further added, "We have grown up discussing diversity issues. We do a lot of discussing, and I think that might be the reason we're so accepting of diversity and respect people's own way of doing things and expressing themselves." Oakley students learn both at home and at school to respect the differences of people and to "let people be themselves."

Teachers use various approaches in the classroom and select materials to address issues of diversity and the various needs of students. As Kevin pointed out, "Our teachers help us talk about topics relating to diversity. They bring up issues that cause us to talk about topics such as racism and sexism. They bring in movies and readings that help spark discussion." Both students gave numerous examples of their teachers addressing issues of diversity through materials and classroom discussions. "This teaches us to be aware of discrimination in our society and to be accepting of diversity," Diane said. Similarly, Mr. Linn explained, "Students have a lot of opportunities to discuss issues of diversity in their classes. It's one of our main goals for the school."

Mr. Linn went on to explain that teachers also address the differences of their students and the broad range of students' needs. He explained,

> We spend a lot of time revising our curriculum and thinking about the way we teach to address the needs of our students. My job is not to prepare students for standardized tests. My job is to teach them physics.

> And I do that by responding to the different and individual needs of my students. I think by and large the staff as a whole has this approach.

Mr. Linn further explained:

> We can attend to students the way we do because we just don't have that tradition of having the state breathing down our necks, because we've done quite well in meeting the standards. We're a good group of faculty as a whole, and so I think the state trusts us. This trust gives us the freedom to teach students in a way they learn best and not to teach them how to take the proficiency tests.

Oakley teachers are trusted enough to create the kind of learning environment where students learn best.

Honesty

"Most of our teachers have a quirkiness to them. They sometimes pull something out of the blue that you don't expect that lets us see how they think about things and they'll have their off days and then they'll have their on days. They let us know what they really think about something and how they feel. This really shows us that teachers are willing to be honest with us about who they are," Kevin explained. Similarly, Diane described teachers as "honest and open with students, not afraid to be who they are."

Teachers are willing to expose their fallibility while they work with students collaboratively to figure things out. By being honest and open, teachers create a trustworthy environment in the classroom for students to feel safe and comfortable enough to take risks. Students are encouraged to share their ideas, understandings and beliefs even when they haven't figured everything out. "When teachers are willing to do this, then it's easier for us to do it," Diane explained. Teachers are open and honest enough to encourage trustful relationships with their students.

Teachers maintain this honesty and openness in their relationships with each other. For the most part, teachers respect the differences of opinion and the differences in the ways they each approach their work. They are not afraid to put differences out in the open so that they can work through them. "No one on the staff is shy about voicing their opinions," Mr. Linn pointed out. Being honest with each other and bringing differences out into the open inevitably cause conflicts and disagreements among the faculty at times that prevent them from working through their differences without a well thought-out process to deal with messy issues effectively. Mr. Linn gave an example of teachers working through their differences:

> Some of the staff doesn't get along with some of the other staff, which is pretty typical. Last year, there were a few teachers who wouldn't talk with each other. Their differences had caused problems with their

> relationships with each other. It really divided the faculty. The principal got so upset with this that he said, 'We're going to address this problem.' So he hired a facilitator and set up this agenda for the staff as a whole to conquer this problem. And we worked on it for a year, and it really has helped. So we've been working on mission statements, goals, and objectives and all that stuff as a faculty group during our waiver days. The state gives us five of these days to take care of odds and ends and not see students. That time has really made us get together a whole lot more and allowed us to conquer the problem that we had with people not talking with each other.

Through this process, the teachers made sense of and worked through their differences, which strengthened their relationships with each other. They were afforded the time that it takes to work on trusting each other.

Responsibility

"They give us a lot of freedom here. I think this helps us establish our own individual way of learning," Kevin said. He went on to say, "I think if I went to a more structured school, one that doesn't give us as much freedom, then I think it would *force* me to learn maybe more, but I wouldn't enjoy learning as much. We have to make a lot of decisions about how we go about doing what we need to do, but that's challenging and keeps us on our toes." Diane agreed that the amount of freedom students have at Oakley enhances student learning. She explained, "Knowing that my teachers have trust in me and believe that I will be successful and give me a lot of room to make decisions makes me want to learn. I feel sort of obligated. I don't feel pressured exactly, but I do want to meet the expectations they have for me. I find this rewarding and challenging." Oakley students have a lot of freedom to make decisions in the classroom context and the larger school community.

With this freedom, students are held accountable for their decisions and actions. "We don't have a lot of rules and people constantly looking over our shoulders making sure we do everything an exact way, but that doesn't mean that teachers let us do whatever. We have to be responsible with this freedom," Kevin explained. Echoing Kevin's sentiments, Diane said, "We are responsible for what we do. We have freedom as long as we handle that freedom in a right way." Both Kevin and Diane agreed that the freedom they have at school makes them more responsible.

By holding students accountable for their actions and decisions, they are provided important learning experiences. As Mr. Linn explained,

> We deal with a lot more problems because we value trust and freedom so much. We have consequences for this, but we always listen to the students. I think that's the nice thing about our principal—he's always listening to and talking with kids. I think it makes it harder because we do

> trust kids. We know they'll mess up sometimes. We know that kids will be late for class, for example, but we don't give them all this disciplinary stuff like suspending them and so forth. There's no feedback to the kid with this approach. The kids never have to live with the consequences of their actions and choices. They get expelled and they don't have to go back to the same situation and encounter people who may be upset with them for what they did. I think it's a very good system here; it's part of the education. When you get in trouble, you face the consequences.

Students are held responsible for their actions and decisions and provided the freedom to figure things out along the way. Through this process, "Kids learn that some things are wrong and you shouldn't be doing them, and they also learn more about living with others," Mr. Linn explained.

A Different World

Most local communities in the United States are further from narrow parochialism today than in the past. Americans are inescapably connected to other communities not only in other parts of the country but also around the world. But this connection to a larger world has impacted relationships within local communities. Pinar (2006) observes that "screens—television, film, and, especially, computer screens—seem everywhere, prosthetic extensions of our enfleshed bodies, dispersing our subjectivities outward, far from our concrete everyday communities into abstract cyberspace and a 'global village'" (p. 19). Similarly, Meier (2004) points out, "The influence of television, computers and other technology, and the vast youth-saavy world of mass entertainment has altered the landscape of our lives, especially for children. … It's not the Big World that kids are cut off from; increasingly, it's the one at their doorsteps—their own communities" (pp. 69–70). For the most part, young people today are cut off from relationships with adults outside their immediate families. Even within families, members juggle spending time with one another with their increased job and life responsibilities in a faster-paced world. In today's world, young people are less in the company of adults than probably at any other moment in our history.

Most Oakley students, however, grow up in a different world. They have close relationships not only with adults in their families but also with their teachers and other adults in their community. In fact, most adults in the community believe that one of their most important responsibilities is "to be part of the raising of our community's children," Mr. Thompson, the president of the school board, claims. He further explains, "What people notice most about our little village when they visit is that we have close ties with one another. We know each other. We look after each other. We support each other in good and bad times. Our kids grow up in a close-knit environment. That doesn't happen in a lot of places, but it's just part of what we're about here." Mr. Thompson and other adults, however, claim that this environment shelters their children too much. Mrs. Malewski, an Oakley parent, observes, "I think we're overprotective of our children too much. We keep them too close to home. We don't allow them to stray too far from the 'bubble' that we've created for them."

Similar to Mr. Thompson and Mrs. Malewski, many adults in the community worry that students are not fully prepared to face the world outside Oakley when they graduate. Many feel that their community is too "closed off" from the rest of the world. This isolation not only has consequences for how prepared students are for life outside Oakley, but it also conflicts with the community's progressive ideals and image.

Many adults in the community resist the idea of Oakley changing in order to be more connected with communities different from themselves. As a result, this resistance allows them to preserve their well-entrenched social class isolation. They do not frame their isolation as such. The clash between their desired liberal identity and their actions to preserve their class advantages are allayed by keeping their class advantages invisible or ignored when their privilege is revealed (Brantlinger, 2003). For example, when the residents overwhelmingly voted not to support a community-wide plan to provide affordable housing to low-income people, most cited their reasons for turning down the plan as wanting "to keep the community small and to keep developers out," the local newspaper reported. Most of the adults in the community frame their isolation and their resistance to change as keeping Oakley a "special place to live," which protects both their liberal self-image and their class advantages (Ricoeur, 1986). In so doing, contradictions between the ideal and the actual are not only disguised but also resolved.

The last time I visited Oakley High was at Diane's and Kevin's graduation. Diane was planning to attend a small liberal arts college about 50 miles from Oakley. She still did not know what she wanted to study in college but believed that "there's no rush to make those decisions that will affect your entire life." Kevin also was planning to attend a small college close to home. His brother attended the same school, which was "a factor in [his] college decision." More selective than Diane, Kevin said, "I didn't have to go far from home to go to a really good school and a place that has everything that I wanted." Kevin continued to waver between psychology and pre-law as his major in college, but, like Diane, he was not "sweating it."

Like Kevin and Diane, several of the graduates were uncertain about their long-term plans after high school. Almost all of them planned to attend college immediately, and most of the other students were planning to take a year or two to travel or work before starting. Beyond their decision to attend college, most students had not made definite decisions about their future plans. From my conversations with teachers and some parents, I gathered that students were encouraged "to be open and explore their options," as one parent told me. An Oakley teacher further explained, "We encourage kids to be kids.

There's an emphasis on college in this community, and there's enough stress that comes along with working toward that goal. But other decisions can wait once they get to college and figure things out more. It's just too much pressure to force students to make every decision now." Their attitudes not only reflect Oakley's distinctively relaxed tone, but also the safeguards in place for students. As a parent explained, "Our kids have plenty of support, and a lot to fall back on. There's not a lot of worrying that they'll not be okay." Students' privileged circumstances give them plenty of leeway to figure things out and not to "sweat" about their futures. Students have the security of knowing, as Kevin explained, that "everything's going to work out."

6
Honoring Traditions

Schools are sites in which social and local values and beliefs are transmitted and reinforced in order to prepare members of the "younger generation" for their eventual adult roles; they are sites that pass the cultural and social baton. An explicit goal of most schools is to educate students in ways that foster positive, constructive social interactions (e.g., "good citizenship," friendship, supportive familial relationships). Conversely, schools can also be sites in which more negative social values and modes of behavior are taught, such as sexism, racism, homophobia, and hazing (Howard & EnglandKennedy, 2006). Within a school milieu, traditions play an important role in transmitting and reinforcing both positive and negative values and behaviors. They provide potent messages to students about who they are, how they should live and relate to others, what is important in life, and what the future holds for them.

The word *tradition* comes from the Latin word *traditio,* which means "to hand over" or "to hand down." Although *tradition* is used in a number of ways in the English language, the word most commonly refers to a custom or practice taught by one generation to another. Tradition is information brought into the present from the past in a particular social/cultural context; information of the past gives form to and guides the present through performance of that information. The concept of tradition, however, refers to more than particular acts or practices, even if they are repeated over a long period of time. Acts or practices, once performed, can disappear unless they have been transformed into some form of communicable information that has historical significance to a particular social/cultural context. A tradition not only brings the past into the present, but also reveals what part of a community's history is important enough to experience again through performance and often celebration. Traditions, therefore, reveal values of a community and play an important role in binding individuals of that community together around those values.

The present and movement toward the future of McLean Academy, the first school described in this chapter, are guided by strong and deeply rooted historical precedents and ingrained ways of knowing and doing. Educators, students, parents and alumni view traditions as solid bedrock for their school community. Even small changes are intentional, calculated, and balanced against their traditions. Traditions are strongly defended and changes often resisted. Sustained continuity of values and standards is performed and honored within this community. Its traditions are carriers of cultural codes (information) that shape students' ways of understanding and influence their actions; they inscribe the *deep grammar* of school culture that transmits (oftentimes symbolically) particular cultural ideologies (McLaren, 1999). By so doing, its traditions play an important role in constructing rather than simply reflecting the deep cultural grammar that reinforces and regenerates privilege.

The Comforts of Abundance

I begin my day around six o'clock to make it downtown in time to catch the train heading south of a large Northeastern city for my 40-minute commute to McLean Academy. It is a chilly morning in early spring. Just a couple of weeks since the last snowfall, the sidewalks and streets are still wet and grimy, and the grass and trees of the urban landscape have not yet started coming back to life. The overcast sky gives indication that it's going to be a rainy day. I board the train at the subway stop just outside my apartment heading toward the downtown station. At this time in the morning, people are shoving their way into the train packed with people in a hurry to get to wherever they need to be for the day. It is a typical midweek morning during rush hour.

A few moments after arriving downtown I board a train with a large group of McLean students who commute from the city to school every day. On my second trip to the school, I discovered that the students ride together on their commute, and I make it a point to join them. As I am boarding the train, I overhear one of the students tell her friends that she forgot to bring money for the fare. A boy beside her suggests asking Mr. Henry, the conductor, if she can pay him tomorrow. She takes his advice, and Mr. Henry agrees to let her pay the fare on another day. She thanks him and promises she will make it a point to remember to bring her money. Mr. Henry accepts her promise with a smile and motions for her to get on board. Mr. Henry exchanges warm greetings with the other students as they board the train. The students seem very fond of Mr. Henry's generous and friendly nature. During the train ride, he walks around the train acknowledging each of the children either verbally or by lightly tapping their heads and makes a point of calling them by their names. Even after he collects our tickets, he does not sit down. He continues walking up and down the aisle of the train talking with the students. It does not take much to discern that Mr. Henry enjoys their company. On my first train ride with them, he noticed that I was paying close attention to what they were doing and saying and told me, "That's the best group of kids there is. If all young people were like this group, we wouldn't have all the problems we have with kids these days."

During the train ride, most of the students are working on schoolwork; only a few are socializing. One group is preparing for their Latin test by reviewing vocabulary words on flashcards. They seem very anxious about the test. A larger group is discussing a novel. They have a paper due today on it and are sharing what they wrote with each other. They are to present their papers in class and are using this time to practice their presentations. Three students closest to me are helping one of their classmates figure out a mathematics problem. The boy who is having trouble seems frustrated that he is "not getting it." Four students sitting in the very back of the train are rehearsing lines of a play that they will perform next weekend. Almost all of the students are busy at work and take a break only to talk briefly with Mr. Henry when he passes them. Shuffling and looking over papers, going over today's schedule, and working on assignments, the students seem more like a group of businesspeople preparing for a day of meetings than a group of adolescents on their way to school. They continue to work on their assignments until we arrive at our train stop.

McLean is a 10-minute walk from the train station along a road on the west side of the tracks. This road borders a residential, middle-class neighborhood in the west section of Highland Heights. When people think of Highland Heights, they envision mostly the community on the other side of the tracks, both figuratively and literally. The modest homes reflecting the various middle-class styles and tastes of the residents and the tree-lined, quiet streets on the same side of the tracks as McLean are a far cry from the harsh, dangerous streets and gray, shabby dwellings on the other side. The east side is a poor, mostly African American urban community with large apartment complexes, several of them uninhabited, with boarded-up windows and doors, among rundown commercial buildings. The residents on the west side are eager to distinguish their community from the rest of Highland Heights.

When the students get off the train, they avoid contact with the local residents waiting at the train stop and quickly make their way to the west side. A student explained to me that they are warned by school officials and their parents to "keep away from the other side." By the time we reach the train stop, it's raining. Fortunately, I brought my umbrella and so did most of the students. Most of them, though, don't walk very far before catching a ride with one of their friends who drives to school. I walk only about halfway before one of the teachers I met in a previous visit stops to offer me a ride.

The Imprint of History

McLean's campus sits on top of a hill, secluded from the rest of Highland Heights. Hidden by wooded boundaries and gated entrances, the land belonging to McLean seems to stretch on forever. Acres of woods and open land surround the three buildings that form the school. Over the years, the main building has been refurbished numerous times but maintains the traditional and graceful architectural style of when it was built in the 1800s. Although not as old, the other two buildings on campus reflect a similar historic quality. These sturdy brick structures in the front quad with ivy growing up the walls and life-size statues of notable men, including the school's founder, let visitors know that this is a school with a long, distinguished history.

McLean Academy is one of the oldest private schools in the country. The school was founded to provide children of the local wealthy families an education that emphasized intellectual and moral discipline. Until the beginning of the 1900s, intellectual discipline was defined by a classical, conservative, and regimented curriculum with subjects in reading, writing, Latin, and mathematics. Extracurricular activities and other subjects such as history had no place in the school. As with other elite schools at the time, "the classical curriculum helped distinguish gentlemen from virtually everyone else and thus defined the difference between an 'educated' man and an untutored one, as well as the difference between high culture and popular culture" (Cookson & Persell, 1985, pp. 73–74). The school's curriculum during these early years was predicated on the belief that students needed to develop a disciplined and trained mind. Although training the mind through classical study was central to the school's mission, it was not the only priority; moral discipline was equally emphasized. Guided by Christian beliefs, moral discipline focused on issues of behavior. Students attended chapel services every morning and were expected to follow particular religious exercises (e.g., reading Hebrew and Christian scriptures, reciting prayers). The school's goal was to impart a commitment to a way of life characterized by honesty, diligence, respect, and concern for others. Students were expected to abide by these moral principles at all times, even when they were not at school.

For the most part, McLean remains committed to the mission established by its founder. The school's classical curriculum has been broadened to include electives, a more diverse selection of core courses, and independent study on and off campus. Students are also encouraged to explore a broad range of experiences by participating in the numerous extracurricular activities offered at the school (e.g., clubs, publications, travel, creative/performing arts) and are required in both semesters of the school year to participate in a sport (football, cross country, soccer, hockey, wrestling, basketball, baseball, lacrosse, or tennis). Their athletic program adheres to the classical principle that physical and mental fitness go hand in hand. "We want our students to be tough, able to withstand the rigors of competition, and willing to endure the pain of hard work so that they achieve something great in the future," the headmaster told me.

Although students no longer attend chapel services every morning before the school day begins, character education remains central to the school's endeavors. The headmaster's address at the beginning of each semester points to the morals and values that pervade the culture of McLean. After his address, students spend the next few days meeting with their advisors to discuss the school's ideals, standards, and rules. Students are expected to abide by the school's firm policies. As the headmaster explained, "If you are a part of this community, then we insist you follow our rules and we make sure we're very clear about how students should conduct themselves." Students are also required to participate in service projects throughout the school year "to build their character." Although most of the students are affluent, the school no longer caters only to the local wealthy families. It offers need-based scholarships to over one fifth of the student body and provides computers for their most disadvantaged students to use at home.

McLean has about 300 students in grades 7 through 12, and approximately 15% of the student body is African American. It is nearly impossible to enter the school after seventh grade. Since the school is committed to being a small community, and very few students leave once they enter McLean, there is a long waiting list for the very few spaces available each year in the upper grades. The school's director of admissions receives inquiries from parents whose children are not yet born and from parents whose children are several years away from seventh grade. Many students and their parents seek admission to McLean for its established reputation as a "feeder school" for Ivy League colleges.

I enter the main building on my way to meet the headmaster, Dr. Whitney, just a few minutes before the school day begins. Dr. Whitney has been at the school for nearly 30 years. Directly after graduate school, he began his career at McLean as an English and history teacher and then held various leadership positions that eventually led to his current position. It did not take me very long to discover that he wields great power at McLean. Everyone, including trustees and families, who hold a great deal of authority themselves, describe Dr. Whitney as powerful—a power that is defined by the traditions and responsibilities of his position, his tenure at the school, his professional accomplishments, and his personality. He takes on the demeanor of the headmasters who preceded him. He is uncompromising and focused in his goals, and holds a firm hand in nearly every aspect of the school. Final decisions about almost everything (e.g., operations, admissions, curriculum) rest with Dr. Whitney. During the school day, he rarely stays in his office or in meetings. He spends most of the day walking around the school to talk with students and to observe teachers. He knows every student's name and talks freely and knowledgeably about their styles, strengths, weaknesses, family lives, and accomplishments. The faculty, students, and their families hold a great amount of respect for him.

Dr. Whitney is standing in the hallway near the doors of the assembly hall greeting the students as they enter for an all-school gathering. He sees me and gives me a schedule that he prepared for my visit. The schedule consists of an interview with an English teacher, class visits, and a meeting with a group of faculty during lunch. He calls one of the teachers, Mr. Thornton, over to introduce us to each other. As indicated on my schedule, Dr. Whitney informs me that Mr. Thornton will be my primary contact for the day and will make sure I get to the places I need to be. Mr. Thornton takes me to the section of the hall where the faculty sits during morning assembly. A few minutes later, a bell rings to signal the beginning of the school day.

Morning Assembly

Morning assembly is the most cherished moment in the school day at McLean. All of the students and teachers come together for assembly every day of the week. During this all-school gathering, there is time for announcements of students' accomplishments and upcoming events, lectures delivered by distinguished visitors and faculty on an assortment of social, political, and moral topics, and performances by students. The assembly hall's stained glass windows, ornate wood carving, and walls decorated with original art work and engraved Latin phrases of classical principles mark the history and roots of McLean.

The students are seated by grade level in assigned sections of the hall, with the seniors up front and the seventh and eighth graders in the balcony. Mr. Steward, the music teacher, begins the assembly with an introduction of an eighth grader who recently won a national piano competition; he is one of the top pianists in the country for his age group. When he appears from behind the stage curtains for his performance, he receives generous applause from the crowd. As he takes his seat at the piano, he has the full attention of everyone; it is his moment to shine in front of his school community. His performance is spectacular and demonstrates years of training and an abundance of natural talent. The audience erupts with applause when he finishes. He stands to face them and takes a bow.

Mr. Steward returns to the stage and announces this weekend's performance of *Joseph and the Amazing Technicolor Dreamcoat*. The musical is part of the scheduled events of the school's anniversary celebration. He then informs us that the cast will perform a 15-minute compilation of the musical and takes a seat at the piano. Several students appear from backstage and are greeted warmly with applause. As they find their stage positions, Mr. Thornton leans over and whispers to me, "We do this for all of the school's events. It lets us know what to expect in the event and gives a little taste for those individuals who are not going to attend it." Mr. Thornton points out that most of the community "tries to attend as many events as possible, but there are too many. You only have so much time with all your other responsibilities." When the show begins, Mr. Thornton stops talking with me to give his full attention to the students on stage. The cast gives us a well-rehearsed preview of this weekend's production.

The student body president, a senior male, leads the meeting after this. Soon after he begins announcing upcoming events and meetings, I am impressed by his ability to speak in front of his school community with such ease and presence. He has a level of confidence beyond his years. "He's born a leader," Mr. Thornton explains. He is referring to the student's status as a "legacy."

Several generations of men in his family have attended McLean, and some have held similar leadership positions at the school. As Mr. Thornton continues to explain, "He's following the footsteps of his family."

The student body president announces a campus clean-up project after lunch, today's soccer and junior varsity football games, a service project at a soup kitchen tomorrow night, a sophomore class meeting with the college advisor after school, and several meetings during lunch. His announcements give some indication of the wide variety of activities offered at the school and the jam-packed schedules that most students keep during and after the school day. All students participate in the mandatory sports program, and most participate in at least two additional activities. Mr. Thornton adds, "Some participate in even more than two if they have their eyes set on getting into a top college." Although students are involved in numerous activities for various reasons, including "transcript packing" (Peshkin, 2001), Mr. Thornton explains that they are encouraged by McLean educators to find "an area that they will excel in and are passionate about." McLean provides a variety of service, artistic, and athletic activities for its students, but students must decide their own focus.

At the end of his announcements, the student body president asks whether there are additional announcements. An English teacher stands to inform us that one of his students won a poetry contest and will be reading his poetry during morning assembly next Tuesday. Another teacher follows with an announcement of tonight's debate competition and urges the community to attend. Several other teachers recognize individuals for their achievement in a variety of activities and publicize upcoming ones. The quarterback of the varsity football team calls on the community to attend Friday night's game. The students respond with a roar of cheers to his request, and the faculty politely claps.

With 5 minutes remaining, the student body president asks Dr. Whitney to come forward and then sits down. Dr. Whitney talks about the schedule of events for the school's anniversary. He explains why participation from the entire community is important. He says, "We are celebrating the long history of our school. By acknowledging our past, we have moments to understand our present more deeply. Through celebration, we honor the traditions that bind the community of McLean Academy together." He ends the meeting asking us to bow our heads for a moment of silent reflection.

A Distinctive Community

I spent the rest of the morning visiting two English classes, one for sophomores and the other for seniors, and talking with Mr. Thornton. In the sophomore class, Mr. Combs, the teacher, facilitated a lively discussion about the significance of gender in F. Scott Fitzgerald's *The Great Gatsby*. Dr. Smith, the other English teacher, gave a lecture to help her students make sense of James Joyce's stream of consciousness in *A Portrait of the Artist as a Young Man* and then followed her lecture with a class discussion. In both classes, the students were fully prepared for class, asked thoughtful questions, and provided insightful comments to the discussions. Although the styles and substance of these two classes differed, both teachers encouraged their students to participate without reservation. In fact, both teachers expected their students to contribute to class discussion, ask questions, and have their own ideas even when those ideas were different than those expressed by the teacher and other students. Students in both classes fully met these expectations. The students faithfully followed a routine in both classes and were praised by their teachers for doing so.

After I observed the two classes, I join Mr. Combs, Dr. Smith, and Mr. Thornton for lunch. We meet in a room adjacent to the main dining hall where faculty meetings are held during lunchtime. On this particular day, there is only one other small group of teachers meeting; the rest are eating lunch at the designated faculty-only table in the main dining hall.

Shortly after sitting down, Dr. Smith asks me about my opinion of McLean so far in my research. I respond by telling the group what I had observed this morning on my train ride and how focused the students were on their schoolwork. I also talk about the close relationship the students have with Mr. Henry. I let them know how wonderful I thought the performances were during morning assembly and how engaged and insightful I thought the students were in both of the classes. I find it easy to talk about the goodness of McLean.

Dr. Smith responds, "I'm glad you were at morning assembly. It gives you a good sense of our community and what we're trying to accomplish here."

Mr. Thornton continues, "It's not only a time to gather as a whole community and inform everybody about what's happening at the school, but—"

Mr. Combs interrupts, "Which is extremely important for maintaining a strong sense of community. We have the chance to get to know one another better and develop stronger relationships by getting together as a whole community every morning."

Mr. Thornton finishes what he was saying, "But it also gives us a moment in each day to celebrate the accomplishments of our students. It's important to recognize their achievements, and we do it on a frequent basis. They deserve to know that we care about all of the success they achieve from their hard work."

"And teachers and the whole community. I think it's important to recognize that students' accomplishments reflect the accomplishments of their teachers. We celebrate what everyone achieves in their work," Dr. Smith adds.

"Yes, of course. But I think our focus is on the student," Mr. Thornton responds. Dr. Smith makes a gesture to let us know that she doesn't completely agree with him, but she lets the subject drop.

I ask them, "Do you gather as a whole community at other times?"

Dr. Smith responds, "The school gathers frequently throughout the year for various assemblies, events, and special occasions. We also strongly encourage both students and teachers to attend the numerous events on campus. There's a lot going on from morning to night, so it's not expected that you'll make it to everything. But everyone keeps a busy schedule. This year we're going to be gathering more than usual to celebrate the school's anniversary. The group of people responsible for the celebration has really come up with some wonderful events and activities for this year. Even though this year is a little different, we still get together regularly. It's just important for maintaining the strong sense of community we have and the close relationships we have with each other. I think these gatherings are also important, and what we do in these gatherings, in keeping the spirit of who we are alive."

Mr. Thornton continues, "I would just add that these gatherings also strive to edify and to entertain. We incorporate learning opportunities throughout school life and continue to emphasize the importance of making what students learn interesting. Learning doesn't just happen in the classroom but in what we do throughout the school. We're a community that values learning."

Mr. Combs responds, "These gatherings are the outward and visible expression of the school's character. We are an intentional, gathered community, which means we are brought together by shared goals and common values. These goals and values give direction to what we do and how we interact with one another."

I ask, "What are some of those values and goals?"

Mr. Combs responds, "One of our foremost commitments is to the development of intellectual excellence. We offer a demanding academic program and want our students to develop the intellectual capacity for rigorous analysis and disciplined reflection. Our school offers an education that fully prepares students for the demands of college work. Our graduates attend the top colleges in the country, and we take our responsibility of preparing them for these colleges very seriously. We also want our students to have a solid moral foundation. We expect students to abide by certain moral principles."

Dr. Smith points out, "I would say that academics is not our highest priority here. It is no doubt that we emphasize a college preparatory program, but I think that we care most about what kind of people our students are. Character education is our most important commitment. We insist that our students follow the school's ideals and standards and live by its rules. We are steadfast to our ideals and principles. If you are a member of this community, then there is an expectation that you will act in a way that reflects the values of this community. It allows us to all get along and to have things run smoothly. It also allows us to create a school community that aspires to the highest ideals."

Mr. Thornton says, "We also want to prepare our students to become tough competitors. Competition is not a dirty word at our school. Instead, we want students to be able to withstand the pressures of competition and be willing to work hard."

Dr. Smith adds, “Competition not only provides motivation for students to work hard but gives them a desire for success. It encourages a strong work ethic and builds their capacities for their immediate tasks and their future endeavors. It encourages them to work on any shortcomings they may have.”

Mr. Combs continues, “Our students love competition and love winning. And they achieve at many things. That’s part of the reason we think it’s important to recognize their accomplishments on a regular basis. It sends the message that we’re not only proud of them and what they accomplish, but also that we support them in what they do. Our encouragement makes them work harder.”

Dr. Smith says, “But we also expect our students not to be wrapped up in themselves, which competition sometimes encourages. We want our students to be concerned for others and sensitive to others, and, to put it simply, be kind and caring people. I think the way competition is understood at McLean is different than at other schools. Students have to find a balance in order to achieve their goals but continue to be good people.”

Mr. Thornton adds, “What I have really liked about teaching here is that we know who we are and what we value. We’re not afraid to stand up for what we believe in, and we’re proud of who we are. And we integrate our community identity and values in our endeavors within and beyond the classroom. There’s a tone and feel at McLean that truly makes this a different and special place.”

Mr. Combs further explains, “And we have maintained our identity and what we value over the years. We have stayed true to our original commitment to academic excellence and character education. Our school community is rooted in traditions that guide what we do. Traditions play an important role in keeping us focused on who we are. Our community gatherings and activities are efforts to remind us on a regular basis and to express who we are as a community and what we stand for.”

“Our traditions make us a distinguished community,” Dr. Smith continues. “This community is not for everyone, because it requires a belief in and commitment to particular ideals and values. How many other schools have remained committed to a mission for as many years as McLean? Not many, if any. This is what makes this truly a unique school and a distinctive community.”

“Our traditions guide what we do on an everyday basis and give meaning to our actions and the overall school community,” Mr. Combs adds.

Mr. Thornton jokes, “They are what set us apart from the rest.”

We stop talking about McLean and spend the rest of lunch casually talking about what books we’ve read recently and our educational and professional backgrounds. We get to know each other more on a personal level. After lunch, we say our good-byes and I head for the train stop. On my commute back home, I reflect mainly on the incredible beauty and seclusion of McLean Academy. I find it difficult to grasp how McLean students become accustomed to the abundance and privilege that most children in this country will never experience in schooling. The everyday realities of McLean’s school life seem distant from ordinary life. It is easy to understand how people might forget about parts of life beyond this privileged environment.

Binding Together

Traditions play an important role in orchestrating the community endeavors and educational practices at McLean. Everything at the school seems to flow so smoothly and evenly. Morning assembly, for example, runs like clockwork. The routines and practices of the morning ceremony have been well established over the years. Everyone knows what to expect because "it has always been this way." Along with the morning assembly, the school community gathers frequently for formal balls and dinners, events and activities to mark the beginning and end of the school year, rite-of-passage ceremonies, and celebrations. Similar to the morning assembly, these traditions represent community and unity, emphasize order and ceremony, and reflect a sense of continuity between past and present. The school's history seeps through the everyday life of the school and is honored through its traditions, which connect the past with the present and give certainty to the future. Educators and students know their place and have particular responsibilities in making things work at the school both inside and beyond the classroom. Traditions guide what happens at the school and make sure things go as planned.

Above all, McLean's traditions bind its school community together and establish a set of ritual practices, which seek to inculcate certain values and norms of behavior by repetition. By transmitting the school's history, ideals, goals, and mission through ritual performance, the social and cultural particularities of school life, or what Peter McLaren (1999) refers to as the school's *cultural equipment*, are maintained. Traditions are embedded in particular ways of knowing and doing that help shape students' perceptions of daily life and how they live it. Traditions send powerful messages to students about who they are, how they should live and relate to others, what is important in life, and what the future holds for them. Students construct a collective identity around these ways of thinking about self and self in relation to others. As a McLean teacher explained, "Our traditions prepare our students for a particular way of life."

The traditions at McLean send rather clear messages about ways of living and doing that reflect their privileged nature. School officials work hard at promoting their elite status—they consider themselves, and many outsiders regard McLean, as one of the best secondary schools in the country. Students and their families choose McLean for this elite status assured that the vast majority of their graduates will move on to selective colleges. McLean's ideals, values, and mission are thoroughly ingrained in its traditions to promote its status and privileged identity. Its traditions communicate the school's superiority, exclusion, abundance, and privilege. The practices of these traditions keep the school's elite character and status healthy and alive through regular exercise. They "set [McLean] apart from the rest," as Mr. Thornton claimed, and remind staff and students on a regular basis that they form a distinguished community. McLean's traditions play an important role in, and provide the cultural script for, reinforcing privilege as a collective identity for the school community.

Beneath McLean's open traditions (those apparent to outsiders and discussed in school publications) lie traditions hidden in student culture. They are traditions that no one openly discusses but that are commonly known within the school community and function in similar ways as do visible traditions by connecting the past to the present and establishing patterns. As Mr. Thornton shared with me, "The students often think we don't know about these traditions, but we do. These traditions have been around for a while, and we've gotten wind of them over the years. But we think of them as adolescents being adolescents. If they are serious enough, then we'll intervene."

In my interviews with students and teachers at McLean, I heard only bits and pieces about these traditions. A student hinted at a tradition of older students hazing younger students. "We mess around with them to show them who's in charge and toughen them up for what's ahead," he told me. He talked about being one of the students "who needed toughening up" when he was a freshman, and being "thankful" for what the older students did to him at the time. Another student told me a little about a "changing-of-the-guard ceremony" that seniors and juniors go through the night before graduation. It sounded more like a party to me, with a few moments to pause for the ceremony once they "had gotten in the right mood." Both students were vague in describing these traditions, even though I tried different approaches to gather more specific information. Consistent with other studies (e.g., Crosier, 1991) on elite schools' hidden cultures, Mr. Thornton talked a little about the alcohol and drug use and sexual activity associated with these traditions. However, like the students, he didn't go into the specifics. During my research, everyone openly and proudly talked about the school's visible traditions and their significance, but they avoided giving details about those hidden in student culture. I was allowed only a glimpse of McLean's hidden traditions.

While researching at Bredvik School, I had a larger view of the community's hidden traditions. The usual silence associated with hidden traditions was broken when a student, Darren, publicly revealed an incident that occurred behind closed doors.[1] Darren broke the rule of "keeping things under wraps," which forced the entire school community to discuss a hidden tradition in public. The incident occurred in the football team's locker room and resulted in the expulsion of the first-string quarterback, Craig, on charges of sexually harassing Darren, who was a newcomer to the team. Backlash against Darren for publicly talking about what happened eventually led him to transfer to another school, allowing the quarterback to return and, simultaneously, reinforcing the tradition of hazing. The reaction of many in Bredvik's community indicates that such behaviors were normally ignored by many of the parents, coaches, and teachers who were aware of them. This permissive attitude changed when the incident was formally brought to the attention of the larger, public audience of the school community.

"Boys Being Boys"[2]

Darren was a freshman at Bredvik and had attended the school since kindergarten. He didn't really like football and admitted he wasn't good at it, but the school's requirement that all freshmen participate in the athletic program forced him to choose a sport. He went along with most of his friends in choosing football. Most freshmen boys selected football because it was considered by the student body to be the most prestigious sport at the school. Since participation on a school-sponsored sports team is required, the students do not have to "try out" to participate in a sport; they are allowed to select a sport that interests them. Although Darren took mostly honors-level courses, he was an average student. Darren was not involved in other school-sponsored activities, but instead spent his free time playing computer games.

One of Darren's football teammates was Craig. Craig was a senior and also had been at Bredvik since he'd started school. Unlike Darren, Craig was considered a "legacy"—his father, several of his uncles, and his grandfather had graduated from Bredvik. Within the school culture, "legacy" is a privileged social category (Eckert, 1989). Legacy parents hold positions of power (e.g., as members of the school board, leaders of school-sponsored committees who establish and oversee financial, social, and academic priorities for the school). Their children enjoy the status and advantages that come from their family's power; one veteran teacher reported that these advantages include grade inflation and turning a "blind eye to actions other kids get in trouble for." Most of Craig's teachers reported that he didn't take advantage of his legacy status. As his English teacher reported, "He's a well-mannered young man. He usually stays out of trouble." Craig gave credit to his parents for his choices and behavior, "My parents don't let me get away with anything; they make sure I'm in line and act decent." Craig did enjoy the status he held as a legacy within Bredvik's student culture. Legacies are the "popular" students; as Darren explained when he referred to Craig's popularity, "Everybody's always looking to get his attention and wants to hang out and be his friend."

Craig was considered "popular" by most students at Bredvik, and therefore, as Darren continued to explain, "He's high up on the food chain" of the student culture's social hierarchy. Craig was also an above-average student who rarely received grades below an A in his classes. He was involved in several school-sponsored activities, such as the student senate, the debate team, and several other clubs; he also volunteered in community service activities. His favorite extracurricular activity was football. He had been the first-string quarterback for the school's team since his sophomore year.

Although Craig and Darren attended the same school and played football together on the school's team, they really didn't know each other, because they belonged to different social groups. As defined and labeled within student culture, Craig was a "jock" and Darren was a "computer geek." Their first (as Darren said) "real" interaction didn't occur until midway through the football season on a Wednesday before a game against the school's local rival. "Of course we knew each other," Darren explained. "But it was like we never paid attention to the other."

Football practices on Wednesdays were grueling. Because games were played on Fridays, the practices on the day before a game were relatively short and light. Wednesday was the coach's last chance of the week to push his players in order to get them ready for the game. This particular Wednesday was no exception. The coach kept the players on the practice field for over 2 hours. After an exhausting practice, the players headed for the locker room.

The locker room consisted mainly of two large rooms with doors leading to several adjoining rooms for the coach's office, hot tub, equipment storage, and showers. Craig, with his fellow upperclassmen and first-string players, had his locker in one room, and Darren and the rest of the team used the other room. Not only were the rooms divided by structural design, but also by social status.

Darren entered the locker room and immediately began to get dressed. He was sitting on a bench putting his socks on when he felt a light tap on his shoulder. As Darren turned his head, Craig, who was standing behind him nude and holding his penis against Darren's shoulder, brushed his penis against Darren's cheek. Darren jerked his shoulder down and quickly stood up to face Craig. "Did you see what that faggot tried to do?" Craig tauntingly asked the group of onlookers standing just behind him. Acknowledging the distressed expression on Darren's face, Craig told Darren, "Don't be such a pussy," as he wrapped his towel around his waist. The group of boys with Craig laughed and joined Craig to head for the showers while Darren continued to stand there. Physically exhausted, embarrassed, and confused, Darren didn't respond.

After a few minutes, Darren broke his tense posture to gather his belongings. Intentionally not looking around to see who had witnessed what had just happened, he rushed out of the locker room to meet his mother for his ride home. Shortly after he got in the car, his mother told Mrs. Roberts, one of Darren's teachers, that she asked him several questions about his day and whether he had a lot of homework. Mrs. Roberts continued, "She told me that he barely answered her questions. She realized something was wrong with him and just left him alone. She thought he was having a 'teenager' moment. When they got home, he went to his room and stayed there the rest of the night. His mom said that he didn't even eat dinner." Darren's mother ended talking about that night by saying, "I just left him alone. Of course, I was concerned but had no idea that he was as upset as I found out later and was dealing with something like [what happened in the locker room]," Mrs. Roberts reported.

Darren later told Mrs. Roberts that he didn't want to go to school the next day. He thought about fabricating an excuse to miss school but eventually decided he needed to go and face whatever teasing and further humiliation awaited him. Much to his surprise, when he arrived at school, no one brought up the incident in his presence. He went on to tell Mrs. Roberts that he felt relieved by what he called "the silence" because "it seemed like no one other than those guys in the locker room knew what had happened," Mrs. Roberts explained. He saw Craig only once in the hallway, just before lunch. Craig was surrounded by a group of friends walking in the direction of the exit to the student parking lot. Craig glanced over at Darren and said, "What's up, man?" Darren didn't respond and kept walking toward the cafeteria. Since Craig had never acknowledged him previously, Darren found his gesture "weird" and intimidating. Darren told his mother, "He was finally being nice to me after treating me like crap. I just wanted him to leave me alone." He elaborated on why he found Darren's gesture intimidating when speaking with one his teachers: "It was his way of making fun of me [for what happened] and being a jerk like he always is," as one of his teachers, Ms. Smith, reported.

On Thursday and Friday during the school day, Darren didn't talk much to his friends or other classmates. He told Mrs. Roberts, "I just didn't want to talk to anyone. I was afraid someone would bring up what happened." He continued to explain how he felt by telling Mrs. Roberts, "I just felt ashamed by [the incident] and hoped nobody knew when I knew everyone knew what happened." He also didn't participate in class discussions and activities. Ms. Smith remarked after the incident became public, "I knew something was up with Darren. He's usually quiet but not as quiet as he was those couple of days."

Darren also kept to himself at Friday night's game. When he entered the locker room, he saw Craig with the other first-string players but avoided contact with him. He remained quiet as he watched the game from the sidelines, and during the game none of his teammates tried to talk with him. Bredvik's team won the game, but Darren didn't join his teammates as he usually did for the victory celebration at the home of one of the players. Instead, his mother reported to Mrs. Roberts, he just wanted to go home. Darren spent the rest of the night in his bedroom alone. As he had been doing since the incident, he avoided his regular routine and activity because, as Mrs. Roberts reported that he later explained to his mother, "I just wanted to be left alone and forget what happened."

On Saturday, Darren's mother decided she needed to find out what was bothering her son. They talked and, during their conversation, Darren eventually told his mother what had happened in the locker room. She immediately called Darren's father, who was out of town on business, and they decided that they needed to contact the headmaster. With Darren's approval, his parents met with the headmaster on Monday morning.

After his meeting with Darren's parents, the headmaster talked with the coach, who said he knew nothing of the incident but promised to investigate what happened. The headmaster then talked with Craig and his parents. Craig was honest with the headmaster and his parents. He told them that he put his penis on Darren's shoulder, made fun of him, and called him a "pussy" when Darren became upset. Craig claimed, though, that he meant no harm to Darren and that the whole incident was just "joking around."

Along with Darren's parents, the headmaster interpreted his actions differently and eventually made the decision to expel Craig for sexual harassment. The headmaster explained his decision by saying, "This type of hazing has been going on long before I became headmaster a year ago. But I'm trying to not only enforce our policy that we will not tolerate physical or emotional harassment, that was developed soon after I arrived at Bredvik, but make this a place where students and faculty are respectful to each other."

When the parents, students, and teachers found out about Craig's expulsion, the school community erupted. There was a group of young female teachers who supported the headmaster's decision and publicly spoke out against the school's long history of, as one of them described it, "keep[ing] this school an old-boys club and not safe for women or others who aren't a part of the club." The majority of the community, however, interpreted the incident as "boys being boys"—that is, as an acceptable and excusable form of masculine joking—and believed that Craig's actions did not warrant expulsion.

For the next few weeks, several parents came forward to voice their disapproval to the headmaster, and some even threatened to enroll their children in other schools if he didn't reverse his decision. The coach and several other teachers also talked privately with the headmaster in attempts to convince him to change his mind. Other teachers, mostly males, talked publicly with each other about their disapproval of the headmaster's decision. As one young, male teacher said in the teacher's workroom to a group of his colleagues, "I think what the headmaster did is political-correctness bullshit. We did stuff like that when I was a student here. It's just part of playing sports. It's just boys being boys. This has been blown way out of proportion."

The group of young, female teachers continued to speak publicly in support of the headmaster's decision to enforce the school's harassment policy in the face of conflict with most of their colleagues and students. Most of their male colleagues interpreted their support as "an opportunity to complain about our school and have their liberal viewpoints heard," as a senior male faculty member described. The female teachers were "not surprised to not be heard at this school," as one female teacher explained. She continued, "We have little say in what goes on here. Our voices are squashed by male egos." She and the other group of female teachers pointed to the inconsistency in "what they say they want this school to be about and what it really is," as one of them pointed out.

The headmaster initially stuck with his decision despite the negative backlash he received from the school community. However, by the following school year, Darren had transferred to a new school to escape the ridicule he'd endured since the incident became public and to make a fresh start, and Craig was once again a student at Bredvik.

Contested Framings

I found the reaction of most of the school community to the headmaster's decision to expel Craig surprising. As I observed discussions and witnessed people express their anger about the headmaster's decision, I wanted to know why the majority of the community was so upset. The answer to this question came in many different forms: Craig's family has a long history with the school. Craig is a popular student and a valued member of the football team. Craig was just joking around and didn't mean any harm to Darren. The incident was just boys being boys. Others pointed out that the headmaster did not follow due process established by school policies because the incident was not brought to the discipline committee to decide a fair punishment for Craig. Some others argued that the headmaster made his decision too quickly, and without seeking counsel from teachers and other administrators. A few teachers talked about the school's responsibility to teach their students "proper" ways of interacting with each other, and by simply expelling Craig without following the school's due process, the headmaster did not fulfill this responsibility.

Although there was no clear consensus of views (even among those on the same "side"), one teacher who disagreed with the headmaster captured the shared opinion of several: "It was just boys doing what they've always done, goofing around. That's just being a part of the team." The majority of the school community, including parents, educators and students, connected this particular incident to past practices and behaviors. Mrs. Roberts, a few other female teachers, and the headmaster wanted to bring about change, while most of the community wanted "to not make a big deal of boys being boys," as Mr. Hanson, one of the older male teachers at Bredvik, explained. The way that some of the female teachers and the headmaster framed the incident was in opposition to how most teachers, parents, and students framed what had happened between Craig and Darren.

During the conversations about this incident, some people mentioned similar incidents that had occurred when students had not been in the presence of adults. No one talked about them openly; rather, these other incidents were brought up in passing. Members of the community did not reveal specifics of these similar incidents, but they acknowledged that, as Mr. Hanson explained, "Stuff like this happens all the time." These incidents remained hidden in student culture, and the rule of "keeping things under wraps" was followed. Mrs. Roberts explained,

"We [teachers] don't know exactly what goes on. Kids just don't talk about them." The *code of secrecy* is followed, Mrs. Roberts added, "faithfully."

Most of the community members indicated, though, that this incident between Craig and Darren represented something bigger. It wasn't just a random act of "boys being boys" or what some considered to be sexual harassment. It represented a pattern of what took place when students were not around adults. Even though most disagreed with what they considered the "harsh" reaction of the headmaster, hardly anyone fully condoned Craig's behavior. Even Mr. Hanson, his closest ally on the faculty, believed that "he needed to be taught a lesson, but expelling him doesn't give him a chance to do that learning." And the football coach who rallied parents and his colleagues to oppose the headmaster's decision similarly understood the incident as "stupid, and when [boys] do something stupid we have to do what we can to make them act better. The headmaster just wanted to give up on [Craig] and didn't give him a chance to learn from his mistakes." Mr. Hanson and the coach, similar to other adults in the community, believed that Craig needed to be taught a lesson about how to be respectful toward others. Most adults in the school community agreed that students should behave responsibly and respectfully so that they are safe and have positive, constructive relationships with each other.

The headmaster wanted to "change the climate and culture of the school" so that "students learn valuable lessons about respecting each other and being accountable for their actions," but, ultimately, his efforts to address this one incident and to bring about change in student culture were not effective. In his response, he avoided addressing the larger issues about what this particular incident revealed about the school community and student culture. More specifically, he ignored the long history of hazing practices that occurred in the school's athlete locker rooms. Like others in the community, he followed the informal rule of not talking about what's hidden in student culture. He remained focused on and therefore isolated this particular incident from the school's historical, social contexts. By not addressing these larger issues and contexts, the headmaster ignored deeply ingrained imperatives of student culture and the school community that protected and reinforced rituals and other practices designed to communicate domination by silencing dissent or nonconformity. His response and the community's discussions needed to penetrate the surface of the issue at hand so that they could all work toward making their school community a more respectful and safe environment, as he indicated he wanted to do.

The football team locker room incident was framed differently by different individuals and constituencies within the school community. These frames reflect differing moral evaluations of the incident. Darren, his mother, and several of the younger, female teachers framed it as an incident of bullying, sexual harassment, and/or sexual assault. Many others in the community (including male teachers and other parents) framed it as "just part of" being a member of a sports team. This framing implies that the act was acceptable—or at least understandable—adolescent behavior and not a type of act that warranted expulsion.

Craig himself, along with others, dismissed it as "joking" or "goofing" behavior, not to be taken seriously. The following sections examine these framings to analyze why community members could not reach a consensus in framing the act and evaluating its moral and educational implications. In performative communications, meaning is mediated by actions and their contexts, as well as relative knowledge about those contexts. In the following sections, I examine how two different versions of framing the incident as a "joke" could have led to community disagreement over how to properly react to the incident. Then I examine how the incident can be framed as "hazing" and a liminoid rite of initiation. This is a form of rite that takes place in a space that is separated from the larger community. The initiates then pass through a transitional phase in which context and information are vague, confusing, or lacking altogether. Unlike liminal, more formal rites of passage, this form leaves the meaning unclear and final reaggregation uncertain. Although I do not consider the concept of *tradition* the same as *ritual,* the body of scholarship on ritual is applicable in exploring the social and cultural purposes and processes of traditions. Both traditions and rituals "thrive in the world of lived experience ... [and] grow conjuncturally out of the cultural and political mediations that shape the contours of groups and institutions serving as agencies of socialization" (McLaren, 1999, p. 38).

"Just Joking Around"—Humor as an Explanatory Frame

When asked to explain his actions, Craig described the incident as "joking around." Most male teachers, who were interviewed, along with most students and parents, similarly defined the act. Jokes are acts of play that are "modeled on acts that are 'not play' [such as sexual harassment], but which are understood not to communicate what would be communicated by these acts if they were performed unplayfully" (Basso, 1990, p. 37). As acts of play, jokes are not intended to cause actual harm (Basso, 1990; Bauman, 1986). In this case, the act can be interpreted (as was argued by most students, parents, and teachers in the school community) as a "practical joke," which involves extralinguistic aspects, such as performances or manipulations of objects. Practical jokes are designed to cause embarrassment or other states of discomfort in the victim. The person in control of the situation (the "trickster") intentionally constructs it to communicate an inaccurate perception of the situation to an unsuspecting individual (the "victim" or "dupe"). The difference between the levels of understanding leads the dupe to misread the situation (or be confused by it) and creates a hierarchy of power that allows the joke to be enacted (Bauman, 1986).

Humor can be used to attack others (Curry, 1998; Jimerson, 2001); this interpretation of the locker room incident as "joke" accords with other framings, such as "bullying," "hazing," "assault," and "sexual harassment." If Darren interpreted Craig's behavior as intended to cause harm, then Craig's unusual act of apparent friendliness in greeting Darren would further confuse Darren as he tried to interpret the incident the following day. Humor also establishes the superiority of the trickster over the dupe (Basso, 1990; Jimerson, 2001); certainly Craig's act reinforced their relative positions in the team hierarchy. However, these aggression-based theories of the uses of humor, although useful in an overarching analysis of the event, seem incomplete as explanations for Craig's act and the responses it received.

Another relevant use of humor is to create or enhance group formation. Jokes and humor also can be used to create in-group solidarity and make friends (Basso, 1990; Bauman, 1986; Jimerson, 2001). Social rules are suspended or inverted in order to highlight and preserve them. Bonding is promoted through "cathartic laughter" and, typically, "shared aggression" (Lyman, 2004, p. 174). Such jokes define group boundaries, indicating who is an "insider" and who is not (Jimerson, 2001) and highlighting relations of power (Lyman, 2004). The framing that the act was "just being a part of the team" and of "boys being boys" implies a belief that it could have been intended to move Darren from the status of outsider to that of insider or "team" member. An act with this intention could have been performed in an atmosphere of playfulness and solidarity while also communicating information concerning social positions and roles. In either case, the performance would serve as an unmarked, relatively informal rite of passage in the form of a practical joke. This would be a performance of aggregation that would presumably unite the members of the team who were in the locker room through their experience of Darren's disempowerment and its reinforcement of the team hierarchy. It would inform them about social roles, expectations, and mores of the group.

Darren may not have been the only team member who did not interpret Craig's act as joking or goofing. The responses of the team members (such as avoiding Darren and not speaking to him at the game) are evidence that they did not read the act as merely playful. Thus, the frame of "joking" does not provide an adequate explanation for the act. It is still possible, however, that the event was intended as a rite of initiation performed within a joking context. The next sections will explore this possible framing as a form of explanation.

Rites and Rituals: An Overview

Rites and rituals serve as performative modes of communication used for instruction (McLaren, 1999). These transmit cultural expectations and behavioral norms, reveal sociocultural conditions and beliefs, and illuminate aspects of culture and worldviews that might otherwise not come under analytic scrutiny (Magolda, 2000). Rites and rituals can be privately or publicly located;

the location affects the form of the symbolic communications within them. In both types of location, cultural meanings of symbols and symbolic acts articulate together (Obeyesekere, 2002). However, in private rites and rituals, communicative acts and the ways in which they are juxtaposed are more likely to have meanings that are idiosyncratic to the group, meanings that can differ greatly from those held by the larger culture.

When new members are accepted into a bounded social group or status, the event may be marked by ritual performances. Rites of passage mark the transition of individuals from one status into another. For example, in a rite of aggregation, a person may move from the status of outsider to that of team member, or insider. Such rites were first described by van Gennep (1960), who named three distinguishable phases: separation, liminality, and reaggregation.

In the first stage, individuals being initiated into a new status are symbolically and physically separated from their old status. They typically move to a location that is separated from the rest of the community and to which access is restricted, such as a locker room. In group rituals, homogeneity and complete egalitarianism are emphasized: Initiates are all naked (as in locker rooms) or are dressed similarly (e.g., in team uniforms), and any markers of differentiation are removed (Turner, 1967). The emphasis of this stage is on eliminating all markers of identity and status; locker room nudity would serve this function. This is often a frightening time for initiates, especially as they often do not know or understand what is about to transpire.

The most crucial stage for identity transformation is the liminal. Because markers of status and social location have been eradicated, personal identity is fluid and can be reshaped to a less individual and more communally defined form. In the larger rite of passage, participants transition from being "newcomers" to part of the group. In Turner's terms, initiates in the liminal stage lie "betwixt and between" the two social roles and statuses. This stage transpires in seclusion, in arenas that are separate from those where social roles are fixed and predictable. Student athlete locker rooms are private sites; access is restricted by gender and membership. Rites and rituals that take place in locker rooms are invisible to other members of the student body and are largely shielded from oversight by adults other than coaches and their assistants (Curry, 1998, 2001; Jimerson, 2001). A "code of silence" or assumption of confidentiality typically applies to athletes' locker rooms (Curry, 1998; Jimerson, 2001; Robinson, 2004; Walsh, 2000). This segregation, secrecy, and lack of supervision make them an ideal location for private rites and rituals that are particular to the group, such as rituals of aggregation (Lienhardt, 1961) or rites of passage (Turner, 1967, 1974, 1985; van Gennep, 1960).

The ceremony's leaders have already attained the end status or an even higher status; Craig's status as first-string quarterback is an example of an end status. The leaders represent the authority of tradition and of community mores and values. Instructors have complete authority over initiates. They can humiliate them or force them to undergo ordeals during the liminal phase, as takes place in formalized hazing rituals and performances (e.g., Guynn, 2002; Nuwer, 2004; Sanday, 1990). Their primary task is to educate individuals whose status is in transition (initiates) about their new status. Initiates may be directly instructed in acts they must perform (Mark & DeJong, 1998) or in how to perform their new role. Cultural symbols (including symbolic acts) are juxtaposed and performed in ways designed to instruct initiates about their new roles and responsibilities.

Symbols, especially key symbols, are vehicles for concepts (Langer, 2002) in rites of passage. As in other rites and rituals, key symbols transmit meaning in school-based performances. Ortner (1973) points out five indicators of key symbols: cultural importance, salience in multiple contexts, cultural elaboration, evocation of emotional response, and summarization or elaboration of key cultural values. Craig's performance included his presenting a key symbol to the group, heightening the emotional and social impact of his act.

A key symbol is considered by the actors to be culturally important, even central. It indicates a fundamental value to which others attach. In this case, a key symbol would evoke and/or reflect a core value of student athletes, such as masculinity. Football is a sport that reflects masculinized and hypermasculinized values (Arens, 1975). The penis of a first-string quarterback (i.e., the team's dominant male) is a quintessential key symbol of masculinity. It is an index of masculinity in that a student athlete would not be expected to consider a person without a penis to be a "real man."

Key symbols are typically presented and/or referred to in a wide variety of contexts that are important to the actors. The symbol might be commonly referenced or displayed in various areas specific to the group (e.g., on the playing field) or in other social contexts in which the group interacts as such (e.g., in shower rooms). Penises as cultural symbols are multivocalic and highly elaborated upon in arenas such as locker rooms (Curry, 1998) and in the wider U.S. culture. Slang referents abound, and males sometimes play competitive verbal games that elaborate upon this organ. Many of these referents and games directly refer to the penis as an instrument of power and violence (Sanday, 1990).

A key symbol is culturally elaborated: A wide variety of terms and symbols are used to refer to it, and members of the group refer to it frequently. This does not mean that members of the group see it as mundane, however. Its use is governed by many restrictions (formal and informal). If misuse is discovered, severe sanctions may be applied, such as expulsion from the community (e.g., the school). Actors respond emotionally to key symbols; the response may be positive or negative but is never indifferent. Notably, emotions are aroused that can catalyze action or crystallize commitment, including commitment to the group or a group value.

Shared Performance and the Power of Embodied Meanings

Shared performances such as this locker room performance link individuals to the group. Even if an individual disagrees with or has reservations about the content of the symbolic action, the individual is complicit in the group action and bears responsibility for participation (Rappaport, 2002). When individuals disagree strongly with the explicit or implicit meanings of a group activity or do not understand what is transpiring, they may experience cognitive dissonance and confusion (Festinger, 1957). This cognitive dissonance can prevent them from feeling connected to the group or from seeking further information. In this case, the emotions and the shared witnessing of the act committed the students to the code of silence that typically surrounds incidents of hazing and other forms of bullying (Curry, 1998; Jimerson, 2001; Walsh, 2000; Wertheim, 2003).

Craig's symbolic action of displaying his penis and using it to make physical contact with Darren added to its power by making the communication performative and embodied. This clearly aroused strong emotions, especially in Darren, whose feelings continued well after the incident ended. The laughter of the other athletes indicates that they were not indifferent to the presentation; Jimerson (2001) indicates that laughter can be a release of stress, especially after an exhausting experience (such as a grueling workout) or before an important event (such as a game against a rival team). The laughter and the failure of the others to communicate with Darren at the game also could reflect the power of the emotional experience in that their avoidance could reflect a long-term emotional discomfort.

Rituals gain effectiveness not through simple, mechanical presentations of symbolic elements, but through being enacted and embodied. Performance locates symbols within their systems of meaning and "socially [constructs] a situation in which the participants experience symbolic meanings as part of the process of what they are already doing" (Schiefflin, 1985, p. 709), such as competing for or displaying status, evidencing masculinity, or sharing a shower after a game. Dramatic elements may be added to heighten the emotional effect; the audience is engaged in the process and responds accordingly.

Craig did not simply display his penis. He performed a symbolic act of approaching Darren from behind and brushing it against Darren's cheek. Coming from behind added to the drama: His behavior could be interpreted as "sneaking up" on Darren and/or as taking the dominant role in an interaction between men; the style of presentation created sexual tension. Darren responded by quickly moving away, enacting his own masculinity by rejecting the sexual display. Craig and Darren performed a contest of masculinity, in which the subordinate backed down rather than challenging the superior. Craig's denigration of homosexuality implicit in the word "faggot" also prevented others from interpreting his action of placing his penis on another male's shoulder as a homosexual act. Craig reinforced his dominant status. Craig's status as a dominant male made his sexual gesture an expression of aggression, toughness, and conquest. Craig exhibited the sort of "*hypermasculinity* that will leave no room for questions about his athletic prowess, manhood, and heterosexuality" (Allan & DeAngelis, 2004, p. 70; italics in original). His domination over Darren emphasized his strength and masculinity.

Symbols and symbolic referents can summarize and/or elaborate cultural values. Summarizing symbols "compound and synthesize a complex system of ideas, ... 'summarize' them under a unitary form which ... 'stands for' the system as a whole" (Ortner, 1973, p. 1340). Complex systems of meaning are collapsed and loaded onto a single symbol. This makes them highly multivocalic. They reference many disparate meanings at once and ground the audience in the fundaments of the relevant system of meaning (Ortner, 1973). As a result, they are not useful for sorting out ideas or understandings. Craig's penis serves as a summarizing symbol, representing systems of masculinity, hierarchy, and relative acceptance within the team community. It therefore interferes with the clarity of symbolic communications within the setting.

Elaborating symbols imply mechanisms for social action and provide categorizations for experience. They serve as cognitive tools for ordering and understanding the world (Ortner, 1973). Because they are more suited to sorting out experience, they are less likely to be confusing to members of a shared culture. This incident did not draw on any elaborating symbols that could have provided clarification. The symbol of the penis was a "scene stealer," presented without context or elaboration. This lack of information opened the discursive space for multiple interpretations and the various framings that resulted.

The meanings attributed to symbols can be shared by the larger culture (i.e., public) or can be particular to the group members (i.e., private) (Ortner, 1973). The meaning of a symbol emerges from the relationships between the symbol itself and all related symbols (Langer, 2002). When symbols and the systems they are embedded in are private, uninitiated persons may not be privy to the private connections between symbols or their relative prioritizations and positions in systems of meaning. As Darren was a newcomer to the team, he might not have known the team's private meanings of symbols or the ways in which they were connected and communicated.

As key symbols are already multivocalic in nature, the meaning of summarizing, private key symbols may be unclear to the uninitiated if explicit instruction is not given. These individuals are therefore more likely to be confused or might "default" to the symbol's more public meaning. Athletes who have been with the team a longer time or have a more central role in the functioning of the team would be expected to have greater information with which to correctly interpret key symbols' private meanings. Outsiders (such as "computer geeks") have significantly less communicative competence with these symbols and may be uncomfortable asking for interpretation.

In a formal, guided rite of passage, a feeling of *communitas*, or fundamental community, is established between initiates during the liminal phase (Turner, 1967, 1985). Bonds formed under these circumstances create camaraderie that is expected to endure for life, even between people who will eventually hold very different social statuses. In the final stage, reaggregation, initiates fully claim their new status (e.g., team member) or have it conferred upon them. They may perform specific acts to formally lay claim to their new status, or may simply enter the role and acquire all its concomitant rights and responsibilities. *Communitas* and reaggregation create a shared ethic that leads to communal action, such as the action of maintaining silence and secrecy about the performances they shared in the bounded, communal spaces.

That Darren did not emerge from the situation feeling he was a fully accepted member of the team indicates that the framing of the incident as "just part of playing sports" and "being a part of the team" is also incomplete and insufficient. Further, there was no clear phase of reaggregation, indicating that this was not a formal rite of passage with a clearly defined liminal stage. A related framing is that the act was one of hazing; this possibility will be explored in the next section.

Hazing

Hazing is a form of initiation that is enacted between peers, without the supervision of an authority who might otherwise direct or prevent the event. Initiates engage in embarrassing, degrading, and/or dangerous events in order to prove their loyalty to the group and be admitted into its membership. In some cases, initiates engage in the process willingly. They give up status and control over the event as a display of trust in the initiated (Guynn, 2002; Nuwer, 2004; Wingate, 1994). In other cases, initiates are "ambushed" by the hazers and are forced to participate against their will or to engage in unexpected acts of humiliation or worse (Gegax, 2005; Guynn, 2002; Wingate, 1994). These events can be psychologically or physically harmful (Guynn, 2002; Hollmann, 2002). They are considered by some to be a form of bullying (Gegax, 2005), an expression of domination over smaller or weaker individuals, specifically designed to intimidate or injure the bullied individual. The reported numbers of injuries and deaths related to hazing incidents have been rising in recent years, despite an increase in the number of antihazing programs and state laws (Guynn, 2002; Hollmann, 2002; Oliff, 2002; Wahl & Wertheim, 2003).

Despite this, parents, teachers, coaches, and authority figures often excuse or ignore incidents until death or extreme injury results from them (Rodkin, 2003). When hazers are punished for their actions, these authority figures often lobby to have the punishment reduced or eliminated (Guynn, 2002; Wahl & Wertheim, 2003). When they have enough collective or individual social power, they succeed, as was the case at Bredvik.

Definitions of hazing vary from person to person, study to study, and state to state (Guynn, 2002; Nuwer, 2004). Guynn (2002) describes two characteristics of hazing that are included in all antihazing state laws:

> [H]azers direct their actions at an individual or group that is attempting to gain membership in some type of organization. … [O]ne dominant group controls which individuals they will permit to join the organization. The dominant group also controls the process by which they allow new members to join. Hazing occurs when the individuals in control focus their attention on a student or group of students due to class status, i.e., being a rookie member of the organization. (p. 3)

At Bredvik, Darren had become a member of the football team by simply signing up, rather than by evidencing enough skill to make the team during a tryout period. He had not yet, in effect, earned full membership in the group as a fellow athlete and held "rookie" status. Craig may have felt that Darren had yet to prove his intent to be a full-fledged member of the team.

Nuwer defines hazing as occurring "when veteran members of a class or group require newcomers to endure demeaning or dangerous or silly rituals, or to give up status temporarily, with the expectation of gaining group status and acceptance into the group, as a result of their participation" (in Oliff, 2002, p. 22). This definition would indicate that the event was not one of hazing, as Darren did not have such an expectation. However, the study performed by Alfred University in conjunction with the National Collegiate Athletic Association, defines hazing as "[a]ny humiliating or dangerous activity expected of [individuals] to join a group, regardless of [their] willingness to participate" (in Oliff, 2002, p. 22). This definition would frame the locker room event at Bredvik as an act of hazing.

The advocacy organization Stop Hazing (see www.StopHazing.org) defines two types of hazing: subtle hazing and harassment hazing. The incident at Bredvik reflects the definition of harassment hazing, which accords with the label of "sexual harassment" given to the incident by some teachers and Darren's mother: "Anything that causes mental anguish or physical discomfort to the [person]. Any activity or activity directed toward a [person] or activity which confuses, frustrates, or causes undue stress" (in Oliff, 2002, p. 23).

Some forms of hazing take place during the liminal phase of a formalized rite of passage, in which older peers take on the role of authority and initiates are put through ordeals (Nuwer, 2000); fraternity initiations often include such forms (Hollmann, 2002; Wingate, 1994). Other cases of hazing, however, can be best understood as a liminoid rite, a type of performance that is often intentionally similar to but performatively different from a formalized rite of passage. The Bredvik case can be analyzed as a liminoid rite of aggregation, specifically as a performance of hazing. Only one of the female teachers referred to the incident as hazing, but within the male-dominated environment of Bredvik this interpretation was silenced.

Liminal vs. Liminoid: Clarification vs. Confusion

Van Gennep's explanation of rites of passage assumes clear-cut markings of ritual time, space, and action; his data were gathered from preindustrial societies, where rites of age and status transition are formalized, intentional, and led by elders or advanced initiates. However, Turner points out that in highly secularized, postindustrial societies, rites of passage (especially age-status rites) become attenuated, and the distinction between ritual and nonritual activities is often blurred or nonexistent. In these societies, the liminal period may be replaced by one that Turner (1974) termed the "liminoid." The United States is typical of such societies; rites of initiation become informalized and take place in routine encounters, rather than in specialized, marked settings. Such rituals are less likely to be overseen by adult or other older members of the community, and communications lack clarity. As no clear meaning concerning status change is communicated, the stage of reaggregation may not even occur, leaving the individual uncertain as to whether she or he is being integrated into the group or further marked as an outsider.

The liminoid differs from the liminal in that there is no clear marking of stages, so the ritual progression is unclear. Individuals involved in such periods of unmarked transition may be confused by events, rather than edified or instructed by them. Indeed, it is possible that initiates do not even realize that they are in fact involved in a period of status transition. If this incident was intended as a means to move an outsider (Darren) into team member status, the fact that it was not formally marked as such would likely have left Darren unaware of its larger meaning, and confused as to why it occurred. The construction of the act as a "joke" by Craig and some parents and male teachers more strongly frames it as an informal event involving play, which could make the meaning even more unclear.

The symbols and symbolic acts involved in liminoid interactions are multivocalic and diffuse, hence multiply interpretable. Different actors can therefore attribute different meanings to communicative acts, both during the actual performance and later, when trying to explain and/or justify them to others (Turner, 1974). This is clearly seen in the multiple framings for the act within the community: as potentially acceptable "joke," or "boy"-ish behavior, and as sexually based, unacceptable harassment.

The day after the incident, when Darren interacted with his teammates, no overt victimization took place in the public settings. The other athletes refrained from speaking about the incident in public, maintaining the type of secrecy typically accorded to in-group interactions and to hazing and initiation situations specifically. Craig publicly greeted Darren for the first time, potentially indicating that Darren had moved to a position closer to the in-group. However, no information or explanation was given to Darren. As he had not been part of the "jock" circle before joining the team, he had no knowledge of other possible private meanings and social mores of this group. It was logical for him to apply only the meanings that his family and the larger U.S. society attributed to such actions; that is, that the actions were assaultive and harassing, solely intended to cause social and psychological harm in order to exclude him from full membership in the group.

Darren's subsequent act of disclosure violated the locker room and initiate-specific norms of confidentiality (Curry, 1998; Jimerson, 2001; Walsh, 2000). His initial reluctance to tell his mother may have simply reflected his sense of "being ashamed," or it may have indicated his awareness of this norm, despite the lack of direct instruction. Breaking the code of silence was a difficult act for him to perform, one that was facilitated by pressure from outsiders, i.e., his parents and an interested teacher. The severity of Craig's punishment underscored Darren's violation of this social more in the eyes of the community. This marked him fully as an outsider, leading to his being ridiculed and to his eventual decision to leave.

Rites, practical jokes, and other symbolic performances reinforce systems of power by reinscribing them on and through social interactions and bodies. Such systems of power can be egalitarian or hierarchical; in this case, a hierarchical system was being reproduced. Within this hierarchy, behaviors that could be interpreted as sexual harassment and homophobic were taken for granted and condoned by figures of authority—specifically coaches, parents of other students, and teachers in the school. This reinforced forms of domination and the views of masculinity of the athletes that facilitated their behavior in the locker room.

Conclusion

Like the hidden tradition of hazing at Bredvik, the open traditions at McLean, as described at the beginning of this chapter, serve as a pedagogical process for teaching students important lessons about how they should live and relate to others, what is important in life, and what the future holds for them. Both open and hidden traditions function to communicate to students, as McLaren (1999) explains, "codified messages which, in turn served both to promote normative behavioural functions and to fashion dominant epistemological frames for students" (p. 218). Their traditions, in other words, provide a blueprint for both thinking and doing. As students engage in the lived experiences and lived meanings of these performances, they absorb and adopt particular ways of knowing and doing; they are structured to think of themselves and others in certain ways. They make decisions about how they should live their lives and form patterns for relating to others. As carriers of cultural codes, traditions supply "terms of reference" (McLaren, 1989, p. 174) which students are expected to follow. These terms are embedded in privileged ways of knowing and doing.

Every school develops a particular milieu with its own traditions, whether consciously enacted or not. In the case of Bredvik, a tradition of initiation into a revered social institution (i.e., a school football team) indirectly informed a new member that it was culturally acceptable for him to feel demeaned. The inaction on the part of the school's officials—and the subsequent fervid defense of Craig—sent the message that humiliation of those lower in the team's social hierarchy was a socioculturally acceptable act. The open traditions at McLean also reinforce social hierarchies by promoting their status and privileged identity. Their traditions communicate the school's superiority, exclusion, abundance, and advantage. The practices of their traditions keep their elite character and status healthy and alive. Both open and hidden traditions at the two schools reinforce and regenerate privilege.

When messages of social status and domination are communicated in isolated and open spaces, students can learn ways of relating to others that interfere with one of the primary purposes of schools: to educate students in ways that foster positive, constructive social interactions. More specifically, these messages prevented Bredvik and McLean from living up to their stated goals for students as outlined in their mission statements and other official documents: to teach students high moral character, integrity, and respect for others, and to prepare students to participate responsibly in the world. Instead, their traditions, serving as conduits for learning power and privilege, embodied and transmitted ideological messages that overshadowed these more positive, productive goals for how students should relate to others.

7
Giving Back

In June of 2006, Warren Buffett, who was ranked by *Forbes* magazine[1] that same year as the second-richest person in the world, made a commitment to give away his fortune to charity. According to Fortune magazine, Buffett is worth $44 billion and plans to donate 85% of this fortune amassed from stock in the Berkshire Hathaway company, of which he is chief executive officer (CEO), to five foundations. He plans to donate $1 billion apiece to the causes supported by his three children, approximately $3 billion to the family foundation named for his late wife, and the bulk of his wealth, more than $30 billion, to the Bill and Melinda Gates Foundation.[2] When Buffett made this announcement, he owned close to 31% of Berkshire Hathaway, but that proportion will ultimately be cut to around 5%. Buffett says the remaining 5%, worth about $7 billion, will eventually go to charities also, perhaps in his lifetime, and if not, at his death. Because the value of Buffett's donation is tied to a future, unknowable price of Berkshire, there is no way of placing a total dollar value on his gifts. The number of shares that he earmarked to be given, however, has a value today of over $37 billion. This amount alone makes Buffett's donation the largest philanthropic gift in U.S. history. If Buffett is correct in his thinking that Berkshire's price will trend upward, the eventual amount given could far exceed that (Loomis, 2006).

Although he is part of a long tradition of business moguls giving to charity, such as John D. Rockefeller and Andrew Carnegie (who each gave what would be about $7 billion in today's dollars), Buffett's beliefs about his wealth and his opposition to the transfer of great fortunes from one generation to the next make him very different from others. For example, he does not believe that anyone has the right to be as wealthy as he is. He describes wealth on the scale he has as "claim checks on the activities of others in the future." He realized early in his life that these claim checks would have to be returned to society rather than passed down to his children. As Buffett explained in an interview:

> Certainly neither [my wife] nor I ever thought we should pass huge amounts of money along to our children. Our kids are great. But I would argue that when your kids have all the advantages anyway, in terms of how they grow up and the opportunities they have for education, including what they learn at home—I would say it's neither right nor rational to be flooding them with money. ... In effect, they've had a

> gigantic head start in a society that aspires to be a meritocracy. Dynastic mega-wealth would further tilt the playing field that we ought to be trying instead to level.[3]

Buffett goes on to explain that passing wealth down across generations "flies in the face of a meritocratic society" and threatens democratic ideals. His charitable act of giving back his wealth to society reflects his commitment to these ideals. One could certainly question whether his generous act justifies having more money than can be consumed in a lifetime while many in the United States and throughout the world live in extreme poverty. In many ways, his wealth goes against the very democratic principles that he claims to advocate. Nonetheless, his act of giving away his fortune to uphold democratic ideals offers new meaning to the concept of "giving back" that many wealthy Americans claim to value.

In protecting their class interests and power, the wealthy are confronted with a particular set of moral, social, and political problems (Weisberg, 2006). Especially in societies that purportedly aspire to equality, they are faced with the task of convincing those in low positions of the legitimacy of their class interests in order to preserve their power. As Brantlinger (2003) points out, "In democracies, dominant groups must have some degree of permission from subordinates to exert control over them; that consensus is achieved by circulating ideologies that obfuscate the rankings and power imbalances that work against equity for peripheral groups" (pp. 5–6). Acts of giving back, therefore, have considerable ideological value not only in diverting attention away from the power of dominant groups but also convincing subordinates that they are concerned for others and are compassionate, kind, and giving. Such ideological messages that place the wealthy in a positive light protect their class interests and power.

Even though many wealthy people claim to hold this value of giving back, research studies suggest that they are not as kind and giving as they want others to believe. For example, wealthy Americans give an average of only 2.9% of their earnings to charities, while those who earn an annual income below the federal poverty line give an average of 5.5% (Mantsios, 2003). Moreover, when tax codes in the United States in the past reduced the benefits of charitable giving, the wealthiest Americans slashed their average donation by nearly one-third. In recent years, with the ability to take a larger tax deduction for charitable contributions, a report from Independent Sector (2001),[4] *Deducting Generosity: The Effect of Charitable Tax Incentives on Giving*, found that the affluent have increased their charitable giving even though they continue to give proportionally less than poor and working-class groups. The giving patterns of the wealthiest Americans also reveal that their acts of benevolence do not typically help the needy. Rather than donate to agencies that provide social services to the poor, the voluntary contributions of the wealthy often go to places and institutions that entertain, inspire, cure, or educate wealthy Americans, such as art museums, opera houses, theaters, orchestras, private hospitals, and elite universities (Mantsios, 2003).

Even though one could certainly question whether most wealthy people are as committed to giving back as they claim to be, the four affluent schools in this book claim to uphold this value by emphasizing "the responsibilities that come with wealth," as the head of Parker explains. In mission statements, curricula, and school publications, they often associate advantage with the activity of giving back. Like those at other schools, the educators and officials at Bredvik, the school described in this chapter, invest a great amount of energy and time in fostering the moral and social qualities that they consider necessary for preparing their students to become civic minded and oriented toward the public good. In part, their commitments to fostering these qualities are connected to what Peshkin (2001) calls the "trickle-down" view of giving back: "provide an outstanding education to the students, who then are prepared to contribute to society through whatever jobs and careers they come to have" (p. 100). They also emphasize a more direct relationship with this value of giving back through community service and service-learning activities.

Summer of Service

It's the beginning of June, a week after classes have ended for summer recess at Bredvik School. I arrive midmorning on the first day of Pathways, Bredvik's academically intensive 6-week program for economically disadvantaged sixth- and seventh-grade students. The students who attend the program live in communities throughout the city and are mostly African American. The program is tuition free and provides students with transportation, breakfast and lunch, books, and supplies such as binders, pencils, and paper. The program also covers the cost of the several field trips students go on during the summer and provides transportation for parents who want to visit the program. Sixty students attend the program this year; half of them are returning for their second and final summer.

The program aims to prepare the students for, and to help them get into, college preparatory high schools. Pathways is not a recruitment program for Bredvik, but several students have gained admission to the school since the program was founded.[5] As the headmaster explains, "We don't intend for Pathways to be a recruiting tool for us, where we take the cream of the crop of the public schools and bring them to a private school. We make that very clear in communicating the purpose of Pathways to the public. There are a lot of good public high schools in the city, and we make sure our students get on the path to those schools." On the average, two students per year are offered scholarships to attend Bredvik, but most of the program's graduates eventually enter one of the public high schools in the city with strong college preparation programs.

The program's application process is time-consuming and competitive. To be considered for the program, students write essays, solicit recommendations from their teachers and principals, submit transcripts, and fill out a lengthy application. Over 300 students apply for the 30 positions that are open each year. The city's school district has buildings with nearly a billion dollars worth of deferred maintenance, one of the lowest average expenditures per student in the state, and a 50% dropout rate. Acceptance to Pathways promises a brighter future for students. As one mother explained, "It gets our kids out of a system that doesn't serve them. It gives our kids chances they don't get at school."

The sun is golden, the air is clear, and there's a gentle breeze. It is a comfortable, magnificent Monday morning in early summer. As I drive into the parking lot, I notice that there are only a few spaces left to park—and none near the entrance of the school. I'm surprised by how active the campus remains when school is not in session. Along with Pathways, Bredvik offers a rich array of educational and athletic programs during the summer for its students and those who have the financial means to afford the expensive fees of these programs. Pathways is the only tuition-free summer program. The list of summer activities is impressive: swimming, soccer, football, wrestling, gymnastics, advanced computer training, mathematics, writing, creative arts, performing arts, and so on. The duration of these programs vary; some of them last for most of the summer and others for a couple of weeks. Although there are some programs for Upper School students, most of the activities are designed for younger students. The majority of Upper School students at Bredvik spend their summers working at internships, attending programs and camps elsewhere, traveling, and doing things that have nothing to do with school. "I want to give my brain a rest during the summer and don't want to think about school," Keegan explained when discussing his plans for this summer. He is spending it at one of his family's vacation homes in the Northeast. Janora, on the other hand, is not having such a relaxing summer. She is working as a counselor at a camp for disadvantaged youth to help her make decisions about her future career plans.

I enter the main entrance of the school on my way to the commons room in the middle school, a centrally located open space where staff training for Pathways is being held. Pathways has exclusive use of the entire middle school during the summer—the only summer program provided with this much space of the campus. Mr. Tappan, head of the middle school, claimed, "We want the students to have plenty of space and to feel like they belong here. We let them take over the middle school; it's their space, their school while they're here. Space is really valuable in the summer because the programs other than Pathways bring a lot of money to the school. Providing this much space to one program shows how much we value and are committed to Pathways." He went on to explain more about the school's commitment to the program, "We really think of the middle school as a year-round school with Pathways, and we treat it that way. We value the program because we know it's good for our school. It shows our commitments to the community and diversity." Mr. Tappan also pointed out that Pathways is provided the entire school to avoid "awkward incidents." He admitted, "We have hundreds of kids here on any given day during the summer, and nearly all of them, except the students who are a part of Pathways, are white. ... The other kids have financial means that Pathways' kids don't. There's potential for some awkward incidents and we do what we can to avoid those problems. People are territorial as it is, and when you add diversity to the mix, it becomes even more complicated." Bredvik officials avoid "awkward incidents" by isolating Pathways' students instead of openly addressing class and racial differences.

All of the teachers of the program are high school and undergraduate college students. The program has 18 staff members working this summer; 10 of them are Bredvik students, and the others come from top colleges across the Midwest and Northeast (e.g., Brown, Harvard, Oberlin, Boston College). The college students are mostly education majors and have been recruited by Pathways to expand the knowledge base of the staff and to take on leadership roles in the program. Half of the Bredvik students just graduated, and the others will be juniors and seniors next year. During the summer, staff members teach one of four core academic subjects offered to students, which are math, science, language arts, and history. They are also responsible for developing curricula and creating lesson plans for their classes, as well as keeping in contact with their students' parents. The program provides multiple opportunities for staff members to experience what it's like to be a teacher in order "to encourage and inspire high school and college students to pursue interests in the field of education."

Staff members are paid a small stipend for the summer. High school students receive $500 for the summer, and college students receive $750. The program offers this stipend to help them with expenses such as driving to and from the program every day. The stipend is not understood as paying the staff for their work, since teaching at Pathways is considered community service. A significant number of staff members even donate their stipends back to the program. As one staff member explained, "I don't need [the pay] and Pathways only has so much money. I would rather the program spend it on the kids instead of on me." Working full-time for nearly 2 months of the summer with no pay, however, makes the staff a homogeneous group for the most part. Except for the two African American staff members and the one college-aged staff member from a working-class background, the staff is white and affluent. Mr. Tappan and other Bredvik leaders are concerned about this lack of staff diversity. "We want the staff at Pathways to be more diverse than it is," Mr. Tappan claims. "But the program has a limited budget. We can only pay our teachers so much." To make the staff more diverse, Mr. Tappan believes, "We would have to come up with more money that could serve other purposes for the program. We need more diversity, but we're not willing to take away from the students to make that possible." Pathways does have a limited budget for what it is trying to accomplish and sacrifices diversity of the staff to provide more services for the students.[6]

The teachers spend the first week attending workshops on lesson planning, promoting study skills, goal setting and evaluation, classroom management, and planning field trips and other activities. They also attend subject area workshops led by experienced professional teachers from partner schools throughout the city. These experienced educators continue their work with the staff after orientation by observing classes and providing feedback, advice, and support. Since most of the staff come from different cultural and class backgrounds than the students, they also receive diversity training during this week to begin a conversation about culture, race, and class that lasts throughout the summer. Between training workshops, there are a lot of activities planned to give them opportunities to get to know each other. The main purpose of this week is to prepare the staff members for the responsibilities and roles they will have this summer as teachers.

I arrive in the commons just a few minutes after training has begun. Beautiful patterns of light and shadow come through tall windows encircling the room to provide natural lighting for the space. Mr. Franck, director of the program and half-time teacher at Bredvik Upper School, is sitting on the floor leaning back with his arms stretched behind him. He notices me walk in and comes over to offer warm greetings. Busy writing, the staff is sitting on the floor in a circle. He informs me that they are writing about their reasons for teaching at Pathways. After a brief conversation about what he has been doing for the past couple of months to prepare for the program, he rejoins the staff, and I take a seat on the floor just outside the circle.

"Just a few more seconds before we come back together," Mr. Franck informs the group. "Finish your thoughts and wrap things up." Some of them bring their writing to an end and others hurriedly jot down a few more words. While a couple of them continue to write, Mr. Franck asks, "Who wants to share what they've written first?" Sonia, a sophomore at Harvard and a graduate of another private high school in the city, volunteers to go first. She tells the group,

> I'm working here for two main reasons. The first is to gain teaching experience. I'm just a couple years away from graduating, and I believe that I need a lot more experience before I graduate. I think this summer will give me this experience. I think that Pathways is really unique because we get to be full-fledged teachers. The other reason is to work with at-risk students. I tutor inner-city kids while I'm at school, and I wanted to continue doing service this summer. I really believe community service is important in helping me become a better teacher.

Mr. Franck responds to Sonia with a nod and smile, and then asks, "Should we just continue with Alexis?"

Alexis, who is sitting next to Sonia on the left, jokes about being the second speaker and then reports, "I've come to Pathways for a lot of the same reasons as Sonia. I think this program gives us a chance to do awesome work and to really help kids who don't have a lot of opportunities in life. I want to eventually be a teacher also, that's what I plan on majoring in in college. I think I'll be exposed to what it's like being a teacher this summer. But the main reason I'm here is because of what Pathways offers to kids."

Claire, a Bredvik alumna who just completed her second year of college, goes next. Claire is one of the African Americans on staff. She began working for Pathways after her junior year of high school and has worked every summer since then. She became involved in Pathways to "deal with" Bredvik better. She explains this to the group by telling them,

> I started Pathways when I was a student here and it really was the only thing at Bredvik that worked with people outside this closed community. To be more frank, it was the only thing that worked with black folks. I was fed up with Bredvik. Being a student of color, I always felt like an outsider here, and this seemed like practically the only way for me to feel a part of the school. Since I've been here since kindergarten, I haven't been a part of a black community, really. Being a teacher here let me deal with Bredvik enough to graduate this place. I also knew that I wanted to be a teacher for kids like the ones at Pathways, so I knew it would give me good experience.

Without a break in the sequence, Galvin, a Bredvik student and a returning staff member, tells the group,

> This makes my second year doing Pathways. I had an amazing experience last summer and really connected with the kids and the other teachers. I wouldn't trade my experiences at Pathways for anything in the world. I've come back to keep involved in the program because I want to keep on making a difference in the kids' lives. I really believe Pathways allows me to have an influence on their futures. I have a very different life than the kids and a lot of advantages they don't have. I'm here because I've been fortunate to have anything I want in my life and want to give back.

The others take their turns and give similar reasons for participating in the program. Most staff members want to become teachers and believe they will gain valuable career-related experience this summer. However, the primary reason for nearly all of them is to spend the summer "giving back," as Galvin puts it, to those less fortunate in their community.

Out for Lunch

After the introductory activity, the teachers attend a workshop on the "basics" of Pathways, which includes the program's mission, history, structure, and rules. Mr. Tappan also welcomes the staff to Bredvik and gives them the tour of the school. Most of the teachers are familiar with the school but listen attentively to the tidbits of information he provides about the school. After the tour, he thanks them for their service to the community. "You are not only making a difference in the lives of the students who will attend Pathways this summer," he tells them, "but you're making a difference in this community." Bredvik's headmaster also welcomes and thanks the staff and talks about the importance of Pathways to their school community. At 12:30, Mr. Franck dismisses the staff for lunch and tells them to be back at 2:00. Mr. Franck informs me that he needs to run errands during lunch and apologizes for not being available. Galvin overhears this and comes over to ask me to join him and the other teachers for lunch. They are going to the food court in the mall nearby. I accept his invitation.

I walk with Galvin to meet the other teachers. They are all standing in a circle just outside the school's entrance deciding who is driving and who is riding with whom. Galvin turns to me and whispers, "This seems too complicated. Do you want to just ride with me?" I agree with a nod. He then announces, "We'll meet you guys over there." Too involved in their discussion, there's no response from the group.

As we're walking to his car, Galvin tells me that he likes to listen to music while driving. He informs me that it helps him clear his mind and take a break from work. He explains, "When the program starts, I try to escape for a little bit after my classes. I just drive around and listen to music to take a break and think about what I have to do in the afternoon. It's my time." With one of those too grown-up sounding responses that afterward I wished I had phrased differently, I reply, "I used to like driving when I was your age." He politely smiles back at me.

Galvin drives a Volvo station wagon that his mother drove for a year before he was old enough to drive. The cargo space in the rear of his car is barely enough for the two large speakers in it. His car is equipped with an elaborate stereo system. His backseat is filled with scattered CD holders. When we get in his car, he proudly gives me an overview of his stereo, speakers, and CD collection. I discover that his car has more gadgets than what's initially noticeable, and he has spent more time and money to equip it with this elaborate system than I could ever imagine spending.

Before driving off, Galvin asks me if I like listening to rap music. I avoid giving another grown-up response that initially comes to mind, "I did in college," but instead answer, "What I've heard I like." He tells me that he listens only to rap and puts in a CD. During the 15-minute trip to the mall, we listen to music without talking much. He decides to play what he calls "clean" rap in order not to offend me. I tell him not to worry, but he insists that I would find most of his music "too much" and "too offensive." He takes the winding back roads of Watercrest. It is a route different than I usually take. We pass some of the largest estates that I have seen in the community. All of the mansions are surrounded by well-tended lawns and gardens and most of them have gated entrances and fences surrounding the boundaries of their property. As we ride past these homes, I ask Galvin how Pathways' students, who live mostly in poor communities, feel when they see all the display of wealth in Watercrest on their bus ride to the program. "It's really difficult for the kids at first. They feel like they don't belong here because it's so different from where they live. They really didn't know people live this way. But then they get used to everything as the summer goes along," he assures me. I find it difficult to fully accept that students "get used to" this environment that is so drastically different from their everyday realities.

We arrive at the mall, and the food court is noisy and overcrowded. The other teachers are already there ordering their food. They took a shorter route to the mall than Galvin. There are not enough available tables for all of us to eat at together. I end up having lunch with just Galvin, which gives me an opportunity to get to know him.

Galvin entered Bredvik in the ninth grade and is about to enter his senior year. His family has lived all over the United States because of his father's career. As his father climbed the career ladder to his current position as CEO of an international company, his family relocated several times. His father is constantly traveling and comes home only a couple of weekends each month. His mother travels with him at times. She spends most of her time, though, taking care of their several homes and Galvin, who is their only child.

Galvin describes himself as a "loner" during the school year. He has a couple of friends but typically hangs out with them only during the school day. He does not usually attend social events or go out on the weekends. He loves sports but doesn't like that Bredvik students are required to play them. Galvin also does not like to participate in any of the extracurricular activities offered at school. He explains, "I just haven't connected with people here. I made friends and got involved in the other schools I've gone to, but not here. People in my class like to go out and drink and do drugs. That's just not me. I just haven't really wanted to get that involved here."

He does continue to volunteer for Pathways during the school year. He regularly tutors, mentors, and plays basketball with a group of male students he taught last summer. He says that these boys are his closest friends in the city and that he "would do anything for them." He also helps with the recruitment of teachers and students, and the preparations for the summer session. He tells me, "Pathways has really changed my life in so many ways. It has helped me find a purpose in my life and with school. I've formed friendships with people who I wouldn't have known without Pathways. I think the program has given me as much as I give it." Galvin has found something meaningful in his life through his service at Pathways.

The Galaxy Awaits

It's the beginning of July and the fourth week of the program. I arrive at Bredvik just ahead of the two buses filled with the students who attend Pathways. It is 8:00 and some of the students have been on the bus for nearly an hour. The staff is gathered at the entrance of the school to greet the students with a welcoming song and cheers. Walking from the bus to the school's entrance, the students give sleepy high-fives to the staff. "Y'all have way too much energy this early in the morning," one of the students tells the staff. But you can tell by their big smiles that the students love the teachers' excitement.

The students have 20 minutes to eat breakfast before their first-period class. They sit at assigned tables in the cafeteria with their advisors during breakfast. The advisors make sure that the students are prepared for their classes and take attendance. Absent students receive a phone call and sometimes a home visit from the director immediately after breakfast. During the application process and throughout the summer, Pathways stresses the importance of attendance. "Having high expectations for students begins with expecting they'll attend the program every day," Mr. Franck explains. He adds, "We do not tolerate students not making it to the program. We make a commitment to them, and we expect them to make a commitment to us." Mr. Franck informs me that on the average, three students per summer are dismissed from the program for lack of regular attendance. Even though he is aware of some of the challenges that Pathways' students face that make regular attendance difficult, he believes, "They must overcome these challenges to be successful in the program." He does work with families to encourage regular attendance but maintains that it is not the program's responsibility to make sure that students attend.

By the end of breakfast, most of the students are wide awake and full of adolescent energy. Mr. Franck stands near the entrance of the cafeteria and raises his right hand in the air, which is a gesture for teachers and students to raise their hands and be silent. It takes only a few seconds from the time he raises his hand for the cafeteria to become a quiet place. With a sea of hands in the air and all eyes directed at Mr. Franck, he announces that it is time for first period and asks them to clean up their tables. The students finish cleaning their tables, grab their belongings, and head to class.

The commons looks very different than it did during staff orientation. The walls are decorated with artwork produced by students and teachers. Two large murals on taped-together long sheets of paper hang from the ceiling on opposite ends of the room. One is a painting of the city's downtown area with "Welcome to Pathways City" across the top. The other portrays outer space with "The Galaxy Awaits" across the center, which I later find out is the theme for this summer.

During orientation week, the teachers select a theme for the field trips, activities in and out of classes, and decorations. During the program, the students visit a planetarium, attend a teleconference with astronauts who are traveling in space, decorate the school with pictures and projects about outer space, and read and write about astronomical topics. The theme is also used symbolically "to send students the message that they have tons of opportunities in life," according to Galvin. During the summer, the students hear motivational and personal presentations about overcoming obstacles in life, visit local colleges, attend workshops on financial aid and the college admission process, and shadow a professional for a day. The students are informed of the possibilities awaiting them.

During first period, I observe Galvin's seventh-grade writing and reading class. He has seven students in his class, two students less than the average class size at Pathways. The program keeps the class size small so that students receive a lot of individual attention and to encourage hands-on learning. By the time the bell rings for first period, all the students are seated at their desks, have turned in their homework, and are ready to begin class. Following Bredvik's guidelines for homework, the students at Pathways have 30 minutes of homework every night for each of their four academic classes. Galvin tells me that the students frequently complain about the amount of homework, but most of them complete all their assignments on time. As with attendance, students are required to complete their homework to stay in the program. Over the weekend for Galvin's class, students read a short story about traveling in space and wrote a short response to the story.

Galvin begins his lesson by telling the students, "Today, we're going on a journey. I want everyone to clear your desks, close your eyes, and get comfortable. Feel free to lie down on the floor or put your heads down on your desks." While the students are following his instructions, he turns out the lights and lowers the window shades.

When the room is dark, a male students jokes, "I'm getting scared."

Galvin smiles at the student and playfully reassures him. He then asks the class if they are ready and waits for them to focus on the activity. They settle down and Galvin continues, "I want you to listen very carefully to what I'm about to tell you to do, and imagine yourself going on a journey." He looks around the room to make sure that students are paying attention and listening to his instruction before he continues. After a brief pause, he goes on,

> You're at your house in your bedroom. You go throughout the house just looking at what's around you. You then go out the front door and step outside. Once you're outside, you begin to float in the air. At first you're not too far from the ground, but then you start to go higher and

> higher. As you travel upwards, you can see your house, then your neighborhood, then the entire city, and then an area that spans several cities and towns. You keep going upwards and now you're in space. You look down and can see our entire planet. You see the shapes of the continents separated by the oceans. You travel in space for a while until you come to the small planet many miles from Earth.

Galvin continues with a detailed description of the planet and then verbally guides the students on a journey back home. He turns the lights on and raises the shades. "You can open your eyes now," he tells the students. He then asks them to prepare for a writing assignment.

For the remaining 10 minutes of class, the students write a story about their journey. For homework, Galvin asks them to draw a picture of their planet and to finish their papers. He gives each of the students a new packet of markers and paper to use for their drawing assignment tonight. After class, I find out that he bought these supplies with his own money. He tells me, "I know that some of the kids have these supplies at home, but I also know that some don't. I just want to make sure that everyone has what they need to complete the homework I assign." Aware of the program's limited budget for school supplies, Galvin purchases most of the supplies that he uses as a teacher. He explains, "I don't want to take money from the program that could be used on other things." He informs me that most of the teachers do the same.

During second period, I visit Claire's sixth-grade writing and reading class. Before class, a group of students are gathered around Claire in front of the room talking about their upcoming field trip. Bidding for her attention, several students are asking Claire questions at the same time. With patience and warmth, Claire tries to answer them all. When the bell rings, the students go to their desks and get ready to begin class.

"When I was really little," Claire begins the class, "I loved to watch cartoons on Saturday morning. How many of us love cartoons?" The students enthusiastically answer to let her know that they share her interest. The students then begin to name their favorite cartoons and characters. Claire interrupts them and continues, "I still watch cartoons."

"You're too old," one of the students insists.

"Hey, hey, watch it now," she chides the student. "I'm not too old. You never get too old. That's what people try to convince you of, but I don't listen to them." Claire finds this a teachable moment to tell her students that they should feel comfortable being themselves.

"But you can't always do what you want," a student questions her advice.

"You're right. You have to determine when you have to do what other people say and when it's okay for you to be yourself. What I'm trying to say is that you should try to be yourself as much as possible, and don't worry about what other people think," she responds.

"You're talking about peer pressure," a student tells Claire.

"That's part of it. But I'm also talking about not letting people hold you down," she tells them. The students are listening carefully to what Claire is telling them. They seem to appreciate what she's saying. Claire says that she tries hard to find moments to give her students lessons about life. "I'm trying to help them not just to become better writers and readers, but also better overall human beings who feel good about themselves and are more confident," she explains. Claire believes that her students aren't given enough advice about how to be successful in school, which she sees as one her most important responsibilities at Pathways.

She continues with her lesson by saying, "Let's get back to cartoons. Even though I love cartoons, I really, really loved it when *Schoolhouse Rock* came on. How many of you have seen one of the *Schoolhouse Rock* cartoons?" Initially, the students say that they don't know the program. Claire explains what she's referring to and almost all of them have seen at least one of the cartoons. One of the students tells her that those are "old-school cartoons." She responds, "You guys are making me feel like I'm fifty years old or something."

Claire tells the students that the ones about grammar are her favorites. She sings the first few lines of the one about conjunctions. "Conjunction Junction / What's your function? / Hooking up words and phrases and clauses," she sings while dancing around the room.

"You're crazy, Claire," one student comments.

"You're right, I am," Claire replies. "I'm being myself and not holding back. Be crazy with me." She then continues dancing and singing the first few lines of several of the songs. Claire invites them to get out of their seats and join her, but the students inform her that they don't know the words of the song. "It's not as fun dancing by myself, so I guess I'll stop," she tells them. Several of the students urge her to continue, but Claire informs them that she will later, when they are working on a skit that they will perform for all the students and staff.

Claire hands out the lyrics to the grammar songs and tells the students that they are going to watch the cartoons on adverbs, adjectives, conjunctions, and interjections. They gather around the television to watch the video. Claire sings along with the video and encourages students to read the lyrics as the songs are playing. One student asks me if I know the song about adverbs that is playing on the video, and I tell him that I do. "I love *Schoolhouse Rock* about as much as Claire," I tell the students. Claire then invites me to join them on the floor and one student asks me to sit next to her. She shares her handout with me so that I can sing along with them.

After the video, Claire talks more about the skit she mentioned earlier. She tells the students that they are going to develop a skit using one of the grammar songs and perform it tomorrow at the all-school meeting. The students are excited about the assignment. They choose the song on interjections. "That one has a lot to work with," one student points out.

Claire and her students ask me to come back tomorrow and do the skit with them. I tell them that I'll be there and join them in their group work. Even as a visitor, it's hard not to get involved in Claire's class. She creates an exciting environment that engages you in the activities. Claire also points out, "Here everyone participates in what we're doing, even visitors." We work on the skit until class ends. "Eeeeeek!" is my word in the skit tomorrow. My homework is to come up with ideas for acting out my word to share with the class.

The students attend two other academic classes in the morning. Between second and third period, the students and teachers gather together for an all-school meeting, a time for announcements and skits about what students are learning in their classes. Students and teachers spend the 20 minutes of this meeting celebrating each other's accomplishments and learning. After lunch, students meet with their advisors for 50 minutes to learn study and test-taking skills and to discuss a variety of issues relating to their lives. Teachers use this time to surface and then address some of the problems that students face in their lives and to help students build skills to overcome them. After meeting with their advisors, the students attend two elective classes (e.g., architecture, African American history, drama, creative writing, art) and then spend the last 40 minutes of the day participating in an assortment of activities, such as playing sports and games. Their favorite activity at the end of the day is swimming in Bredvik's huge, indoor pool. A few of the students use this time to work on their homework. Students who did not complete their homework meet with Mr. Franck during this time to discuss their reasons for not completing their assignments. At the end of their meeting, Mr. Franck establishes a "contract" with students for completing homework assignments on time. At 3:15, the students board buses to go home. As students get on the buses, the teachers send students off with the same displays of excitement as when students arrived to the program. After students leave, the teachers go back inside for meetings to plan the next day. They still have over 2 hours of work to accomplish before they call it a day.

Resistance

Although Claire and Galvin share the desire and the sense of obligation to give back as other participants in the program, their other reasons for involvement in service stand out from the rest. Most of the students participate in the program as a way to demonstrate to others their commitment to service and to gain a rich array of work experience. The high school students are interested in demonstrating this commitment to service and in acquiring work experience to help them gain admission to college. Similarly, participation in Pathways for the college students is beneficial for working toward entry into graduate school or a career. Even though the participants emphasize the amicable reasons for their service (i.e., to give back), they reap particular benefits through their involvement in Pathways, and these perks certainly influenced their decision to participate in the program.

Claire and Galvin seem not very focused on these perks. They are, of course, aware that involvement in Pathways "looks good on college applications and gives me some clue what it means to be a teacher," Galvin explains.. He claims though that "I'm not here for those reasons. I could have done a lot of things that take less time and a whole lot less effort if all that I wanted was something that looked good on my application." Claire similarly explains, "I'm just not interested in the superficial benefits that you get from being here." Unlike others in the program, Claire and Galvin are committed to the idea of stepping outside and resisting privileged ways of knowing and doing. It is through their involvement that they attempt to construct and negotiate a sense of self that resists privilege. The program provides them an alternative cultural and social context to the ones in their lives that reinforce and regenerate privilege.

Resistance has been theorized elaborately by several scholars (e.g., Giroux, 1983a, 1983b; McFadden, 1995; McRobbie, 1991). In this body of work, resistance theorists have recognized "the ways in which both individuals and classes assert their own experiences and contest or resist the ideological and material forces imposed upon them in a variety of settings … [and] the ways in which both teachers and students in schools produce meaning and culture through their own resistance and their own individual and collective consciousness" (Weiler, 1988, p. 11). These theorists contend that "people forge their own meaning systems in response to the societal position they face and its material implications" (Holland & Eisenhart, 1990, p. 32). For example, Giroux (1983a) argues that it is crucial "to understand more thoroughly the complex ways in which people mediate and respond to the interface between their own lived experiences and structures of domination and constraint" (p. 108). In examining anthropological studies of schools and classrooms to develop a theory of resistance, Giroux found that poor students often behaved "badly" as an expression of resistance. Students knew, at some level, that the way their schools responded to them limited their life chances. Therefore, their resistance to this injustice, in Giroux's view, can be considered as healthy rebellion against an oppressive system because their response is rooted in "moral and political indignation" (Giroux 1983b, p. 289), not individual psychological problems such as lack of self-discipline and laziness. Giroux insists that oppositional behavior be critically examined and that resistance be mined for its broader significance.

One of the studies that Giroux examines in developing his theory of resistance, and one of the most seminal studies on resistance (see Dolby & Dimitriadis, 2004), is the work of Paul Willis (1977). In his examination of schooling practices and students' resistance to them, Willis demonstrates how lived culture contributes to the shaping of the structures of power and privilege, yet how these structures conclusively determine individuals' roles and experiences. In his study, Willis finds a major division between students. Most students in his study are the "ear'oles" who comply with the rules and norms of the school. Willis, however, directs almost all his attention to understanding the counterculture of the "lads" who reject the school's achievement ideology, subvert authority, disrupt classes, and mock the "ear'oles." Willis found that the lads use whatever means possible to display open opposition to school.

According to Willis (1977), their resistance to school is partly the result of some insights into the economic condition of their social class. The lads believe that their chances for significant upward mobility are remote and, therefore, conforming to school norms is pointless. As MacLeod (1987) explains, "The lads repudiate schooling because they realize that most available work is essentially meaningless and that although individuals are capable of 'making it,' conformism for their group or class promises no rewards" (p. 17). Within a capitalist society that values, among other things, formal education and class-based control, Willis claims that working-class groups' cultural attitudes and practices are not necessarily reflective of structural determinations or dominant ideologies. Although the mode of production powerfully influences individuals' ways of knowing and doing, they do not simply respond to forces bearing down on them with passivity and indifference. Their response is often marked by contestation, resistance, and compromise. According to Willis, subordinate groups can produce alternative cultural forms with meanings relating to their own cultural sphere. As Weiler (1988) explains, "Individuals are not simply acted upon by abstract 'structures' but negotiate, struggle, and create meaning on their own" (p. 21). This active and transformative process has the potential to catalyze class solidarity and collective action. Nevertheless, despite their resistance, the lads' rebellion against school rules and activities ultimately reinforces their oppressed positions. The potential of these cultural penetrations are limited by the lads' acceptance of their subordinate economic fate.

Although some have argued that resistance "is not a working-class specialty," (Bernstein, 1994, p. 104), the focus of the literature on resistance to this point has been almost entirely on oppressed groups and their resistance to the status quo. As Alpert (1991) points out, "Research on resistance seems to ignore less overt resistant phenomena that appear routinely in the daily lives of students and teachers who come from the same social-cultural groups" (p. 350). Some have argued that this focus makes resistance more about understanding failure than understanding students' conscious resistance to the dominant ideology of society (e.g., McFadden, 1995). Galvin and Claire's conscious efforts to resist the cultural processes that regenerate and reinforce privilege, therefore, provide an opportunity to extend the scope of this scholarship.[7] This is not to suggest that affluent students face the same consequences for their resistance as members of oppressed groups. For example, Aggleton (1987) found that middle-class students who resisted schooling continued to enjoy advantages in the labor market. Aggleton's middle-class resisters did not face the same consequences as the lads in Willis' study; that is, their aspirations were not leveled by their acts of resistance. Similarly, resistance does not lead to failure for Galvin and Claire, as research on resistance has demonstrated that it does most often for working-class children. Even though they experience problems at Bredvik, both of them are successful. As Alpert (1991) found in his study of resistance in affluent suburban high schools, students "conform to educational expectations and are actively engaged in achieving academic success" (p. 350). Claire entered college directly after graduating from Bredvik with no problems, and Galvin has gathered the necessary credentials to gain acceptance to a selective college. However, as with oppressed groups, their expressions of resistance result from cultural penetrations into unjust conditions and a response to domination.

Outsider Status

Both Claire and Galvin describe themselves as "outsiders" within Bredvik's community. Claire explains that when she was a student at Bredvik, she "never fit in with others." Similar to what others have pointed out about the experiences of African Americans at predominantly white academic institutions, Claire remained an "outsider within" (Collins, 1986), even though she had been a student at Bredvik for 13 years. Claire explains, "Being practically the only black person in school for 13 years makes you stand out from everybody. You never quite fit in no matter what. It doesn't matter who your family is, how much money you have, or if you have all the right stuff to fit in—you still don't." Since her family is wealthy, she never experienced the double marginalization (i.e., class and race) that many have focused on in the literature (e.g., Cookson & Persell, 1991). Her shared class status with others at Bredvik, however, did not equate acceptance. Race functioned to influence her school experiences at Bredvik even though her family is wealthy and she describes herself as the "whitest black girl you'll ever meet." She further explains, "They always saw me as different. No matter how much I acted like [a white person], I was still black. I was always on the fringes at Bredvik."

The social stigma of acting white has been addressed in great detail (Bergin & Cooks, 2002; Spencer, Noll, & Stolzfus, 2001). However, similar to what Gayles (2005) found with high-achieving African American males, Claire seemed not impacted by the notion of acting white. Even though she acknowledges that she expressed behaviors characteristic of whites (Fordham & Ogbu, 1986), she claims, "I didn't *try* to [act white], but it was unavoidable. I was doomed to act like the people I have been around most in my life." She believes that her actions, behaviors, and outlook on life have been profoundly influenced by "growing up in a white world." She further explains, "I read in one of my [education] courses that black students at white schools act white to be successful. That really wasn't my experience. Except for my family, of course,

I have only been around white people. We live in a white neighborhood. I've been at white schools. My whole world is white. … It's all that I know. It wasn't a matter of acting; it was just who I am." She claims that race is typically not a major factor in her life as it was at Bredvik. She explains that her family is "accepted more in other places. Call it 'color blindness' or whatever, but we're not treated differently elsewhere; it's very unique, at least for us, with the people at Bredvik. Maybe they're more racist. I don't think so, but they certainly had some issues [with race]."

Even though she was relegated to the status of different/outsider in the white world of Bredvik, she claims, "I never really wanted to fit in. Well, I guess there was a part of me that did because I had a pretty shitty time in school. I didn't really like the people. I never thought I had a lot in common with them. [Other Bredvik students and I] never saw eye to eye. I wasn't interested in getting to know them." She believes that she contributed to her status as "outsider," because, as she explains, "It wasn't worth doing what I would have needed to do to fit in with that crowd. I just wasn't willing to give up who I am to be liked by [members of the Bredvik community]." She said that she often "acted more different from [individuals at Bredvik] than I actually was to make it clear that I wasn't one of them. I didn't want to be one of them. I wanted to be very clear about that." She says that she frequently expressed "radical" beliefs and displayed "bizarre" behaviors at Bredvik to make herself more of an "outsider." She further explains, "They thought that I was weird and I loved it. I wanted to be weird if being normal meant that I had to be like them." She believes that it would have compromised her beliefs and sense of self if she had attempted to fit in at Bredvik. Furthermore, even if she had been like others in the community, she believes that this would not have automatically equated acceptance. As an African American in a world dominated by whites, she believes that she would have remained an "outsider within." While a student at Bredvik, Claire resisted this status by further distancing herself from the school culture. Similar to what Proweller (1999) found, Claire managed "*race on [her] own terms,* rather than having race *managed for [her]* on the conditions set by the generalized culture of the private school [Bredvik], that is to say, white, mainstream culture" (p. 801; italics in original).

Certainly, Galvin, as a white male, does not face the same challenges at Bredvik as Claire. His racial identity does not refract him as "other" (DuBois, 1961) in Bredvik's white culture. However, like Claire, he claims that he is an outsider in the school community. Galvin explains, "I've never got along with people at Bredvik. I've gone to other schools and no problem, but at Bredvik I've always had difficulties. I just don't fit in there." Galvin reports that his status as an outsider causes him problems. He claims that most of his teachers do not "like" him and treat him "unfairly" compared with other students who are "typical Bredvik kids." He feels that he does not have close relationships with adults in the Bredvik community from whom he can draw support and who would advocate for him. He also has very few close relationships with his peers at Bredvik. He explains, "I don't hang out with anybody at school. Well, there's a couple of people I hang out with during the day, but we don't do anything outside school. I hang out with people at other schools." He describes his experiences in school as "lonely," but, "I deal with it."

One of Galvin's teachers agrees that he has problems "fitting in" at Bredvik. His teacher explains, "He keeps to himself most of the time and does just enough in his classes to get by. … He's really smart but a troubled kid." Similarly, one of Claire's previous teachers remembers her as an "outsider and troublemaker." Her teacher says that Claire "always caused problems for herself and others … [and] she wasn't easy to get along with." Both teachers cite "family problems" as reasons for Claire's and Galvin's difficulties in school and their status as outsiders within Bredvik's community. Claire and Galvin admit that they have problems in their families, which mostly result from their parents being away from home on a regular basis. Although most likely they carry some of their family problems to school, they believe that these problems are separate from the "issues" they have with Bredvik. Both of them believe that the "environment" of Bredvik creates the problems that they have at school. They acknowledge the impact that their family problems have on different aspects of their lives, including education, but argue that their outsider status has more to do with "disagreeing, at the core of my being, with the shit [at Bredvik]," as Claire explains; and, as Galvin claims, "want[ing] nothing to do with those people." Moreover, both of them believe that Bredvik has an "unsupportive" environment, which makes it "impossible to deal with any problems you have here or outside of here," Galvin points out.

Galvin claims that although he feels like people treat him as an outsider, he makes a "conscientious effort" to separate himself from those within his school community. He claims, "I've never wanted to fit in [at Bredvik] and because I don't want to [fit in], I don't. I'm like there but not really there. I'm invisible to most people, which is fine by me." He says that being "invisible" does not bother him because, as he explains, "I would have to be something that I'm not in order to be accepted. I'm just not like that. I'm not going to be something and act a certain way to get along with people here." Galvin claims that he is not willing to change in order to fit into his school community. His lack of social networks with adults and peers at Bredvik occurs, in part, because he positions himself as independent (Fairbanks & Ariail, 2006).

Whereas Claire admits that she expresses behaviors characteristic of whites, Galvin claims that "a lot of people [at Bredvik] think that I try to act black." He claims that his behaviors and language are perceived by most of his white peers at Bredvik as dipping into black cultural forms. Several researchers have explored the motivations behind the cultural appropriations of white students who dip into black cultural forms by "tr[ying] on fashions, linguistic dialects and communication styles like Black Vernacular English typically not their own" (Proweller, 1999, p. 799), which has been referred to most commonly as "acting black" (e.g., Fordham & Ogbu, 1986; Peshkin, 1991). It has been argued that white students "act black" to fill themselves with culture, something that they feel is missing in their lives as white people (Haymes, 1995). Even though Galvin admits that he shares some of the mannerisms and fashions with his closest friends, who are mostly African Americans and not students at Bredvik, he maintains that he is very aware of his racial identity and does not need "to act like something I'm not." He goes on to explain:

> I do listen to rap music, but everybody else does also [at Bredvik]. It isn't like everybody here listens to classical music or country music. I dress like most of my best friends, who don't go here. But this is also how [Bredvik] guys dress. So I'm really not that different from other guys here. What makes me different is that I hang out with not only people outside this school, which is a big no-no here, but they're also black. When they say that I'm trying to act black, what they're really saying is, 'You're hanging out with the wrong people.'

Galvin believes that how his peers characterize his actions and language reflects their racist attitudes and the dominant belief at Bredvik that "you should only hang out with people at this school," as he explains.

Galvin also believes that he is perceived as acting black because he inverts the *white* public, polite language of race (Proweller, 1999). He explains, "Because I talk about racism a lot, most people don't know how to deal with that. They think only black people talk about those issues. They don't know what to do when a white person talks about how racist things are. It's like talking about things that don't concern you." Galvin seems to hold a position different than most white students at Bredvik, who have a tendency to defend race privilege and escape any responsibility or connection to the history of white racism (McIntyre, 1997). He reports that he talks openly about racial issues in a "straightforward" way that acknowledges racism and white privilege.

He gives credit to diversity training he attended a couple of years ago for his awareness of his white privilege and his knowledge about racial issues. He explains, "That [diversity] workshop changed my life. It opened my eyes to how racism works and how we have to talk about these issues and do something about them." Even though white students typically do not avoid talking about and dealing with racial issues, research studies have found that most students selectively engage with these issues in ways that protect their privilege (Proweller, 1999). Galvin, however, claims that he takes "every opportunity" he can find to talk about racial issues and privilege. He says that he is chastised at Bredvik for taking these opportunities and for not following the class-based norms of civility and propriety that normally govern conversations about these topics. Galvin reports that he is seen as deviant or bad by overstepping the bounds of what has been determined to be the proper way of talking about racial issues. He chooses to break from practices of omission and silencing that *white out* talk (Doane & Bonilla-Silva, 2003) about race at Bredvik. He challenges and resists the prescriptive class and race codes that keep whiteness hidden and unexamined (see Proweller, 1999). In so doing, he is further defined as an outsider within the community.

Reasons for Involvement in Pathways

For Claire, race, again, played a role in her decision to participate in Pathways. As indicated in her statement earlier in this chapter, her participation in the program allows her to be "a part of a black community for a change." She thought that the program uniquely offered her opportunities to establish "meaningful relationships with other blacks" and to explore her racialized self. As she explains, "I felt like I needed to do something that puts me in different situations, that gave me a chance to figure things out about who I am or really who I wanted to be. I had a lot of questions about my culture and didn't have a lot of options to get answers to those questions." She recalls that when she heard about the program, she became immediately excited about the possibilities at Pathways for self-exploration of her racial identity. She claims, "Pathways was also about self-discovery, for a lack of a better way of putting it. I was mixed up on a lot of things and I thought this would help me sort some of what I was struggling with about being black."

She claims, however, that she became involved in the program "more than for what I thought it would do for me personally. I was interested in what I thought it would do for the school. I really wasn't doing the program to only focus on myself. It was about a larger issue." Claire believed that the program would offer the Bredvik community opportunities to engage in work and discussion related to race and class issues. She recalls, "When I heard about the program, I was excited. I thought it would help people at this school deal with diversity issues more because they couldn't avoid it. They couldn't avoid sixty-some poor, black kids running around the school. Bredvik has some issues—some real big issues when it comes to dealing with diversity. I thought it would help change this place, and I wanted to be a part of that change."

Similarly, Galvin remembers feeling that the program would be a "wake-up call" for the school community and decided to participate in Pathways to be a part of "something that raises awareness of social justice issues" at Bredvik. He explains, "They couldn't sweep the fact that not everybody has the same opportunities we do [at Bredvik] under the rug. I had high hopes for the program. I thought it would have us take on some important [racial and class issues]. The school just wasn't talking about diversity but they were actually doing something about it."

Both Galvin and Claire believed that by starting a program like Pathways, the school was demonstrating a commitment to be more critically responsive and responsible to those outside the Bredvik community. They became involved in the program to work toward the change in school culture that this commitment promised.

Both Galvin and Claire, however, believe that the program has had "little effect on Bredvik," as Claire explains. Galvin claims that "there's a lot of reasons why it hasn't changed anything here. But the main reason is that the school hasn't lived up to their promises to the program. They haven't made the program a part of the school like they said they would." He believes that Pathways has not been integrated into the community in the same way as the other programs offered at the school. He explains, "The other programs have all white kids participating in them and they have no problem fitting in here. Even when [the children who participate in these programs] aren't Bredvik students, they have no problems fitting in. But it doesn't work this way with Pathways. Black kids aren't accepted so easily." Claire similarly explains, "The school claimed that the kids in the program would be a part of the community, but they didn't make sure that happened. It was good [public relations] for them. The program made the school look really good, [but] the program is like in its own little world and not a part of [the Bredvik community]. They didn't do what they should've done." When I ask Claire what the school needs to do to integrate the program more into the school community, she replies, "Treat the kids [in Pathways] the same way they treat the rich white kids in these other programs."

In addition to wanting to be involved in the program for its potential to change Bredvik's culture, Galvin and Claire claim that another main reason for their involvement was to step outside of that culture and establish what Galvin calls, "real connections" with others. As outsiders within Bredvik's community, they looked forward to the possibility of finding a space at Bredvik where they could be, as Galvin describes, "myself and be accepted," or as Claire put it, "not ignored for who you are." Galvin expands on this point:

> I wanted to get away from all the bullshit and hypocrisy at Bredvik. I wanted to get away from it all and put my energies somewhere more positive. I found myself too negative, and I'm not like that. I wanted to make new friends and find real connections [at Pathways]. I wanted to meet new people and let them know me without all of this bullshit standing in the way. I wanted to be more of myself and not have to put up a front to deal with [what happens at Bredvik].

Similar to Galvin, Claire explains, "I just wanted to make this place more bearable and find something meaningful to do. I was excited about meeting new people and knew that I would have different kinds of relationships [at Pathways]. It was the glimmer of hope for making it through this place without going completely crazy." Both Galvin and Claire believe that the program has offered them these opportunities for developing close relationships with others and finding something meaningful at Bredvik.

Resisting Privilege[8]

Galvin and Claire claim that like most private schools (see Cookson & Persell, 1985; Proweller, 1999), Bredvik wants students to develop a purposeful identification with the school culture. They believe that Bredvik places tremendous pressure upon students to give up significant parts of themselves in order to develop this connection. They claim to resist giving up who they are for a culture that they believe preserves privilege. Galvin explains, "People don't respond too well to you being an individual here. They think something is up if you don't fit in. They can't imagine that some of us don't want to fit in. They frame it as having pride in the school, but it's something else ... It's about keeping up a front and keeping this place the same." Claire adds, "It's like a country club. There are benefits to being a member, and everyone is extremely interested in keeping those benefits." Although Claire is not specific about the benefits that Bredvik offers its "members," she elaborates on this point by saying, "It has to do with the extreme wealth that's here and very powerful people [at Bredvik]. The school embraces that [wealth and power]."

Although both of them acknowledge that they have benefited from attending Bredvik, they feel not only disconnected from this culture, as discussed previously in this chapter, but also "hate what this place stands for," Galvin explains. Claire similarly holds a feeling of "disgust" for Bredvik's culture. Both of them claim, however, that few escape valves exist for them to express their feelings of frustration and anger against it. Claire elaborates on this point: "You're trapped in a world where there's no way to express your true feelings. You keep it bottled up inside you and feel like you can burst at any moment." Like Galvin, she believes that Pathways "allowed me to escape this little world" and "to find a way to express how pissed off I was at how things are [at Bredvik]." Claire reports that she could talk openly about her feelings about Bredvik's culture with participants in the program. Similarly, Galvin feels that he can be "himself" at the program and, as he explains, "don't have to watch what I say. I can be honest about my feelings [toward Bredvik]." Although Galvin has a "difficult time pinpointing what makes me feel so comfortable [at Pathways]," he goes on to say that "it has to with what the program is about. The program isn't like the rest of Bredvik. It's about something entirely different." Both Galvin and Claire claim that because they are different, they are provided a space by Pathways to express their conflicts with Bredvik's culture. They are not just simply complaining about Bredvik in this space (even though they admit that they complain often), but are also finding a way (an escape valve) to step outside the privileged ways of knowing and doing that pervade this culture. For Galvin and Claire, Pathways provides them a space for resisting privilege.

In describing their conflicts with Bredvik's culture, Claire and Galvin emphasize the sense of "oblivious entitlement" (Horvat & Antonio, 1999) of most students. As Claire explains, "It's that selfishness and it's the all-about-me attitude. It's that attitude that 'I don't care about others' or most of the time 'I don't even acknowledge others outside my little world.' They barely care about people in their *own* world, let alone people who aren't. All they care about is themselves." She also believes that most Bredvik students "expect the world to be handed to them on a silver platter. When it isn't, then they go ape shit. They expect to get their way no matter what." In similar ways, Galvin believes that most Bredvik students "could care less about anybody except themselves ... [and] expect to get what they want." He goes on to point out that most of the time for students, "things go the way they want. Their whole world makes sure of it." Galvin believes that this sense of entitlement and selfishness are "normal" for the culture of affluence.

Even though Galvin comes from one of the wealthiest families in the program, he thinks that wealth creates "a separation from most people." He adds, "No one gets to know you for who you are. They only look at how much money you have, and that's all they care about. They just see the surface and nothing else." He says that he does not "flaunt" his family's wealth "in front of people at my school or my friends [who do not attend Bredvik]." He claims, though, that "they all know how much money my family has, and there's no escaping that image that you're like everyone else who's got money. They think you don't care about others and all you care about is your money. They think you're stuck up until they get to know you. But most of the time people don't even try to get to know you." He admits that at times he tries to hide his family's wealth. He explains, "I never take anybody to my house or have them meet my parents. They know where I'm from, so it doesn't matter if I take them [to my house] or not. They know [that my family is wealthy], but I don't want them to see it." He believes that markers of affluence stand in the way of developing "real" relationships with people outside his class.

Claire, on the other hand, does not care when others are aware of her family's wealth; but, like Galvin, she wants to form relationships mainly with individuals outside her class. Both Galvin and Claire report that they find it difficult to develop close relationships with members of their own class because their values run counter to those that pervade the culture of affluence. As Claire explains, "I just can't relate to people who all they can think about is themselves."

Galvin and Claire claim that Pathways provides them opportunities to develop close relationships not only with individuals outside their own class but also with other like-minded affluent people. Even though they think some Bredvik students participate in the program mainly for the perks, they believe that most participants are "truly faithful" to the purposes of the program and "helping others." As Claire explains, "Most of [the participants at Pathways] aren't like, 'Look what I'm doing.' This is a whole lot of work, so if they're only interested in being in the spotlight, there are a hell of a lot easier ways to be the center of attention. Most are truly faithful to what the program is about. They're truly interested in helping others." According to Galvin and Claire, participants' genuine interest in helping others runs counter to the strong sense of entitlement, materialism, and selfishness of most Bredvik students. Within this community, Claire and Galvin find the space and support they need to resist the privilege that is deeply woven into the fabric of Bredvik's culture.

There were other students at the four schools described in this book who expressed resistance to norms of their school culture. For example, Shannon (discussed in chapter 4) did not conform to the role defined for female students in Ms. Perry's classroom or in the larger culture of Parker. Shannon challenged the "feminine role" through her assertive behaviors toward male students who dominated classroom interactions and discourse. She displayed open opposition to the sexist norms of the classroom and school culture. Although affluent students like Shannon, Claire, and Galvin express their resistance differently than, and do not suffer the same consequences for school opposition as, poor students, their acts of resistance stem from a critique, implicit or explicit, of school-constructed ideologies and relations that reinforce domination. The "logic" of their resistance is grounded in a struggle against, rather than submission to, domination. As such, this logic has possibilities for interrupting the cultural processes that reinforce and regenerate privilege.

More so than other affluent students described in this book, Claire and Galvin seem to hold some level of critical awareness and a desire for social justice. They are positioned, however, in a context, both in school and in Pathways, that does not provide opportunities for them to develop a deeper level of critical understanding and a social justice orientation. They are left on their own to develop strategies for interrupting privilege, which limits the political possibilities of their resistance. As McLaren (1999) points out, "Students are unable to invent the multiple strategies to overturn fixed ideological positions and reveal their anchorage in practice" (pp. lii). Even though Galvin and Claire actively work toward rejecting privileged ways of knowing and doing, their resistance, unaided by a critical consciousness (Freire, 1970), is a reaction primarily to cultural processes of privilege and not their transformation. Such expressions of resistance are not sufficient "to free that aspect of agency subsumed to the larger determinations that position individuals in the world" (McLaren, 1999, pp. lii–liii). Transformational efforts, on the other hand, offer the greatest possibility for social change (Solórzano & Delgado-Bernal, 2001).

Transformational Service

Pathways is just one of the several opportunities for Bredvik students to be involved in community service. In the classroom, several teachers use service-learning activities to connect academic content with real-life problems and to create hands-on learning experiences for students. These activities extend beyond the confines of the classroom to integrate curriculum with participation in thoughtfully organized community service activities (Harkavy, Puckett, & Romer, 2000). Outside the classroom context, students participate in a variety of service activities facilitated by the school's full-time director of community service, such as raising money for charities and volunteering at local service programs. Additionally, Bredvik suspends classes for a week during the school year to have all students participate in well-organized service activities throughout the city. Although Bredvik does not require students to participate in service, they emphasize the importance of service to support their stated mission of preparing students to become participating citizens and responsible leaders.

The other three schools described in this book place a similar emphasis on community service. In fact, completion of a certain amount of hours of service is a graduation requirement at these other three schools. For example, Parker requires students to complete a minimum of 30 hours of voluntary service to a "needy" community outside the school. The primary goal of these service projects is to assist, express care for, or in some way enhance the quality of life for people and/or living creatures in need without expectation of reward. The projects require that students spend the majority of the 30 hours in direct contact with, for example, people who are physically handicapped, mentally disabled, or physically, financially, or spiritually in need. Students may also volunteer to care for animals that are either housed in shelters or are recognized as endangered species. After students have completed their service projects, they are required to submit a verification of completed hours and a summary (minimum 500 words) covering specified guidelines, which include a description of the project, the reason for the choice, problems and successes, and personal reflections on the experience. As with Bredvik and the other schools, Parker emphasizes the importance of service to support its mission and values statements.

In the last decade, an emphasis on service-learning and community service has become increasingly popular at all levels of education. According to a study sponsored by the National Youth Leadership Council (Scales & Roehlkepartain, 2004), 44% of high school students, 31% of middle-school students, and 22% of elementary school students are involved in service learning, and even a larger number of students at all levels are involved in community service projects and organizations. Like thousands of schools across the United States, the four schools in this book engage students in community service and service learning in hopes of fostering civic responsibility and acceptance of diversity, developing leadership skills, helping students move on to assume roles in their communities as committed and engaged citizens, and increasing the likelihood of lifelong community service and civic altruism. Even though several scholars have noted the need for more research on the educational outcomes of service learning in K–12 settings (e.g., Furco & Billig, 2002; Tannenbaum & Brown-Wiley, 2006), there is no shortage of studies that suggest that these outcomes can be achieved when students engage in service (e.g., Giles & Eyler, 1994; Melchior & Bailis, 2002; Rockquemore & Schaffer, 2000; Shumer & Belbas, 1996; Waterman, 1997).

This body of research demonstrates that participation in service has the capacity to rebuild civic society and even communicate the goals of social justice (Melchior & Bailis, 2002; Rocha, 2000; Rockquemore & Schaffer, 2000). Involvement in service also offers the conditions for participants to examine social issues critically and to be engaged in an intentional and thoughtful process of understanding self and self in relation to others (Eyler & Giles, 1999). However, as Robinson (2000) points out, the service activities at most schools do not "espouse the kind of system-challenging service-learning that would be necessary to achieve such goals" (p. 144). Like Pathways and the other service projects at Bredvik, most service activities follow a "charity model" instead of a model that promotes social transformation. Linking individual students to charitable service projects (e.g., teaching at Pathways, tutoring inner-city students, serving food in a soup kitchen) allows students to give back—that is, help others who are less fortunate—and to be "do-gooders" (Puka, 1993), but this is not guided by or grounded in the transformational aims necessary for social change. For affluent students, these service activities do not provide the conditions necessary for interrupting privilege.

In fact, the goals of the charitable model of service reinforce privileged ways of knowing and doing by embracing certain unpleasant assumptions about people, especially those different from the service providers. One basic assumption is that any group of people would function better if only they would act like the service provider. Another assumption is that there are no connections between those who provide service and those who receive service, that they are more different than they are similar; this assumes that their lived experiences, hopes, dreams, and aspirations are so profoundly different that difficulties can be resolved only by finding the one right answer. These attitudes are expressed clearly in the practices and policies of Pathways. Although the program offers exceptional services to disadvantaged students, the goals of the program are to save them from their impoverished environments and educate them "the right way." Pathways' students and their families have little say in determining the practices and policies of the program. The service providers have all the answers to solving the problems that the students face in gaining academic success. In this context, service is mainly about the nature of the activity and the work of the service provider, not about the needs of the entire community.

Transformational service learning, on the other hand, contextualizes service within an educational environment where all participants are learners and teachers. As Kendall (1990) explains, "All parties in service-learning are learners and help determine what is to be learned. Both the server and those served teach, and both learn" (p. 22). This form of service does not seek to make individuals see, understand, or appear the same. Rather, it seeks to foster uniqueness, individual contribution, and an understanding based on compassion. For Pathways, this would mean creating opportunities for the staff members to step outside their privilege in order to learn from those whom they serve. When the relationship among participants involved in a service project like Pathways is defined by equality, all persons develop, rather than being given, the voice necessary for stating one's needs, goals, and responsibilities. The service providers no longer exclusively determine what students need to be successful in school and life; the students and their families have a voice in articulating their needs and goals and how they are addressed. The staff members are provided opportunities to understand and appreciate different ways of knowing and doing. They are provided opportunities for encountering and coming to understand competing definitions of the common good, different perspectives on the causes of social problems, and questions about who and what knowledge is for (Enos & Troppe, 1996).

John Dewey (1916) put this notion of equal participation within the context of democracy when he pointed out,

> A democracy is more than a form of government; it is primarily a mode of associated living, of conjoint communicated experience. The extension in space of the number of individuals who participate in an interest so that each has to refer his [or her] own action to that of others, and to consider the action of others to give point and direction to his [or her] own, is equivalent to the breaking down of those barriers of class, race, and national territory which [keep] men [and women] from perceiving the full import of their activity. (p. 87)

Dewey calls our attention to the importance of reciprocity in establishing standards for service and learning. The standard of judgment is the checking of one's actions in reference to other's actions in the service project. Stated otherwise, the mutual benefit of all participants becomes the reference point for judgment. Dewey calls for the use of this reference point in consideration and reconsideration of the service-learning process. This consideration and reconsideration form the reflection, which is integral to a process guided by transformational aims.

Both these components of reflection require knowledge of the content and nature of the service experience, and knowledge of the participants in the experience. As Apple and Beane (1995) maintain, "Knowledge is that which is intimately connected to the communities and biographies of real people. Students learn that knowledge makes a difference in people's lives, including their own" (p. 102). This refers to both knowledge of the mutually beneficial outcomes and the daily work of the service experience. Consideration stated differently is what Max van Manen (1991) refers to as "anticipatory reflection" and "anticipatory imagination." He explains "planning and thinking things out beforehand, we make ourselves pedagogically available in a meaningful way" (p. 103); in the context of service, individuals make themselves mutually available to all participants through careful "anticipatory" consideration. Van Manen cautions, however, that inflexible planning or consideration prevents the flow of creative, spontaneous experiences. Avoiding this rigidity requires all participants to come together to decide how "we are going to deal pedagogically with a challenging, difficult, puzzling situation" (van Manen, 1991, p. 103). This can happen only when individuals involved in service activities view each other as learners and teachers, when they recognize that each person (including themselves) has much to learn from each other.

Reconsideration, as part of reflection, is the identification of what has been learned so that further experiences can be constructed. Without that reconsideration, participants in service have done the activity and move from that activity to the next one without realizing the full potential for learning that exists within the experience, without constructing what Dewey (1916) names as an "educative experience." This component of reflection provides a means for participants to reconsider their assumptions of the world and their actions. This reconsideration provides the educational opportunity to make sense of their experiences so that they can develop new understandings of their place in the world, their sense of self, and their relationships with others. This process of developing new understandings engages participants in a struggle with their prior assumptions that relate not only to the particular contexts of the service activities but also to personal and ideological matters (Purpel, 1999). This struggle puts the focus of service less on the activity itself and more on transformation.

I want to avoid being critical of the current practices of service, even those guided by the "charitable model," to the point of not recognizing the amazing work students do in service projects across the nation like the kind I witnessed at Pathways. I want to acknowledge and support the well-intentioned, concrete efforts of the many students and teachers who participate in service. They are making significant contributions to address unmet social and community needs. The growing presence of service learning and community service in our nation's schools is providing more students the opportunity to be involved in their communities in meaningful ways. The dominant model of charitable service learning, however, does not take full advantage of the potential that participation in service has to interrupt privilege and to prepare students to be their own creators of democratic culture. Service that is guided by transformational aims provides greater possibilities for drawing one's attention toward the relations between people, toward the process of living a democratic life, and toward a celebration of one's place with others.

8
Outsiders Within[1]

> It's maybe like a plant in a whole bunch of weeds. The plant is in a weed garden and the weeds are trying to choke you each minute. But you got to keep growing like a plant.
>
> **Janora, Bredvik School student**

Janora's symbolic representation of her experiences at Bredvik (as described in chapter 3) typifies the experiences of most other African American students at the schools described in this book. Although there are few studies of the experiences of African American students at predominantly white and affluent schools, this body of research has documented the various ways that institutional arrangements, policies, and practices in these settings place African Americans at a disadvantage (e.g., Proweller, 1999; Tatum, 1987; Zweigenhaft & Domhoff, 1991). These studies offer a textured composite of the disadvantages, discrimination, cultural conflicts, and struggles that African American students negotiate daily in these school contexts. Institutional racism—that is, the values, practices, and understandings that work against students of color—encroaches on the everyday experiences and relationships of African American students in the classroom setting and the larger school community. Unequal social relations and institutional arrangements are woven into the fabric of their educational experiences.

The data generated from my research at the four schools documented the various ways that institutional racism powerfully influenced the experiences of African American students.[2] In approaching the task of giving form to clumps of categorized and organized data through writing, I became concerned with representation. As Geertz (1988) points out, researchers are not ventriloquists. We do not speak for others, but instead capture others' lived experiences. We describe and interpret cultural behavior through our research and writing. As writers, our work is to make another's world accessible and understandable by respecting the particulars and locating the recurring themes of that world. In representing another's world, we need to acknowledge that our interpretations are culturally constructed and our knowledge is partial, positioned, and incomplete (Magolda, 2000). I was mindful of the limits of my own privileged cultural situatedness (Asher, 2005) in accurately and fully representing the experiences of African American students at these schools.

I discussed my concerns with an African American parent at Bredvik. I told her that I was having difficulties writing about what I had found through my research. She immediately responded, "I could write that chapter for your book." We both chuckled at her suggestion and then she continued, "Seriously though, we all know black students have a really tough time at private schools. What I think folks don't know is why we decide to send our children to those schools. We also don't get too many opportunities to voice our concerns and offer our suggestions." She urged me to extend the focus of my inquiry to include the voices of African American parents. She also urged for me to "devise a way to work with us in getting a better sense of what our children go through and experience at a private school." She added, "We know what's going on with our kids and can get to the heart of the issues they face and what we do about those issues." I took this parent's advice and decided to expand the scope of my inquiry. By the end of our conversation, I had begun to make plans with her to collaborate with a group of African American parents to explore the experiences of their children at predominantly white and affluent schools. Past studies of parents' perceptions and feelings have contributed important understandings of the educational experiences of children from different social class and racial groups (Brantlinger, 1985; Brantlinger, Majd-Jabbari, & Guskin, 1996; Tatum, 1987). Similarly, I intended to include the voices of parents to understand and represent what I had witnessed as a researcher more fully and accurately.

Participants, Approach, and Context of the Discussion

I eventually decided to facilitate a group discussion with parents instead of conducting individual interviews. As one of the eventual participants explained during the selection phase, "I think you'll get us talking more if we have each other to bounce ideas off of." I took this parent's advice. The coleaders of an organization, the Network of African American Parents in Independent Schools (NAAPI), assisted me in sending out requests to participate in the discussion. Nine parents, including two men and seven women, from seven households agreed to participate in the discussion. As a whole, the parents' children attend or attended six of the seven private schools located in a midsize Midwestern city, including Parker Day School and Bredvik School.[3]

All of the parents are college educated, and seven of them have graduate degrees. Of the seven households, three identified as upper middle class, three as middle class, and one as upper class. Dr. and Mrs. Williams' three daughters graduated from the same private school and currently attend colleges in the Northeast. Dr. Williams is head surgeon at the city's largest hospital. His wife is a part-time administrator of a local, nonprofit organization. Before their daughters graduated from high school, Mrs. Williams served on the school's board of trustees for several years. Mr. and Mrs. Miller's son and daughter graduated from the same private school. Mrs. Miller is a nationally known writer and consultant. She has received several awards, including honorary doctorates, for her work. Her husband retired early after a very successful career as a civil engineer. He works now as a part-time consultant. Mrs. St. John's two sons graduated from the same private school, and her daughter graduated from a suburban public school. She is a professional volunteer. Her husband is an executive at a large company. Ms. Johnson and Ms. Daniels are sisters and single parents. Both of them work in social service fields. Ms. Johnson's son and Ms. Daniels' two daughters attend the same school and receive need-based scholarships to help with the costs of the school's tuition and fees. Mrs. Cullins' daughter has attended the same private school since first grade. Mrs. Cullins is a school counselor at a public school, and her husband is a dentist. Mrs. Keen's son and daughter attend single-sex private schools. She is a health administrator. She described her husband's occupation as a "businessman."

I facilitated the discussion at a church located in a predominantly African American community of the city. Several of the parents suggested this location, because as one parent explained after I suggested we hold our discussion at one of the schools, "I think we would feel more comfortable at the church. If we met at the school, we would be focusing on who knows we're having this discussion and do they know what we're talking about. We just couldn't focus our attention on the discussion." I discovered early on that the parents didn't feel completely comfortable being honest and open about their children's educational experiences at any of the schools. Unlike parents of dominant cultures who are "loud and influential" (Brantlinger, 2003, p. 28), the parents felt that they had been traditionally silenced in "talking about what African Americans experience in these schools," Mrs. Williams explained. They felt that there were consequences for voicing their opinions. "Our kids already have a tough time at these schools," Mrs. Williams added. "The last thing I want to do is add to that by causing problems. I fear my kids would pay for my actions and words." Since all of the schools are located in predominantly white, affluent communities, they wanted to hold the discussion outside any of the schools.

Before the discussion, I collaborated with the parents to develop the questions I would ask them in my facilitating role. During this collaboration, some parents offered specific questions and others suggested general topics. The parents made it very clear that they didn't want to participate in a discussion about how racist and bad their children's schools were, even though, as you will read later in this chapter, they did discuss these issues. They initially wanted the discussion to focus on their reasons for sending their children to private schools and to offer suggestions on how these schools could improve. The guiding questions that were developed for the discussion, therefore, focused on these two areas. After the discussion, I continued to collaborate with the parents in revising the transcript and identifying the main themes that emerged from our discussion. They worked with me during all stages of the research process, from developing the guiding questions for our discussion to the analysis of that discussion. Rather than "giving voice" to only the stories of others (Lather & Smithies, 1997), the parents collaborated with me to determine how their stories and voices were represented in the following sections of this chapter.

Perception That Private Schools Are Better

For over four decades, the educational and other benefits of private versus public education at all levels of schooling have been debated (Suitor, Powers, & Brown, 2004). Both scholarly and popular literature engaging in this debate has focused mainly on the question of whether private schools provide a higher quality of education. This higher quality has been gauged by such factors as class size, records of student achievement, test scores, and college admissions (Coleman et al., 1981). Judging quality of education by these indices, the general opinion is that private schools are better. This general opinion, whether accurate or not, has led many parents to the belief that their children will have broader academic opportunities and learn more if they attend private schools. Parents also believe most often that private schools provide an educational environment that will encourage their children to focus on academics as well as character development (Badie, 1998; Folmar, 1997). Although earlier studies (e.g., Coleman et al., 1981; Sandy, 1989) provided an inconsistent report of the differences in actual academic achievement between private and public school students, more recent work on parents' choices finds that a major factor in school selection continues to be guided by the belief that private schools are a better choice in terms of academics. The general opinion among parents is that private schools provide better academic programs than public schools, even though there is little empirical evidence to support such a claim (e.g., Bickel & Chang, 1985).

Another question that this body of work has explored is whether private schools provide a better social environment for students. Highly publicized reports of violence in public schooling have led many to the conclusion that public schools in general are not safe places. In recent years, as concerns about violence and drugs in schools have escalated, private school enrollments have increased due to perceptions that they provide greater security on these issues (Suitor et al., 2004). Again, the question remains whether private schools actually provide a safer environment for students than public schools. Without the support of empirical evidence, the common perception, however, is that private schools are safer places.

Most of the parents during the discussion offered similar reasons for sending their children to private schools. Their comments about why they decided to do so are consistent with what others have found in examining parents' school choices (Suitor et al., 2004). They believed that private schools offered a better academic program and a better overall environment than public schools. Some of them developed this belief from "bad" experiences with public schools. Mrs. Miller, for example, explained why she and her husband decided to transfer their son to a private school from a public suburban school:

> We were committed to public education, but we didn't have a very good experience with public schools with our children. We transferred our son to a private school because we decided that he needed a different kind of learning environment. He was in a public school in a suburban district where he had a number of behavioral issues. He was receiving failing grades and very low grades, but he had tested at a genius level IQ. Nobody was paying any attention to him at all. So we sent him kicking and screaming to a private school by the eighth grade. He was not happy to be with 'privileged, snotty people.' But he did do much better than when he was at public school. His private school just provided a better overall academic program and a better social environment for him.

Even though the majority of the parents did not have similar experiences and provided very little specifics about public schools, all of them expressed great concern with the city's public schools. As Dr. Williams explained,

> With public education, I think there are problems in virtually every large city, and I don't think this city is unique in that regard. I attended public school and so did my wife. We were committed to public education. However, the landscape of the city's public schools had changed. The schools were no longer the same as when I had attended them. I felt like they were teaching different things and their reputations were different than when I was in the schools. They used to be known as really good places, where students got a solid education. But a school that may have been highly regarded years ago was not necessarily thought of that way now. We just didn't have faith that they provided a solid education as they once did.

Like Dr. and Mrs. Williams, all of the parents had attended public schools themselves and were "open to the idea of having our kids be in public schools also," Mrs. Miller claimed. Most of them had even attended public schools in the same city but believed that the public school system "is not what it used to be," as Mrs. Cullins added. Most of the parents agreed that the public schools in their city and other large cities did not have the same good reputations they once had with the general public.

Mrs. Keen further explained that this bad reputation was a major factor in deciding against sending her children to public schools:

> The reputation of the public schools in this city has not been that good, so we always felt that we would send them to the parochial schools. When our son came, we decided that he seemed to be very bright, more exceptional than normal, so it became important for us to send him to a private school because we thought he would get a better education, even more so than at a parochial school. But then he started experiencing some problems at the school. They were showing some differences, so much so that my son, who was in the second grade, came to me and began to ask why he couldn't go to certain things or why couldn't these things be done for him. So we decided to take him out of that school. We then put him in a parochial school where he did well, and they actually gave him advanced courses, which is what we actually wanted for him. The school had a good academic reputation, and so he went there and did well there. Sending him or our other children to public schools was never an option. We wanted to do more for our children.

Even when parents had negative experiences with private schools, and almost of them had at some point in their children's education, they still held firm to the belief that private schools were better than public schools. Mrs. St. John believed, "You have more control of your child's education at private school. You know what's going on more than you do with public schools. Even when something bad happens, you can address it or do something about it. It doesn't work the same way with the public school system." All of the parents agreed that they felt more in-control of their children's education at private schools. Ms. Daniels added, "Your child can get lost easily in the public school system. It's too big and you don't get individualized attention as you do at private schools. Your child can have problems and you don't even know about it. That doesn't happen in private schools because you can keep in touch more with what's going on with your child."

The parents recognized that private schools faced similar negative influences, such as drug use and bullying—the two problems they emphasized the most during the discussion—as did public schools, but they felt that private schools had the resources to deal more effectively with these issues. Mr. Miller addressed this point by saying,

> I think that the assumption that a private school is a perfectly safe, perfectly behaved environment is insane. There are drugs in private schools, just like there are in public schools. To some extent, maybe they are different kinds of drugs, but still drugs. There are social conflicts. Teenage boys will fight; I don't care where you put them. I mean, that's just part of the growing-up dynamic. I guess teenage girls get into squabbles just like the boys. So I don't think that those problems go away in either environment. I think that the private school environment can better deal with them because of the smallness of the numbers. There's a distinct

> advantage in the learning and socialization factors in both environments, but private schools have an advantage just because it's not thirty in a class, it's twelve or ten. When these issues come up, just because of the numbers of people that have to be dealt with, the private school has the advantage. I also think, though, that private schools have the ability, because of their finances, to offer more opportunities for social skills building. They have the funds to offer students more field trips, whether it's to space camp or whatever. Those numbers of programs and those things that get kids together in order to interplay and interact and build on social skills can occur because of just the funding.

All of the parents believed that public schools did not have the resources to address problems as effectively as private schools. "They barely have enough resources to provide the basics, and sometimes they don't even do that well," Mrs. Miller added. "You can't do much without resources, and public schools don't have a lot of resources."

The parents also agreed that the level of parental involvement and teacher dedication at private schools is greater than at public schools, and this allows problems to be better resolved when they arise. Mrs. St. John explained,

> I think the parental involvement at a private school is much greater. I think the dedication of the teachers is much greater. When you look at the salaries—and I could look at the salaries because I served on the board for nine years at my son's school—the salaries were lower than in the public schools. But these teachers were eager and excited about teaching and about stimulating students. I see that as the greatest difference. When we had parent meetings at my son's school, they had to have police there to direct traffic because the parking lot was overflowing every time. I see that as being the greatest difference between the public and private schools. When you have this type of dedication to education from teachers and parents, you can deal with situations when they arise. I'm not saying that private schools are perfect; they have their problems. Everyone in this room knows that. But they have the resources, and I'm including human resources in this, to give your child the best possible education.

There was consensus in the group that sending their children to private schools, or some parochial schools, was a matter of wanting the best possible education for their children. Above all, they believed that private schools offered educational opportunities to their children that were not available at public schools. Mrs. Cullins said,

> I want the best educational opportunities available for my child. I think that I'm no different than any parent. I want the best for my child. I just didn't have the faith in the public school system that I needed, to know that this was the best option for my child. I know my child has

> opportunities at a private school that she just can't get at a public school. I want those opportunities for her.

For some of the parents, it was "tough in terms of affording private school education," but they did "whatever it took to make sure my child had the most opportunities," Ms. Daniels explained. Ms. Johnson added to this point,

> We were attending school on a scholarship and it wasn't something I was ashamed of. It was an opportunity that wasn't available in the public system, which made me frustrated and desperate, and I was willing to do whatever it took to get my child a decent education. And from that perspective, my experience at private school was good because I got the education my child needed in order to make the next step and compete on an even playing field when he got to his first year of college. Those were my basic goals. I was determined to meet those goals for my child.

Even for some who did not receive much financial assistance from scholarships, it was difficult for their families to afford the tuition of a private school education. Mrs. Cullins explained,

> We didn't receive much financial assistance for our daughter to attend. Some of my black friends would ask, 'Well, is she on scholarship? How are you affording that?' I would always say that I'm making the sacrifices to invest in my child's future, and it's worth the sacrifice. But a lot of people look at the price tag and don't understand why you would pay all that money if you're not extremely wealthy. My husband and I decided it was worth the investment in our daughter's future to sacrifice whatever to make that happen for her.

The parents' decision to send their children to private school was also a "tough one because our children don't always agree with the decisions we make about their education," Mrs. Cullins further remarked. Except for Mrs. St John, who allowed her children to be a part of the decision to send them to a private school, the other parents made the decision for their children. As Ms. Daniels explained, "Our children don't always know what's best for them at the time. You have to make those hard decisions as parents and hope that everything in the end turns out to have been the best for your child." Mrs. Miller added to this point,

> I think that you make a decision about your child's education and where is the best place to send them. You make a choice; whether you're going to give them a good educational opportunity or whether you're going to provide a holistic life for your child. I think our decision was: 'Down the road, it will be okay.' We wanted the best education possible for them so we made the decision to send them to a private school. We might have

> been wrong, but we knew that it wasn't going to be a happy social experience. We had to make that tough decision.

One of the main reasons that the parents made these tough decisions, oftentimes with financial sacrifices and going against their children's wishes, was because they were not confident in the quality of the public school system "to know what kind of education we were getting" and to make sure "our children were getting the best available education," Dr. Williams explained. Parents believed that the purposes of education and the curriculum of private schools made more sense to them. "You know what you're getting at private schools," Mrs. St. John remarked. "We weren't so certain what our children would be getting at a public school." Dr. Williams added to this point,

> We tried public schools for our kids first in elementary school. And with the public school system, it's just really hard to figure out who's teaching what at any particular school. The school that we had our older two daughters into was a Montessori school, which was very good for the younger one and very bad for the older one. And when it appeared that that didn't work out, I tried to figure out from the public school system where to send them from there. Because what I wanted was a basic education: Learn how to read, write, count, and speak English. I couldn't figure out which school did it. Then, also, figuring out that they wouldn't be able to go to school in the neighborhood, we would have had to take them out of the neighborhood to do the best we could in terms of assuring that they got a good foundation and a basic education. And then we were just lucky enough to be able to afford to send them to private school. We knew what we were getting with private school. We knew our girls would get the kind of education that we wanted for them.

All of the parents were confident that their children learned more and had broader academic opportunities because they attended private schools.

Conflicted Cultures

Despite the fact that around 20% to 25% of the students at the schools that the parent's children attend or attended came from cultural backgrounds other than white, the parents described the dominant culture of the schools as white, wealthy, and marked by a sense of "taken-for-granted entitlement," as Ms. Johnson explained, which is akin to Coles's (1977) concept of "narcissistic entitlement" found among the children of the very wealthy (p. 366). This narcissistic entitlement is based on a feeling held by wealthy children that they will receive "an inheritance the world is expected to provide" (Coles, 1977, p. 366) and, as Mrs. Miller observed, "get whatever they want in life even if they don't work for it or, to be blunt, don't really deserve it." Similar to what Horvat and Antonio (1999) found in their study of the experiences of African

American girls in an elite high school, the dominant members of their children's school communities did not acknowledge "the diversity within their midst and assume[d] that all members of the community function[ed] in society in the same way that they [did], with significant class resources and a sense of privilege based on their color (white) and class" (p. 326).

Most of the parents said that they were "naive" about this culture and in their thinking that "our presence in the communities would make a difference to the culture of the school," as Mrs. Miller pointed out. Ms Johnson elaborated on this point:

> I don't think I went in with an open mind. In other words, I wasn't expecting all that comes with the white culture that was there. In this culture, I was kind of set apart from everyone and everything else at the school. It was something that I really wasn't ready to deal with and didn't fully expect. I discovered that the values of my child's school were so totally different that it became a struggle in trying to keep the values of your home from conflicting with the values of all the homes of those people who were a part of the school.

Most of the parents agreed with Ms. Johnson that they too were unprepared for the struggle between their values, which they described as typical for African American families, and the values of the school, which "are embedded in everything these white environments are about," as Mrs. Miller described.

Ms. Johnson further explained her unawareness of these differences of the values between home and school:

> Nobody warns you about these differences—not other African Americans and certainly not white folks at the school. And if you're out of touch with your child, then you have a tendency to lose your child in that environment. I think it's important that we provide each other with information that could be helpful. A little bit of information was shared, and a lot of it was just shocking to me. Some of the experiences I had and some of the things that I knew went on were just overwhelming. I had to learn about these differences through experience. I wished that I had known more before these experiences to help my child more.

Mrs. St. John added, "These values are so normal at these schools that they're hard to recognize. They get hidden in a lot of ways by how well accepted they are and how they are part of everything. It's hard to keep your children focused on different values than the ones at their school that are so celebrated and cherished."

Most of the parents agreed that it was difficult to inform other African American parents about the culture of the schools. "You think it's unique to your child's experiences," Ms. Johnson recalled. "It takes a while for you to figure out that what is happening to your child and what they're experiencing, other African Americans are experiencing." One of the major ways the parents tried to educate other African American parents about the culture of the schools was by forming a family-like relationship with other African American families. These relationships were a source of support for themselves and other African Americans. "We get to know people and can establish lines of communication to let people know what's going on in these schools and try to figure out what we can do to support African Americans in these environments," Ms. Johnson explained.

The parents agreed that these relationships were formed mostly through their involvement in their children's schools. They became involved not only for their own children but also for other African American students. As Dr. Williams observed, "I think most of the African American parents try to create a family atmosphere within that group and I think they did a pretty good job of that, both in terms of the parents helping new parents learn the system, learn the ropes and in having parenting or village-type of relationships with other people's children. I think within the black parents we tried to develop family-type relationships."

All of the parents are involved in the various parent groups that are very well established at the schools. Mrs. Keen noted, "There are a lot of groups for parents at these schools, everything from ones that focus on curriculum to sports to fundraising. It seems like there's a parents group for every aspect of the school." All of their children's schools also have groups specifically for African American parents, and all of them are actively involved in these groups. Ms. Johnson explained, "These groups are getting more established at my son's school out of necessity. We want to institutionalize the ways African American parents work together and build strong relationships with one another." Mrs. Keen is one of the parents who started such a group at her daughter's school. She explained,

> At our school, we set up a parent group for both fathers and mothers. It is a very private school thing to do to have a mothers group. But we wanted a group for both parents. We have fathers who are very much involved with their children and they attend our meetings regularly. We decided to form our own organization that includes fathers and to try to become a recognized organization within the school. We call ourselves 'Parents of African American Daughters,' or PAD. We're tried to become a recognized organization just like the Mothers Club, to maybe open their eyes. We want to be a presence in this school, because we have things we want to bring to the table. We want to make a difference in the school.

The parents believed that most of the time fathers, including African American fathers, are less involved in their children's schools than are mothers.

"You will see these parent gatherings and a whole room will be filled with parents, but there are no fathers in the room," Mrs. Williams observed.

The two fathers in the group acknowledged that they were less involved than their wives but still found it important to be involved for their own children and to form relationships with other African American families. Dr. Williams explained,

> I try to socialize or incorporate myself with the other parents, but a lot of times you go to parents' meetings, and parents, like their kids, will compartmentalize in various groups. You sometimes get the feeling that this was a continuation of a conversation from earlier in the day. I didn't really aspire to belong to any of those groups. So, I didn't feel like I was incorporating into the larger school's family. I was there mainly for my kids and to show the school that I was interested and concerned about them. I also thought it was important to form good relationships with other African American families, but most of the time these relationships couldn't be formed in larger school gatherings. We had a chance to form those in other settings. Now, my wife spent a lot more time there than I did and knew people a lot better. She was more effective in navigating the social scene of these larger gatherings than I.

Like Dr. Williams, Mr. Miller wanted to have a presence in his children's school. He did so, however, in a more aggressive way than Dr. Williams. He explained:

> I think sometimes that you have to go in situations and say things that normally you feel that you shouldn't have to say. I find myself telling people often, 'Look I'm black. Don't tell me how black people behave—I'm black.' I did that at my kids' school and maybe it's because I tried to avoid having problems down the road. I made things perfectly clear up front. I did that with our son and had to come back later on and do that same thing with our daughter in junior high. I wanted to make sure everyone knew that if they were having problems, then I was going to be there to help them solve those problems.

Wanting to have this presence in their children's schools was a common theme during the discussion. "You being there lets others know that you know what's going on," Ms. Daniels remarked. More than what message their involvement sent to others, all of the parents felt that they had to be involved in order "to look after your kids in these environments," Ms. Daniels added. Most of the parents believed that they needed to be involved in their children's schools in order to protect their children and other African American students. As Mrs. Cullins explained:

> I think the need for protecting your children and other black students should be the reason for parental involvement in these private schools.

> There are a lot of things they are exposed to. There is a lot for these children to figure out in terms of cultural differences between the school culture and home culture. You have to be involved. I was also involved from the very beginning. I was part of room mothers and went on all the field trips. That was just part of it. I would have done the same had my daughter been in a public school. You just have to be involved. It is a responsibility you have.

Similarly, Mrs. St. John explained,

> I became involved immediately. I took part in everything. I became president of the mother's club and president of the women's club. I also sat on the board for 9 years. Our kids were nearly the only African Americans from preschool throughout. I knew I had to be there for them and to be there in a visible way in order for my kids to succeed, and that's what I did. I tried to do it for all those parents who were not able to be there, because I thought it was important that the schools not mistreat the African American kids. Therefore, I was very much involved. After a while they do listen to you. You have to be very blunt in a very nice, gentle way in order to address some of the issues.

Mrs. Williams added,

> Parental involvement happens on different levels, and I think that it happens at different ages for the child. I also think that it may happen differently at different schools. The culture and nature of private schools is that parents are involved: 'Doggonit, I'm paying my dollars. I'm going to be here, and I'm going to question everything that goes on.' People are involved, and in that sense, you become a family of parents who are concerned about the well-being of your child. Now, having said that, there are tensions. Different people have different priorities and concerns and that sort of thing, but because parents are involved, you do get to know people, you do get to know kind of where they are coming from for their child. That's where we as parents make decisions.
>
> Over the course of 15 years at a school, I got to know people. I got to know where they are coming from and what they value. And what all these people value is education for their kid, and there's a common understanding that they are there because they want to get their kids not only through high school but also into college and into a life path, a career path that's going to allow their child to have a decent quality of life as an adult. You figure out where you find common ground with other parents at the school.

Most of the parents could not be involved in their children's school at the same level as Mrs. St. John and Mrs. Miller because of other life and work responsibilities. In many ways, the parents' level and type of involvement in their children's schools reflected their social class status. The more affluent parents in the group held higher status and more powerful positions at the schools (e.g., board member) and spent more time being involved in a wider variety of events and activities at their children's school. All of the parents, however, considered involvement in their children's schools and forming family-like relationships with other African Americans priorities in order to become more familiar with the school culture, to address problems when they arose, and to have a voice in what happened at the schools.

The parents also formed relationships with other African American parents and families to keep their children "connected to African American values," Mr. Miller explained. Regardless of how the parents individually were situated in terms of residence, friendship networks, and class status, they shared with other African American parents a sense of a "we" feeling. Above all, the parents identified themselves as African Americans and wanted to make sure, as Ms. Johnson explained, "that our children know and are proud of this identity." Ms. Daniels elaborated on this point:

> I think there's a very intentional cultural significance to why we get involved in our children's schools and get to know other African American families. There are deep levels of culture, and to me culture is beyond the type of food or what you wear or where you go. It is about common life experiences and values. In a sense, we re-created these basic cultural beliefs and values through our cultural bonds with one another. We're able to get together and re-create that sense of family for those students who were there. So what you have is a set of relationships based on a common commitment. Even though we're not blood relatives, and as a parent I'm responsible to care for and look after my own children, the success of one student was no better than the success of others, and no one really succeeded unless everybody succeeded. That is a totally contrasting value system than what is inherent at these schools.

All of the parents agreed that their reasons for being involved in their children's schools and forming relationships with others in the school community were different from those of white parents. For the parents, their involvement and their relationships were about survival in these white environments. Ms. Daniels explained:

> I didn't really socialize and go to the luncheons that I was invited to, but I did participate in whatever meetings that parents invited me to be a part of. I found that is what really is essential in being able to provide a support system and being visible. I wasn't there to network and build friendships. Most of the parents, white parents, that is, went to these events for social reasons. I had a different purpose. If I'm going to have

> my daughters enrolled in the school, then I'm going to be a part of it, too. I'm going to allow myself to experience enough to at least be able to know what my children are experiencing with the whole emotional climate of the school. I thought that was very important to do. I think there is a cultural dimension and it's very important that we pay attention to it—even if the school is not aware of it.

The rest of the parents agreed that it was important for them "to be in touch and to experience the best you can what your kids are going through in their school," Mrs. Williams added.

The parents found a great importance in understanding the culture of their children's school. Mrs. Williams explained, "You have to know these places well enough to respond to these different values in ways that you can teach your children the ones you want them to have." Mrs. Miller added, "I agree. It's extremely important that you have an understanding of what these places are about. But gaining this knowledge isn't easy. You have to spend time at the school, interacting with people and trying to understand the details of your children's experiences." Understanding the social and cultural particularities of these school communities was difficult for the parents because, as Mrs. Miller continued, "It is so different from your own understandings of how things are and work." Most of the parents, however, felt that they had enough understanding of their children's school culture to make sure their children "aren't sucked up in this culture to where they forget who they are," Mr. Miller explained. He continued,

> When you get in an environment like their school where affluence dominates, there are no values in that environment. Material things are all that matter, and if I tear up this or tear up that it doesn't matter 'cause my mama and daddy will buy me another one. We as a group of people have different values than that, I believe. I don't want to sound racist myself, but we place value on things. We work hard for what we have, and we're not materialistic, but there is a respect for property—your property and other people's property. In those affluent environments, kids have a tendency not to have those values. I'm not trying to knock anybody, but when you put your kid in that environment, you have to remember to tell your kids to respect things and to respect your belongings and so on or they'll lose it.

Mrs. Williams added, "And respect other people."

Mr. Miller continued, "Right, respect other people. Those values can get lost. We had to constantly remind our kids about the values that they got at home. Those values at home are so different than the ones they faced at school."

Dr. Williams responded,

> To add to that, we tried to emphasize to our kids that you can't have everything you see the kids at school have. We're just not able to provide you with that kind of lifestyle in terms of home, car, money, and travel and all the things that those kids do. It was important to try to emphasize early on that there is a difference, and we're not going to be able to compete or provide you with a lot of things that you may see other kids at school have. I think we were lucky that our kids understood that early on, and it wasn't a problem of saying, 'Well, somebody's parents bought them this or gave them that, why can't I have that?' or be ashamed of their origins. We were very lucky in that regard.

Most of the parents shared this same sense of pride in their children's decisions and actions. "I think you're hearing us say that we're very proud of our children," Ms. Johnson added. "They're no angels; I think we all would admit to that. But they face difficult challenges in these environments and do well."

Ms. Johnson and Ms. Daniels found it less difficult than the other parents to keep their children aware of their family values because their children entered private schooling later in their educational careers than the other parents' children. Ms. Johnson said,

> I want to say that my daughters had an awareness about our family values because they came to the school later. By having that awareness, they were set apart and they made decisions that didn't always allow them to be included in the social gatherings and events. I watched them struggle with the isolation and deal with it. They identified with those values they learned at home. They were confronted with choices that required them to decide whether they wanted to be a part of the group and at what cost. What does it mean to me socially and personally if I decide not to participate in some of those lifestyles?

Ms. Daniels responded, "My son faced similar questions, because he didn't enter this environment until later. He knew what our family values are and he could recognize when his experiences at his school didn't match those values."

Mrs. Williams replied, "I think all of us really have to help them answer those questions. They are just kids and don't have the maturity to make the decisions we always hope they'll make."

All of the parents agreed that their children encountered situations when they needed to decide between family values and those embedded in school culture. Mrs. Miller explained, "Unfortunately, they face these dilemmas needing to sort out conflicting values more often than I think we fully realize. We only see a glimpse of what they experience and go through, even though I think you've heard us say that we do our best to keep in touch with what's going on with our kids."

The parents all agreed that white students at these schools did not face these same dilemmas. Ms. Cullins remarked, "These are white, affluent environments with white, affluent values. The majority of the children at these schools don't face the same situation as our children because there's not a conflict between what they're experiencing at home and at school." Mrs. Williams added to this point,

> Many of these children are the offspring of extraordinarily wealthy people, and they will never have to look for a job. Unfortunately, they will not even have to come in contact with certain people if they don't want to. Not from the school's point of view, but from the family's point of view, they see no value in, or no reason why, their child has to learn how to relate to other people and to learn about other people different from themselves. If it's not going to be on the SAT and it's not going to help them with the AP test, then why should they learn it? What happens for my child, then, is a whole different story. My children have to understand others in order to thrive in these environments and in life in general. They're going to have to be ready to deal with a whole lot of different kinds of people, but I'm not so sure that some of those other kids are going to have to do that.

Ms. Johnson responded, "They become societal misfits. They may be good in their own world and can sit back in their little corner with their money, but they'll never blend in in society. They don't have to, but our children have a different reality."

In fact, all of the parents believed that their children's experiences in these schools prepared them well for the realities of life. "They know how to deal with people different from themselves and especially how to deal with people who have a lot of money and are powerful," Mrs. Miller said. "Hopefully, they also learned how to stay true to who they are and that they don't have to do what everybody else does." Dr. Williams added to this point,

> For me, diversity, for lack of a better term, was important. Because, when I grew up, I went to segregated schools in the inner city up to the ninth grade. I went to an integrated school in the ninth grade; it was the first time that I had ever seen anybody white up close. I was in awe for a long time. What I really wanted for my children was to be demystified about white people at a very early age so that they could see that they had similar faults and similar imperfections and not feel inferior to them by having seen them up close and personal.

Even though the parents wished that their children's schools did not exclude values outside those embedded in white, affluent culture, they believed that their children's experiences in these environments were educating them about this culture. They believed that this education was important for preparing their children to confront the racism they would face throughout their lives. "Like the saying goes, knowledge is power," Ms. Daniels proclaimed. "And our kids are gaining a lot of knowledge at these schools."

Gender Differences

Most of their children's private schools that are now coeducational were formerly all male. Even though these schools have been coeducational for around 30 to 40 years now, the parents believed that the all-male legacy has shaped the culture of the schools in powerful ways. "In a lot of ways, you just know that this school was once an all-boys school," Mrs. Miller pointed out. Mrs. Williams elaborated on this point,

> The school my daughters attended was at one point an all-male school, and those male cultural roots are very deeply embedded in the school's culture. Even when teachers talk about things, they use sports language, male sports language, in talking about things and giving examples. I'm trying to think of another example that comes through, but it's difficult because it's very subtle, but the girls pick up on it and they can point it out to you and tell you what's going on. I think that's why the boys have a good time at these schools and girls struggle more.

Although the parents described the impact of institutional racism on their sons' experiences, they emphasized the estrangement and alienation their daughters endured within these predominantly white environments. All of the parents believed that girls faced more difficulties socially and academically at their children's schools. Mrs. Miller further explained,

> I think that it's a gender issue when you look at our children's experiences in these schools. Of course, it's difficult for them to be African American in these places, but our girls face more challenges academically and socially. I don't think there were very many social benefits for our daughter at her school. There were social benefits for our son in that he went out with people and made associations he still has. Our daughter kind of gets left out of things. I noticed that when she got to the age where people were coupling off, you know, where people were dating, she was left out. But you make the trade-off and say, 'Well, getting the education is better and more important. It is a priority at this point in life, and then later on she'll catch up with other parts of her life.'

All of the parents who have daughters agreed that they chose "a better education over a good social experience [for their daughters]," Mrs. Keen added. She continued,

> For African American girls in a private school setting, I'm hearing all of us agree that it is very difficult. Boys often are able to socialize a little

bit better because they get involved in sports or other kinds of things, so they build camaraderie differently than girls do. Some girls get in sports and some don't, that's just what some girls just don't do. They just don't find the same opportunities to build camaraderie like the boys.

There was disagreement in the group on the social benefits that boys receive by "being pigeonholed as athletes more than as smart young men," Ms. Johnson observed. Some of the parents recognized that although African American boys were "acknowledged more for their athletic ability than their academic ability [in these schools]," as Ms. Daniels pointed out, their involvement in sports allowed them "to find a connection with the school community," Ms. Daniels added. The other parents believed that this "only reinforced stereotypes that black boys are only good on sports fields and not in the classroom," Mrs. Cullins believed. Most of the parents said that although they did not support the idea that African American boys were valued more for their athletic abilities than for how well they perform academically, they believed that sports did provide an avenue for boys to make connections within the school community. "It opened the door for them socially," Mrs. Williams explained. "It gave them a chance to make friends and establish connections with others—not only with other students but the overall school community." All of the parents believed that girls did not have this same opportunity to establish relationships with others and their school.

The majority of the parents agreed with Dr. Williams' observation that African American girls begin to experience social difficulties within these school environments during middle school. He recalled,

With each of our daughters somewhere around the seventh grade is when the lines of friendship get redrawn. Without any warning, people just sort of just abandoned their friends, and kids don't do anything well or tactfully. They abandoned one set of friends and started to congregate with people of more alike backgrounds, whether it was the jocks or the country club set or whatever. The lines got redrawn, and it was very painful I think for all three of our daughters when people they thought were their friends suddenly were not anymore.

Although the parents did not fully explain why these friendship lines "get redrawn" at this point, several believed that "this is the time when kids begin to notice differences more and they always can't deal with those differences," Mrs. Miller observed. The parents agreed that their children's (both boys and girls) social experiences at school changed during their middle-school years. "The beginning of adolescence is a difficult time, and the world changes for kids during those years," Ms. Daniels pointed out. Most of the parents agreed that the change in their daughters' relationships with their peers at school correlated with typical changes in behavior during adolescence.

Mrs. Miller and Mrs. Williams also described the estrangement and alienation their daughters endured from the white notions of beauty prevalent within school culture. Mrs. Miller explained, "It's the cute little blue-eyed blond who is valued in these communities and who is considered pretty and likable. Our daughters, of course, don't fit this mold. They're different and stand out because there's a particular look for girls that is valued in these communities." Similarly, Mrs. Williams said, "Our daughters aren't appreciated for their beauty, because their beauty doesn't fit into the narrow way it is determined by people. This narrow way has serious consequences for African American girls in how they see themselves and how they value themselves."

The other parents agreed that African American girls were negatively affected by what was considered beautiful within these school communities. "It really does have a negative impact on their self-esteem and self-respect when the people around you every day don't like the way you look," Ms. Daniels added. The parents all agreed that understandings of what was beautiful and likable, and what was not, within these white environments significantly affected African American girls' self-regard, self-esteem, and self-respect in ways that made it very difficult for them to develop into strong, independent women.

A Need for Change

Throughout the discussion, the parents offered suggestions for how their children's schools could realize more equitable school experiences for African American students. As others have argued (e.g., Proweller, 1999), the parents emphasized the need for curricula and pedagogies that affirm and critically engage all members of the school community. They believed that the process of working toward a genuine, collective effort against racism, sexism, and other forms of prejudice must begin with school leaders. The leaders must be "genuinely committed to fully incorporating diversity throughout the school," as Mrs. St. John explained, and be willing to work with African American parents in order to facilitate a process that engages the school community in dialogue about multiculturalism and diversity. The parents agreed with Mrs. Miller when she remarked that "the leaders of the school have to believe that this is a priority for everyone and not just for African American students." Mrs. St. John added to this point:

> The majority of the population is getting shortchanged by not providing a foundation for them to respect and appreciate diversity. When you look at the hiring of an administrator, then you should look at a person who is really committed to building diversity from the bottom up. I mean, everyone throughout the building should buy into that philosophy. The administrator needs to make it more than just an agenda item or something that sounds good. It needs to be a real commitment that every individual is respected. That's the only way you're going to

> be successful at creating an educational environment in a school that is truly committed to diversity. You have to build diversity and multiculturalism in your curriculum year-round, and to celebrate people. You don't have to have a special week or month. You build it in your curriculum, and you respect everyone. You have to be genuinely committed to fully incorporating diversity throughout the school.

Mr. Miller responded,

> You don't need to make it something special. When you start making it the Black History Month or the Black History Week instead of an issue confronted every day, it takes away from its significance. I mean, there are black people who were in history. They didn't just come around in the month of February. But that's what a lot of schools, including the public schools, do with talking about diversity and so forth. We are more than a 1-month-a-year people. We need administrators who consider us and our concerns and these issues more than just 1 month out of the year. They have to continuously work on these issues.

Most of the parents agreed that in order to bring about "long-lasting, effective change," Mrs. Miller believed, "you can't address it every once in a while or on special occasions. It must be a part of how you do business and what you're about."

The parents believed that school leaders were in the ideal position to change "business as usual" (Sleeter & Grant, 2003) at these schools by raising questions and initiating dialogue about discrimination and the experiences of African American students and providing the space for African Americans to have a voice in the school community. Dr. Williams continued,

> Those leaders at the schools have to send a very clear message telling everybody else in this school, This is what we'll tolerate, this is what we won't tolerate, and these are the things that I want you as a faculty and administration to incorporate into what we do every day—in the curriculum, how you treat people, what kinds of things we will and will not tolerate in terms of behavior. Rather than say, 'Well, we're for this,' and then it just sort of ends right there with just the words or a document and nothing else happens, they need to reinforce that or to make it very clear to everybody there that this is the direction that we're going to go.

Although all of the parents agreed with Dr. Williams that leaders' messages about the importance of addressing issues of diversity throughout the school community must be clear and firm, most of the parents disagreed that this alone would bring about change. Mrs. Williams replied to her husband's statement, "I think that's the way it should be and that's a great theory, but it doesn't happen like that. I will use an example that has nothing to do with race or culture. Our daughters' high school has a dress code, but they don't wear uniforms. And young ladies are supposed to wear dresses at a certain length and tops that aren't too revealing. There's a laundry list of things they are supposed to not wear, and young men are supposed to dress a certain way and not wear certain kinds of T-shirts and wear pants a certain way. And guess what?"

Mr. Miller replied, "It's a joke."

Mrs. Williams continued,

> It's a joke. It has always been a joke, and the reason it has been a joke is because it's not enforced. The top people say, 'We got this dress code and blah, blah, blah,' but as soon as Susie Little walks in the door in a tube top that she's wearing as a skirt because she couldn't find a skirt that morning, and then the teacher, head of upper school or whoever says, 'That's a violation of the dress code and you're going to get a detention,' Susie Little says, 'So, give me a detention and then I'll tell my daddy,' and then so much for the dress code. It does have to start at the top with the board, the culture of the board, and then the headmaster and so on, but it doesn't happen. It just doesn't.

As previously noted in this chapter, the parents described the culture of the school as marked by a strong sense of entitlement, and they believed that this sense of "getting what I want needs to change before anything else changes," Mrs. Williams added. "You don't have rules in this environment," Mrs. Miller explained, "or at least ones that are followed." Most of the parents pointed out that it is difficult to insist on any kind of behavior if "it's not what the majority of the people already want to do," Mrs. Miller added. Most of the parents believed that this entitlement embedded in school culture had to change before these school communities truly respected diversity. Mrs. Miller continued, "It would just be another example of putting down words on paper without any follow-through. You have to convince people that these issues are a benefit to the community."

Unlike Mrs. Miller, most of the parents had little faith that individuals at their children's schools could be convinced that issues of diversity were important without "a major overhaul of the school culture and people's attitudes and lifestyles," as Ms. Daniels put it. She continued, "You'll never convince people that these issues are important without having consequences for their actions and making sure you actually hold people accountable, because they will want to know how this benefits me individually. I just don't believe most of the individuals at these schools care about others enough to take on what they would consider other people's issues."

All of the parents felt that educators and other members of these school communities were not invested in issues of diversity. Even though all of their children's schools "say they are committed to diversity," Dr. Williams observed, "[they] don't back up verbal commitments with deeds or actions that reinforce the words." Ms. Johnson responded, "They ignore diversity issues. They say they care about diversity and want diversity in their schools. But they don't. They do nothing to demonstrate that they want to create an educational environment where all students can be successful."

All of the parents reported that their children's schools had included commitment to diversity in mission statements and other official documents, but, as Ms. Keen observed, "There's no follow-through with the elaborate plans and beautiful words that they come up with." Ms. Daniels added:

> The head of my daughters' school has adopted this core character and diversity platform. They then need to translate that into some behaviors that are built into the evaluations of teachers and set up some sort of incentive-based promotion system that incorporates the demonstration of some of these behaviors as part of the criteria for promotion and advancement in the school. I think the school has attempted to incorporate diversity in the school culture through individual staff who don't have the maturity of understanding of what it really means. So you have tokenism that takes place in the same way as it did in the past.

Mr. Miller responded, "They need to take a much more aggressive role with these issues. If you're talking about trying to improve private schools from a diversity standpoint, and while you're at it from an academic standpoint, then you have to make some serious changes and hold people accountable for making these changes."

Most of the parents agreed that individuals at their children's schools needed to be held accountable for "making [the schools] places where all children are successful, not just white and affluent kids," as Mrs. Williams explained. Mrs. Keen added,

> I think we need and the schools need to operationalize the idea of having a diverse school and then decide what exactly that means. If we want to have a diverse school, then it means this, it means that, and then making sure those things get accomplished. I think one of the ways of doing this is through performance evaluation. Teachers should do certain things and they are going to get evaluated for it.

Mr. Miller responded,

> It's hard to cross over the line and tell teachers that you have to do x, y, and z to the point you are almost writing their lesson plans. But students go through 4 years of high school and have the background in English and creative writing, but they haven't been given an assignment in reading Langston Hughes or Paul Laurence Dunbar, the old black poetry, which is some of the most eloquent writing that's ever been done. These

> works are ignored. Teachers are failing at their jobs to make sure that the curriculum is diverse. We are a nation of various groups of people, and they should be represented in the curriculum. Education for most people is preparation for life, and the real world is not all white, not all black. And if schools aren't going to prepare these kids with anything but two plus two equals four, then they are really falling down on the job.

Similar to what many have argued (e.g., Delpit, 1995; Sleeter & McLaren, 1995; Tatum, 1997), the parents emphasized the need for multicultural education to provide African American students opportunities to learn about the intellectual and historical legacies of their own culture and to promote the strength and value of cultural diversity for all students. Most of the parents agreed that the schools "are failing to provide this diversity in the curriculum" and "are, therefore, failing to live up to their promises" of creating school environments committed to multiculturalism and diversity, as Mrs. Keen noted.

The parents acknowledged that addressing issues of diversity and multiculturalism was a "time-consuming and difficult ongoing process for everyone," Ms. Johnson remarked. Most of them also agreed with Ms. Johnson when she further explained, "We, as African Americans, have an important role in this process, but we have to be given the voice and be allowed to have a meaningful role in the process." She continued,

> Problems in the schools reflect problems in society that we all are familiar with. A lot of the people who run the school and are a part of the school have the same problems outside the school that they have inside the school in terms of understanding and relating to us as human beings and dealing with diversity very successfully. I think it takes an effort from parents and the people at the top to come together and work together. We have to get to know each other. Spend time getting to know each other. I don't think that the people I met at my son's school actually understand who I am as a person, what my values are, and what my needs are. They don't understand the needs of our children other than their academic needs, but our children have other needs. I think they need to get input from someplace other than a book. It takes dialogue. It takes conversation.

Ms. Johnson responded, "The concept that it takes getting to know people is simple in a lot of ways but it takes intentional efforts, a plan to gain this knowledge." Most of the parents felt that their children's schools did not know them or their children. From their perspective, this lack of knowledge stood in the way "of our children being educated and feeling proud of who they are and where they come from," Ms. Daniels added.

As Ms. Johnson observed,

> One of the problems I saw at the school was that the environment became less motivating for our children. Our children had no incentive to do well or even do their best. It was a frustrating thing because I couldn't put my finger on it. But there was just no drive to do well. And I know that's not just necessarily a private school thing, but I think private schools should address it because they are there to provide a higher level of education. The longer I spent time at my son's school, the less motivated I saw our children being. It was just so frustrating knowing that we had talented, beautiful children who for some reason felt no desire to do their best.

Mrs. Williams replied,

> Doing well was not rewarded. Kids are kids. I can't remember my Psychology 101 class, but when you are rewarded for doing your best, then you're going to continue to do your best. You can get some of the needed encouragement from home, but if you're not encouraged in the classroom to do your best, then you're not going to do your best in the classroom unless you're just that exceptional kind of kid who can work outside of whatever's going on around him or her. There are some children like that. But everyone wants their strokes, everyone wants to be recognized. If they aren't getting that in the classroom but they are getting it from somewhere else, then that may be the road they take.

All of the parents agreed that one of the most important ways to encourage African American students both academically and socially was for school communities to celebrate their culture. "This celebration not only sends the message that African Americans are valued in these schools but also that people are putting forth the effort to get themselves educated about our culture," Ms. Daniels explained. The parents believed that these celebrations would demonstrate that schools cared about and respected African Americans and their culture.

Most of the parents reported that they had made efforts to be involved in different and, for some, numerous activities that celebrated African American culture at their children's schools so that "these communities got to know who we are," Mrs. Miller explained. She continued,

> I did go to my children's school and participate in diversity activities. I taught the kids to cakewalk. I brought sweet potato pie and things that were part of our culture. That is the kind of understanding that a staff needs to have to be effective. There has to be some way of teaching people to appreciate diversity, to feel comfortable enough to draw from those who are around them. And I don't think that is there at my children's school. Instead, I think there's a kind of "we're in this place with all these rich people" and diversity is a window dressing.

Most of the parents disagreed with Mrs. Miller that these types of activities were effective in teaching the community about African American culture. As Mrs. Williams pointed out,

> When we go and participate in these events and share our culture with them, how do they incorporate what they've learned about African American culture in the learning environment so that everyone benefits from that perspective? All the schools seem to be stuck on food, fairs, and festivals. I mean, they can't get beyond that. I look forward to the day when diversity means more than food, fairs, and festivals.

Most of the parents agreed that multicultural education needed to be more than "food, fairs, and festivals," but instead, as Ms. Daniels explained, "a process that puts important issues on the table—issues that don't necessarily make everyone feel good, but more importantly issues that challenge people's thinking and the way they do things. It has to be more than a 'by-the-way' approach to diversity."

The entire group believed that it took intentional, ongoing, and sincere efforts to be a school community committed to diversity. The parents also agreed that if schools were not willing to make these efforts, then "they don't need to say they're committed to something and don't do the work it takes to do that," Ms. Johnson stated. Mrs. Keen responded, "Once our students are in the door, they don't continue to demonstrate that they have a commitment and actually want African American students at the school. They just enroll African Americans because it's like something they have to do, but they really aren't showing any commitment that this is something they want to do. There's a feeling like they don't have to do any more than just have our children there." All the parents agreed that their children's schools made considerable efforts to recruit African Americans but not efforts "to make sure they're successful in these schools," Mrs. Miller added. She continued, "I think the school and their leaders have to decide if indeed they want to have a diverse population in their school and if they're prepared to provide everyone with a quality education. If it isn't about providing African Americans with a quality education, then there's no point in them being there." Most of the parents agreed that their children's schools, as Mrs. Williams added, had "a long way to go" in providing a quality education to African American students.

Disharmony in Diversity

For the most part, private schools have discontinued their formerly exclusionary practices in admissions. The number of students of color in private schools in the United States demonstrates how far they have traveled from the days when their graduates were almost entirely "soldiers for their class" (Cookson & Persell, 1985, p. 26) and "Christian gentlemen who followed the footsteps of their fathers into the corporate board rooms with little knowledge of all those

Americans who lacked the privilege" to attend private schools (Armstrong, 1990, p. 15). Most private schools in this country are no longer places only for wealthy, white, Anglo-Saxon, Protestant, male students in terms of enrollment. For example, in the 2005–2006 school year, 21.2% of total enrollment in member schools (both boarding and day) of the National Association of Independent Schools (NAIS) were students of color.[4] While private schools are not diversifying at the same rate as public schools in the United States (Proweller, 1999), they have made considerable efforts to recruit and enroll the broadest possible constituency.

Even with the shifting demographics of student populations in these institutions and the great efforts they make to recruit students of color (Fordham, 1991), African Americans remain outsiders in these school cultures; to quote Collins' (1986) apt phrase, they are "outsiders within" (p. 14). That African Americans are a part of these communities does not mean that racism is a relic of the past. As revealed throughout the parents' discussion and similar to what many have found (e.g., Proweller, 1999; Zweigenhaft and Domhoff, 1991), African American students are marginalized within these school cultures. Their experiences at these margins reveal that the center of these institutions remain unchanged. These school cultures continue to be embedded in white, affluent cultural ways of knowing and doing.

As the parents noted, their children's schools, through mission statements and other official documents and plans, acknowledge the need for addressing difference but do not work toward disrupting or dismantling institutional systems, practices, and arrangements that place African American students at a disadvantage. These school communities engage in a discourse of "harmony in diversity" (Proweller, 1999), which keeps the center of their school cultures unchanged. As Mohanty (1990) observes,

> The central issue, then, is not one of merely acknowledging difference; rather, the more difficult question concerns the kind of difference that is acknowledged and engaged. Difference seen as benign variation (diversity), for instance, rather than as conflict, struggle, or the threat of disruption, bypasses power as well as history to suggest a harmonious, empty pluralism. On the other hand, difference defined as asymmetrical and incommensurate cultural spheres situated within hierarchies of domination and resistance cannot be accommodated within a discourse of 'harmony in diversity.' (p. 181)

Proweller (1999) adds that although the discourse of "'harmony in diversity' preserves the liberal commitment to transcending cultural particularities … , it fails to dismantle ideological systems that persist in reproducing systemic inequalities in our schools and society more broadly" (p. 802).

Consistent with what the parents pointed out, it is not enough to acknowledge differences; the school culture needs to change. White, affluent cultural ways of knowing and doing need to be decentered, and conflicts that arise from differences within schools communities need to be engaged, rather than suppressed, in order to begin working toward establishing a school culture where African Americans are no longer "outsiders within." In order to realize more equitable school experiences for all students, the cultural center of school communities must be redefined to "become more critically responsive and responsible to the breadth and depth of human experience yet to be heard, listened to, and affirmed" in these communities (Proweller, 1999, p. 803).

9
Privileged Perceptions of the Subjugated Other

> I think students [at Parker Day School] are more successful in school because we work harder. Just from the stories I've heard from people who used to go to public schools, students there just sit around and don't do anything. They don't do homework and don't work in class. They don't listen to teachers. Most of them sleep during class instead of paying attention. It's totally different here. Students work hard 'cause they want to be successful in school. We want to get into good colleges and know we have to work our butts off to get into the really good ones.
>
> **Scott, Parker Day School student**

Sara Lawrence-Lightfoot (1983), in her study of "good" high schools, observed during her research at the elite St. Paul's School that "the incredible beauty, seclusion, and abundance of St. Paul's makes it seem far away from the reality most people know. … It is easy to imagine that people might quickly forget the ugly facts of life beyond this serene place" (p. 228). Consistent with her observations as well as those of other researchers (e.g., Peshkin, 2001), the "ugly" facts and realities of poverty and those living in poverty seem very distant from the life and schooling circumstances of those in the four school communities described in this book. As elsewhere in the country, individuals within these affluent schools are clustered in isolated, class-segregated communities. Isolation is fairly consistent in the various spheres of these students' lives. They have little contact with the "ugly" school and life circumstances of Others.

During the course of my research, I discovered that although most students at these four schools were isolated and had little contact with those outside their closed communities, they were aware of the class divisions of the larger society and within their local communities. They were also aware of their own life and school advantages. They acknowledge social class differences and have some ideas as to why these differences exist and persist. Their awareness, however, is limited by their class-segregated life and schooling circumstances. Students are too isolated to have understandings of social class differences and their own advantages that are not bound by their own taken-for-granted realities.

Two Parker students, Nicole and Scott (introduced in chapter 4), showed more interest and were more frank and open in discussing social class differences in schooling than were other students. Most likely, they were more eager to discuss these issues because during that time I was also conducting a research study at Reed High School, a public school with mostly poor students.[1] Nicole and Scott were very curious about what I was observing at this other school and freely offered their opinions about the differences between Parker and Reed students and the reasons for their own advantages in schooling.

Far Different Realities Nearby

Reed High School is located about 30 miles southeast of Parker Day School just outside the limits of Owensville. When I first drove through Owensville, I was reminded of the small, rural communities in Kentucky where I lived during my childhood. The town has a restaurant, grocery store, post office, town hall, and two gas stations. One of the gas stations has a sign posted that changes daily announcing birthdays with closings that usually read, "Love, Mom and Dad." It is a town where residents know each other and strangers are easily spotted.

Owensville is one of the several small communities in Reed County, which is one of the poorest counties in the state. The residents are almost entirely white (98%), Christian, and working class with strong Appalachian cultural influences. Most residents of the county are employed either in industry or in agriculture, but nearly one fourth of the population is unemployed. When I first met the superintendent of the Reed County School District, he described the county as the "land of illiteracy." He told me, "Once you get about 10 miles east of [the city where Parker Day School is located], you can't find an educated person. You enter the land of illiteracy; no one around here cares about education." He was referring, in part, to the high percentage of the county's adult residents who did not complete high school (nearly one third of the population) and the school's history of a high dropout rate.

There are about 600 students at Reed High, and the average income per family of the student population falls within the range of poverty. Consistent with Kozol's (1991) extensive study of the "savage inequalities" in school funding between the affluent and the poor, the average expenditure per student at Reed High is significantly less than the state's average and far from what is allocated for each student at the public school in the neighborhood where most Parker students live. The below-average expenditure at Reed High results from the small amount received from local income and property taxes, which are the primary sources of funding for schools in the state. Residents have consistently voted not to increase funding for the county's public schools over the years. "People just won't give us the financial support we need. We can't get a tax levy passed around here," the superintendent complains.

Academically, Reed ranks as one of the lowest counties in the state in terms of students' scores on the statewide mandated proficiency test. At the time I conducted research at Reed, only 16% of the students taking the proficiency test for the first time passed. After five attempts, 79% of the students passed all five parts of the test. Of the state's 611 school districts, Reed ranks 547 for average student attendance. On average, 17% of the students attend one of the four vocational schools within the district, and the rest of the students take a general academic course. The school does not offer a college preparatory program.

Reed High's one-story, rectangular-shaped brick building is surrounded by farmland and at first glance appears to be in the middle of a field. The school building is surrounded by only a few trees and sits a good distance from the two-lane road in front of the school. Similarly formed, the county's middle school is beside Reed High but not connected. Parking lots are located in front and in back of the schools. The athletic facilities are about a half-mile from the school, but not within sight of the building. During my visits, I observe mostly Ms. Conlan's tenth-grade English class and follow a faithful routine. Unlike my visits to Parker, where I was free to roam the campus buildings and grounds, Reed has a firm policy for all visitors. Visitors are required to let the main office know where they are in the building at all times and must wear a name tag. Since I frequently visit the school, I am excused from one of the rules, which requires all visitors to be escorted by a school official to their destination. I arrive at 8:00, go to the office to sign in and get my name tag, and wait until 8:13 for the bell. At this time in the morning, the office is filled with students who are either late for school or waiting to talk with Mr. Bradley, the assistant principal, for disciplinary reasons. When the bell rings for second period, the hallways immediately become crowded with students rushing within the 2-minute interval to their next class and teachers who hall-monitor between classes.

Much like a student, I too jump up and head in the direction of Ms. Conlan's classroom at the cue of the bell. Her classroom is in the east wing of the school, where the rest of the English department is located. From the office, a long hallway leads past the gymnasium, library, distance-learning lab, and smoke-filled boys' bathroom to her classroom. Several years ago, a group of local businesses furnished the distance-learning lab with a fax machine, video cameras, televisions, and a computer so as to provide students with more educational resources to prepare them for the workplace. The school received only initial funding from these local businesses and has not been able to maintain the lab financially. Filled with broken and outdated equipment, the room is unused. Even though there are hall monitors dispersed throughout the school, there are never teachers present in the hallway directly leading to Ms. Conlan's classroom. Because of this, the male students designate the boys' bathroom located along this hallway as the smoking area. Neither the bathroom nor the stalls have doors. Smoke flows out of the bathroom, creating a haze throughout the hallway.

In Ms. Conlan's classroom, the students' desks are arranged in rows facing the chalkboard. Covered with stacks of books and papers, her desk is in the back of the room. Two small bookshelves stand nearby to store the overflow from her desk. Looking out the windows of the classroom, one sees the farmland surrounding the school and a small river running beyond the length of the building. The walls are covered mostly with movie posters. Ms. Conlan changes the posters in her room on a regular basis to keep up-to-date with the blockbuster hits. Along one wall of the classroom are workstations with computers that the school received as a corporate donation, on which graduating seniors could write resumés and letters to assist them in seeking employment.

During my initial meeting with Ms. Conlan, she warned me about one of her students, Jason, who she described as a "very lively character who is always telling outrageous stories during class and keeps things very interesting around here." When I meet the students, I immediately identify Jason without the need for formal introduction. He walks in the classroom rapping a song that is filled with curse words. Ms. Conlan, who is sitting at her desk working on papers, acknowledges Jason with a disparaging look but does not say anything to him. A group of students gather around his desk to listen to his animated account of last night's activities. When the bell rings, Ms. Conlan continues working at her desk, and the students remain captivated by Jason's storytelling. At this point, he has the full attention of the entire class. About 4 minutes into class time, Ms. Conlan gets out of her chair and says, "OK, Jason. We've heard enough."

Jason responds, "My bad. It's just crazy, Ms. Conlan," and the students take their seats at their desks. Shortly thereafter, she has the attention of all the students and begins class.

Unlike the majority of his classmates who have always lived in Reed County, Jason entered Reed High School at the end of his freshman year at the age of 15, when he moved from New York, where most of his family continues to live. Jason's parents are divorced, and he has met his father only twice. His father is a truck driver and his mother is unemployed. His mother moved to the Midwest in hopes of finding employment. It has been nearly 4 years since they moved, and she has yet to find work.

Jason is now 18, almost 19, and is making his third attempt at sophomore English. When he was eligible during his second year at the school, he entered the vocational school in the culinary arts program with the hope of eventually becoming a chef. During his first year at the vocational school, he was dismissed for disciplinary problems relating to his drug use and subsequently returned to Reed High School. Jason is now enrolled in the school's dropout program, which provides basic courses in the morning and employment in the afternoon. A teacher supervises the student's work, and upon satisfactory completion of a work assignment, the student receives credit toward graduation. Jason has remained in school to participate in this program. "I would have dropped out when I could," he explains, "but they get me jobs. I get steady work keeping here." Students do not have to maintain a certain grade point average to remain in the program, but they are required to attend academic classes in the morning regularly. In other words, they need to show up for school, but they do not need to do work.

Jason has brought a pillow to make his nap during class more comfortable. Ms. Conlan reminds Jason that she told him not to bring it to class, but he ignores her. Trying to draw the attention of his classmates, he fluffs the pillow and situates it on top of his desk in an exaggerated way. He lays his head down and sleeps for the remaining time in class. Ms. Conlan leaves him alone. During class, Ms. Conlan gives the other students a worksheet on last night's reading. She hands out the worksheet and returns to her desk to grade papers. Students mostly socialize for the 55 minutes of class time and then half-heartedly finish the worksheet in the last 5 minutes of class. When the bell rings, a student sitting near Jason wakes him up.

After class, I approach Jason to ask him for an interview. He agrees, and we schedule a time during my next visit. The following week after my observation of Ms. Conlan's class, I meet Jason for our first interview. I sit with him in a small room located in the library. Before I have the chance to ask him questions, Jason tells me, "So, you're here to find out just how bad our school is and compare it to that rich school."

Taken aback, I ask, "That's what you understood from what I explained about why I'm here?" In my initial meeting with the class, I explained that I was comparing their school with Parker and gave them some information about Parker.

"Well, you said it in a different way, but that's what you're trying to tell us," he responds. "You're just trying to say it in a nice way." I explain the purpose of my research to him again, attempting to reassure him of my intentions. I sense, though, that he's still suspicious of me even after my explanation.

We spend most of this first meeting getting to know each other. He asks me nearly as many questions about my life, past educational experiences, and understandings as I ask him. I realize that the traditional approach to interviewing research participants that I had been trained to conduct in graduate school isn't going to work with Jason. He wants something different. He wants us to engage in dialogue about the issues of my research. He wants to know what I think and what I've experienced. He wants to know as much about me as I want to know about him.

During our dialogue about the influences of social class on education, I discover just how acutely aware Jason is of the educational inequalities between the poor and the affluent. He tells me,

> At the rich schools, kids never fail. They'll get tutors or whatever it takes to be successful. Their teachers also give more attention to them because they've got money. They have to care about them because their parents are paying good money for them to care. But around here, there ain't no shit like that. And it's because it has to do with money. Everything revolves around money because that's the way our socially economic society works. If you're poor, then you're shit out of luck, and if you're rich, then top of the world to ya. And it works like that in school, too. Our teachers ain't pressed to do shit because they don't have to be. We don't have all the stuff at school that rich kids have. We don't get attention or the other stuff.
>
> A lot of kids here have maybe decent potential but fall through the cracks. The principal kicks kids out of school if they sneeze too hard. They don't deal with shit; they just kick you out. I mean sometimes people don't get a chance. It's because we're at a lower social structure than that private school you're looking at. Everybody knows that, and especially this school. Our school doesn't prepare you for life like it needs to because nobody cares about us rednecks. Our school is preparing us to be farmers and to do jobs our parents do. It works the same way in the rich school. Those kids are being prepared for jobs that their parents do. They're being prepared to be rich.

Jason's insights penetrate the myths of school as a neutral territory where all students have equal opportunity and meet on an equal footing. He believes that schools reflect the cultural and economic divisions of the larger society and, consequently, prepare poor students for different positions in society than affluent students. By relating social class distinctions in schooling to society's class stratification, Jason not only identifies the inequalities in schooling between the affluent and the poor (e.g., resources, academic achievement, educational expectations), but also surfaces the economic, political, and social consequences of these differences. Jason's understandings reveal a class consciousness—that is, an awareness of the everyday realities of particular class positions that shape our lives—of his educational experiences.

Leveled Aspirations

Summer vacation is just 2 weeks away at Reed High School. Administrators and some of the teachers are helping seniors find work and finalize plans for life after graduation. Military recruiters have been at the school frequently for the past couple of months. With limited employment opportunities in their community, military service promises one of the best chances for students to be employed after graduation. According to results from a school-administered survey, 30% of the seniors plan to attend a postsecondary institution, mostly 2-year colleges, and the remaining 70% plan to seek employment immediately after graduation, with a significant number joining the military. The number of Reed High seniors planning to continue their education is just slightly below the national average of poor students attending college, which is 36% (Howard, 2002). Since the school does not offer a college preparatory program or college counseling, I find nearly one-third of the graduates going on to college surprising.

I arrive at the school for my last interview with Jason. Ms. Conlan informed me the week before that Jason was failing all of his classes this semester. "It's such a shame. He's a bright guy but has let drugs get in the way of his doing well. He could do much, much better in school if he focused his energy on it as much as he does on having a good time." I agree somewhat with her assessment but believe that his lack of interest and effort in school has more to do with his seeing school "as a holding cell that tides students over until they hit adulthood" than his simply wanting to have a good time outside of school. After getting to know Jason, I am inclined to accept his explanation for abusing drugs and alcohol as his way of "dealing with all the shit in my life." I am convinced that Jason's "bad decisions" reveal his efforts to cope with the everyday realities that he faces living in poverty.

We meet in our usual space in the library, the tape recorder going. He asks me, "So, did you find out anything new?" I reply by going over some of what I plan to tell the entire class in a couple of days about the findings of my research. To answer his question more directly, I tell him that my research has found a lot of what other studies have documented about the differences in education between the affluent and the poor.

Not satisfied with my answer, Jason cuts to the chase by asking, "What did the rich kids have to say?"

"About what?"

"Did they say they're better than us and smarter?"

"No, not really. They didn't say they were smarter. They said they work hard and care about school and really try to do well so that they can go to good colleges. They also said that they care a lot about school, and their parents pay a lot of money for them to go to a school like they do."

"Do you think they work harder?"

"I think their school is a place where students get a lot of encouragement to work hard and get rewarded for that work. I did observe most students there working a lot in school. They want to get into good colleges and do well in their classes and participate in a lot of activities to help them get into good schools. They did what they were supposed to do." Although I don't tell him that I think Parker's students work harder than the students at Reed, I'm sure Jason understands my response as saying that.

He replies to my observations, "Then you come over here and us hilljacks don't do any work. We just sleep and fuck around."

"Why do you say that?"

"I'll only speak for myself, but I think if I went to a rich school and my daddy and mommy were rich, I'd have a different outlook about school. I think I'd give a damn about school and do what I had to do to get good grades. But I don't have a rich mommy and daddy, and I'm stuck at this school. I just want to get out of here and don't give a good goddamn about anything that has to with this school. I mean, I hate this school, man."

I ask, "Do you really think that you would like school more if it were like the other school in my research?"

"Probably, but I don't want to think about that too much. I'll just get more depressed about shit," Jason replies.

"Depressed about what?"

Our conversation pauses for a moment while Jason, looking down at the table, contemplates my question. He eventually responds, "Like I've told you before, me and my mom have it pretty rough. She doesn't work, and we're just making do by the skin of our teeth. I know it's always going to be this way."

I ask, "What way?"

"I'm always going to be strapped for money. I'm never going to get out of here and back to New York. I'm stuck here. That's why when I think about being rich or something, it's so depressing because I know that's never going to happen. I know if I cared about school and did my shit, then I could do things."

"What things?"

"Not be poor. Get a job. Maybe go to school and learn how to be a chef. You know what I'm talking about. You did what you had to do to get ahead in life. You played the game right."

"You're right. At your age, I did whatever it took to get out of poverty."

"It seemed like it all worked out for you, but I just don't want to do that shit. I just don't want to do all the shit it takes to get where you're at. I don't think it would work out the same way for me."

Reflections on My Conversations with Jason

Since Jason failed all of his academic courses during the year of my research, he didn't move closer to graduation. Midway through the following school year, he dropped out of high school and began working at a fast-food restaurant. Ms. Conlan and other school officials cited his drug abuse and family problems as the main reasons for his failure in school. They all described him as "very bright" but claimed he was unmotivated, lazy, and undisciplined.

What I learned about Jason through our conversations led me to an alternative understanding of his failure in school. Beneath his drug abuse, his lack of effort, and his unwillingness to fulfill his academic responsibilities was an awareness of the deeply seated structural inequalities in society. Jason did not accept the individual achievement ideology (i.e., the notion that people can get ahead if they work hard). He was conscious of how the education offered to him leveled students' aspirations. Skeptical about his chances to get out of poverty through education, he actively rejected school.

Jason's actions of subverting teacher authority, disrupting classes, displaying open and hostile opposition to schooling, and sleeping during class were attempts to legitimate his own right to control his time and space. Jason's actions were consistent with what Michael Apple (1982) explains about students who doubt schooling will help them get ahead in life, "Their rejection of so much of the content and form of day to day educational life bears on the almost unconscious realization that, as a class, schooling will not enable them to go much further than they already are" (p. 99). Powerless and isolated, Jason's individual acts of resistance forfeited his chances for social advancement. Consistent with what other researchers have found (e.g., Fine, 1991), Jason's resistance to the context at his school eventually led him to drop out.

Understanding and Justifying Advantages

Similar to Jason, Scott and Nicole at Parker Day School acknowledge the differences in schooling between the poor and the affluent. Although both of them claim to have had little contact with schools with predominantly poor students, they believe that their school has better teachers and more resources and offers an overall better education than schools with poor students. Like Jason, they too believe that students at their school are being prepared for different occupations and positions in society than poor students. Unlike Jason, though, Scott and Nicole indicate that the disparities in schooling result from differences in the efforts, attributes, and attitudes of students and their families. They believe that affluent students have better schooling than poor students because they work harder in school and care about being successful and their families pay more for education. They justify their advantaged schooling without relating the meanings and practices of Parker to social class divisions in the larger society.

We Work Hard in School

Scott and Nicole attribute academic achievement to individual effort. They believe that affluent students are more successful in school than poor students because they work harder. Scott's statement prefacing this chapter captures this sentiment. He clearly feels that students at Parker have strong work habits, such as paying attention in class and completing their assignments. These work-habit strengths lead to academic success. For Scott, students are personally responsible for how well they do in school by the amount of effort they put into their schoolwork. He believes that most students at public schools, which he repeatedly equates with poor students, are not willing to do what it takes to be successful there—"They don't do homework and don't work in class." As he further explains, "Students decide how well they do in school by how much they're willing to work in school."

Looking at his own academic success, he says, "I really just try to do my best, and if I know that I tried my hardest throughout the quarter and I got a grade, then I think that's what I deserve cause that's what I got. So I just try to do my best, but if I don't do my best, then I get disappointed with the grade I get because I know it's my fault. I haven't worked hard enough to do as well as I know I can." He goes on to say that his work-habit strengths allow him to maintain his high grade point average. He believes that he has *earned* his good grades and deserves academic success for his work.

Similarly, Nicole believes that success in school is a result of individual effort. She maintains,

> I think students at Parker just work harder than students at poor schools and public schools. We also have a lot of really smart students. Almost everybody wants to get good grades because they want to go to a really good college. So we work a lot in our classes. To do well here, you have to really work a lot. We all pretty much do what it takes to make good grades. I don't think it works the same at poor schools, because students just don't work that much.

Elaborating on this point, she explains, "Everybody here wants to go to college and we know what it takes to get there. That's what makes this school different than other ones. The schools with poor kids just don't have too many students wanting to go to college." Both Scott and Nicole believe that individual effort, motivated by the aspiration to attend a "good" college, precipitates academic achievement. In their opinion, poor students don't have the same motivation to work hard as affluent students.

We Care about Education

"We work hard in school because we care about education," Scott explains. Both students believe that academic success rests on students caring about their education. They contend that affluent students work harder in school because they care more about their education than do poor students. Scott's and Nicole's belief that poor students and their families do not care about education reverberate through their discussions about social class differences in educational outcomes. As Scott says,

> Most students and their families at Parker really care about getting a good education. Education is one of the top priorities in the families here. I don't think it's the same priority for poor people. I think the schools they attend are a lot different than this one. They develop a routine that has an idea that they're not going to go to college. They don't really care about going to college. They don't want to succeed. They just want to stay there and just live and survive. I think the schools take that into account. I think it's bad that we have different education than poor

> people, but honestly I think it has to do a lot with how much students care about education. This school knows we all care and so they take that into account.

Scott believes that poor students "don't want to succeed," because, as he explains, "they don't really care about going to college." He believes that poor students' preoccupation with the day-to-day aspects of life and survival outweighs their drive to succeed. Scott's conclusion that affluent students care more about education is couched in his narrow understanding of "success" as going to college. Like Scott, Nicole believes that poor students aren't concerned with going to college, which results in poor students caring less about education.

Along with students caring about education, Nicole and Scott contend that their teachers express more care than teachers at schools with poor students. As Nicole explains,

> Our school has a smaller community. It is more academic. The teachers here care more about their students. Well, I mean, it's hard to find a good teacher in poor schools, and here there's a larger majority of good teachers. There's a tighter knit community, there's a feeling of community in private schools because people just seem to care more and they know each other more. At least everybody has seen each other's face, and at most poor schools there's not even that. They have a lot more students to deal with. Teachers don't even know their students well. and this makes it more difficult to care about the students the same way they do here.

In addition to community size, Nicole believes that teachers at Parker care more about their students because "they know the students and parents care about their education." Likewise, Scott maintains, "Teachers at our school care because we care about school. Teachers couldn't be here if they didn't care about their students. The families just wouldn't put up with it. There's not that same pressure at poor schools."

We Pay More Money for Our Education

Nicole and Scott also believe that they receive a better education than poor students because their families are willing to offer the necessary financial support for them to attend good schools. Although they recognize that families at Parker are financially capable of paying more for education than are poor families, they nonetheless feel that since education is not a priority for poor families, they do not make the financial sacrifices to ensure that their children receive a good education.

Scott points out the failed levies to increase funding for the city's public schools as an example of the unwillingness of poor families to support, financially, the schools that their children attend. He says,

> It costs a pretty hefty sum to go here. Our families pay a lot of money for us to go to this school because we all value education. In the poor areas, people don't value education the same way and aren't willing to provide money for schools to make sure that they have the needed resources for a good education. The last election proved this point. Poor families may not have as much money as the people at our school to spend on education, but they can show their financial support in other ways. The city's public schools need a lot of money. Everybody knows that. But people aren't willing to make sure that they get more money through taxes. The schools ask for more money at every election, but they never get it. This is a way for poor families to support their kids' schools financially, but they don't.

Scott is asked to consider, "How about the voting patterns of poor people? Since not a lot of poor people vote, at least compared with the affluent, do failed levies really indicate poor people's unwillingness to financially support the schools that their children attend?" He responds, "Again, if they cared about their kids' education, then they would vote and make sure that schools got more money. Just like voting against giving more money for schools, not voting at all still sends a message." Scott doesn't acknowledge that there may be other reasons why people living in poverty don't vote; that it's not simply a matter of poor people "not caring" about their children's education.

Nicole embraces the notion that "you get what you pay for." She associates educational opportunity with one's family financial circumstances. She explains,

> Our parents just have more means to send us to a school like Parker. There are expectations that if you go to this school, then you're going to go to a good college. Kids here are expected to have better jobs and make a certain amount of money. It's just the nature of different social statuses and the way kids are educated. We just have more opportunities because of our parents. Like, our counselor is really good. She's an excellent college advisor. She gets you where you want to go and helps you realize what you want to do. So it depends on the parent if they want their kid to get into college. This school has parents who have the means and kids who want to learn. Parents want their kids to come here because the teachers are good and the school has the needed resources to prepare us for college. Everybody knows we have a better school. It's just the way the world works. It isn't fair, but you get what you pay for when it comes to education.

Nicole attributes class distinctions in schooling to what families are capable of affording. With facile liberal, egalitarian sentiments, she expresses the unfairness of the differences in education between the affluent and the poor, but concludes, "It's just the way the world works." In her perspective, affluent students have more opportunities because their families have the means to provide them with those opportunities.

Like Scott, though, Nicole also believes that poor families do not value education and deliberately choose not to support, financially, the schools that their children attend. She explains,

> Most of the kids here are wealthy, so there are certain expectations that are different than at other schools. And I guess it's because of the students' backgrounds, just what their parents have done and like the neighborhood they're in. In the poor areas, most of them haven't gone to college and they just have those kinds of jobs. The community is people who do labor kinds of jobs which don't pay that much. Here, it is totally different. Most of the people here come from wealthy families where we don't have those kinds of jobs, those labor kinds of jobs. Because of that, people in poor areas don't put the same emphasis on education. Since they aren't going to college, they don't see the need to make the financial sacrifices to have their kids go to really good schools.

Scott and Nicole allude to conditions beyond personal control in discussing resource disparities in schooling between the poor and the affluent but, in the end, attribute educational advantage and disadvantage primarily to individual actions and choices, not to systemic or structural forces or circumstances.

Privileged Identities Revealed: Ideological Operations and Frames

Like the narratives of Brantlinger's (2003) affluent mothers, and Bonilla-Silva's (2003) white subjects, Nicole's and Scott's narratives reveal a variety of ideological operations and frames at work—all of which serve to shape and mediate their own privileged identity. First, and perhaps most obviously, Nicole and Scott use legitimation ideological modes (representing relations of domination as legitimate) to justify a sense of worthiness for their own social class group and to position Others as unworthy. Because Scott and Nicole equate academic success with merit, they establish the worth of affluent students with their patterns of academic success. In turn, by attributing school failure to lack of effort and bad decisions, they establish the unworthiness of poor students who they feel do not achieve academically. In legitimating their own worthiness, they rationalize their advantages in schooling by discrediting Others. They do not, however, establish a relationship between their advantages and the disadvantages of poor students. Although they believe that they attend a "better" school with more resources and consider their teachers "better" than the teachers at low-income schools, they attribute their advantaged schooling to the higher financial support their families provide for education than do poor students' families. Echoing Peshkin's (2001) findings in his ethnography of an elite private school, Nicole and Scott feel they deserve the schooling advantages they have.

In fact, they use both legitimation and dissimulation ideological modes (obscuring relations of domination) to attribute social class distinctions in schooling to the decisions, attitudes, and actions of poor students and their families to divert attention away from their own school and life advantages. They fully attribute their advantages to their intentions and deliberate choices of caring about their education, working hard in school, and investing financially in their education. They attribute success in school to individual merit, and failure to personal inadequacies. Consistent with Brantlinger's (1993) in-depth examination of affluent and poor students' perceptions of their educational experiences, Nicole and Scott frame social class differences in schooling in the abstract liberal ideology of "personal choice"; that is, they attribute the differences to individual merits, efforts, and choices rather than to societal circumstances or biased institutional structures. Their comments are also consistent with Bourdieu's (1984) observation that affluent people assume that poor people prefer their disadvantaged lifestyles. These ideas, of course, also reflect the use of both naturalization and cultural stereotype ideological frames.

Although Nicole and Scott have little contact with poor people, the lower class is symbolically visible in their narratives as a problematic group who make wrong decisions about their lives, particularly decisions about education, and who share virtually no commonalities with their own social class group.[2] Nicole and Scott position themselves, and other Parker students, as superior to poor students, even though their narratives reveal that they have no firsthand knowledge of the educational circumstances of poor students: They are, in fact, both physically and socially segregated from poor people. Unification ideological modes (embracing individuals in a collective identity) surface in their narratives to reinforce solidarity with others in their own social class, while they use fragmentation modes (dispersing others capable of mounting a challenge to the dominant group) to differentiate themselves from poor people. Regardless of what individual differences Scott and Nicole may have with each other and other Parker students, they emphasize the similarities of those within their social class group while highlighting how dissimilar Others are from themselves. They differentiate themselves from the "bad" decisions and actions of poor students. They emphasize the positive traits of those within their social class group and the negative attributes of Others. Simply put, they construct a social class dichotomy that separates the affluent from the poor.

While neither Nicole nor Scott fully establish a cultural deficit position to explain the differences in achievement patterns between affluent and poor students—that is, they do not make reference to the intellectual abilities of poor students—they cognitively lump together low achievement, indifferent attitudes toward education, laziness, and lower social class. Scott and Nicole claim that poor students do not value education and are less motivated to do well in school than affluent students. They therefore employ what clearly appear to forms of reification ideological modes (representing a transitory historical state as natural and permanent) and naturalizing ideological frames.

In Brantlinger's study (1993), poor students claimed that affluent students taunted them with epithets of "stupid" and "dumb," even though the affluent students in her study never used such labels for poor students. The affluent students in her study, however, communicated that poor students were less advanced academically than students of their class. Similarly, Nicole and Scott never directly identify poor students as less intelligent than affluent students, but they continually point to the distinction in academic achievement patterns and levels between poor and affluent students. Both of them feel that affluent students are simply more advanced academically than poor students.

I argue elsewhere (Howard, 2000) that affluent students often refrain from expressing certain views and using derogatory language to project a politically correct image; they have been taught ways of talking about Others to avoid being seen as prejudiced (cf. Bonilla-Silva's [2003] conception of "color-blind racism"). Nicole, for example, demonstrates such reluctance by emphasizing how "really smart" Parker students are in her explanation for why affluent students achieve higher levels of academic success than poor students. Although both Nicole and Scott are openly critical of poor students and their schools, they constrain the ways they talk about poor students by pointing to poor students' choices and actions rather than talking about poor students' abilities. Once again using reification ideological modes, they do, however, make it a point to call attention to the high abilities of affluent students in their explanations for academic success. Intelligence, therefore, for Nicole and Scott, is signified by achievement and attainment.

To some extent, Scott and Nicole acknowledge the unfairness of the disparities in schooling between the affluent and the poor. Their narratives give some indication that they understand that poor students do not have the same schooling advantages as they have. They demonstrate awareness of the social class influences in schooling. They conclude, however, employing a naturalzing frame, that even though social class distinctions in schooling are unfair, "it's just the way the world works." They accept unfairness as natural and unavoidable. As others (Mickelson, 1990; Olson, 1983) have found, Nicole and Scott accept and even expect their own advantage in schooling, even though they speak of fairness. In their narratives, they straddle an ambiguous position on social class distinctions. Glimmers of their awareness of social class inequities in schooling are overshadowed by ideologies that divert attention from and justify their advantaged schooling.

In sum, the ideological frames and modes embedded in Scott's and Nicole's narratives constitute an array of available cultural meanings for understanding the world around them and stabilizing themselves in that world (Dolby, 2001). These ideologies reveal how an interwoven collection of ideas rationalize their schooling and life advantages, construct between-class divisions, establish within-class solidarity, and discredit Others. The ideological operations and frames they use provide legends for their cognitive maps that are replete with markers that guide their taken-for-granted interpretations and understandings of their place in the world, their relationships with others, and who they are. Their cognitive maps point to some of their knowledge, values, dispositions, and beliefs that insulate and regenerate their identity. Their understandings and interpretations of self and Others reveal a privileged identity that they both inherit and re-create.

Ideological operations and modes are not simply methods or competencies that Nicole and Scott know how to use, however; they are also formative elements of their respective identities. The ways they conceal and rationalize their advantages reveal the medley of forces that construct their senses of self. Their cultural construction of meaning is interconnected with the development of their identity. Ideology and identity meet at the boundary between their inner and outer worlds. Their identity is produced in relation to and in coordination with their ways of thinking and knowing. Through this coordination and relationship, their identity is not a given, but an activity, a performance, a form of mediated action. This activity/performance is one of coordinating the values and views that form the foundation of Nicole's and Scott's immediate social context with those that underline their ideologically mediated identities. As revealed in their narratives, "meaning in the service of power" (Thompson, 1984, p. 7) is firmly situated as a central aspect of who they are and what they do in the world in which they live.

10
Interrupting Privilege

Contradictions often arise in what schools *say* they want their students to learn and what they actually *teach* them. Students learn both intended and (purportedly) unintended lessons that are often in conflict.[1] In part, this conflict results from the myriad factors that influence student learning such as social contexts, organizational structures, institutional rules, curriculum, community influences, norms, values, and educational and occupational aspirations. These factors often give shape and life to the unintentional lessons, even when educators and parents *say* and *claim* they want their children/students to learn other lessons. Frequently, these unintentional lessons end up being the ones that are the most consequential for students' lives. Because these lessons often reflect and are parallel with the norms of society, they are experienced as the way things are or perhaps should be even when these norms support oppressive conditions (Kumashiro, 2002). The everyday nature of these lessons allows them to remain hidden as they pervade students' educational experiences and reinforce powerful messages to students about who they are, how they should live and relate to others, what is important in life, and what the future holds for them. The impact on students' lives is far reaching, influencing how they think about others and how they view and feel about themselves.

Just as the term *hidden agenda* conjures up something covert, deceitful, and undisclosed, the hidden nature of unintentional lessons "suggests intentional acts to obscure or conceal—a conscious duplicity that may not always be present" (Gair & Mullins, 2001, p. 23). However, because these lessons often are framed as "normal" and every day, they are not usually hard to detect. In most cases, they are taught in plain sight and repetitively. The contradiction of something open being hidden not only legitimizes these lessons but masks the cultural processes behind them. By way of analogy, this allows the "white elephant in the room"[2] to remain unrecognized, disguised, and not talked about. The commonsense nature of these lessons functions as a barrier to exposing the meanings and purposes embedded in them, which often reinforce domination. As Apple (1995) explains, what gets defined as common sense may appear to be just the way things are, but they are actually social constructs that function to "confirm and reinforce ... structurally generated relations of domination" (p. 12). Their commonsense appearance, as Kumashiro (2002) elaborates, "not only socializes us to accept oppressive conditions [and I would add, cultural processes of domination] as 'normal' and the way things are, but also to make these conditions [and processes] normative and the ways things ought to be" (p. 82). These norms function to suppress alternative versions of what ought to be.

Within the context of affluent schooling, these "unintentional" lessons play an important role in normalizing and hiding in plain view the cultural processes that reinforce and regenerate privilege. They have an everyday presence that keeps them both known and unknown to insiders of these school communities, which validates and supports the cultural processes that they reinforce and regenerate. The unknown, even when it is partially known, cannot be combated. Protected by lessons that make these cultural processes seem how things ought to be, privilege is perpetuated, regenerated, and recreated (Wildman, 1996). These hidden lessons of privilege, therefore, must be brought to an overt level and made less unknown in order to expose the concealed and sophisticated processes involved in the cultural production of privilege (Howard & Tappan, 2007). In the next section, I summarize the findings of the research reported in this book to surface these lessons that reinforce and regenerate privilege.

Lessons of Privilege

All four schools described in this book are as different as they are similar. Their communities hold different political orientations (conservative/liberal), different forms of social status (old money/nouveau riche), and different types of relationships with their local communities (detached/connected). Oakley is a public institution, while the other three are independent schools. Each school has its own distinctive mission statement, customs, set of rules, requirements and policies, and ideals. Most teachers, students, and parents at these four schools would argue that my list of differences is just a starting point. The four school communities take great pride in their distinctive qualities. Even though there are differences, these communities take similar norms for granted as natural and legitimate. These norms reflect core values—academic excellence, ambition, trust, service, and tradition—that are expressed in a variety of ways and contexts (e.g., in their ideals, missions, and standards; in and outside classrooms; in their school culture; in curriculum) and guide ways of knowing and doing that both create high standards for their educational programs and reinforce privilege.

On one hand, these values reveal their excellence. They promote student success, trust within the community, choices, the importance of service, and the value of connecting the past to the present to give certainty of the future. The schools are places where excellence is the order of the day and students and educators are really good at being good. Of course, their abundance of resources also contributes to their excellent qualities, but all that is good at these four schools does not entirely result from their affluence. The confluence of motivated, dedicated, and hardworking educators and students significantly contributes to the "goodness" (Lawrence-Lightfoot, 1983) found at these schools. However, on the other hand, and often not as apparent to outsiders, the values by which the schools define their excellence also encourage win-at-all-costs attitudes, unhealthy levels of stress, deception, materialism, competition, white ways of knowing and doing, selfishness, and greed. Their values validate "unintentional" lessons that teach students that:

- There's only one right way of knowing and doing.
- Success comes from being superior to others.
- Do whatever it takes to win.
- Fulfillment is gained by accumulating.
- Others are too different from us to relate to.

These lessons and the values behind them embrace particular norms, perspectives, dispositions, ways of knowing and doing, and ideologies that reinforce and regenerate privilege.

There's only one right way of knowing and doing. In pursuing academic success, students at these schools describe what they do at school and what it takes for them to gain academic success as playing a game. Attempting to win the favor of their teachers, participating in the right amount of service and academic and athletic activities, and playing to win are some of the rules of this game. Most students at the four schools abide by these rules and are really good players at the school game. They are hardworking and talented, get good grades and top scores on college entrance exams, and are involved in numerous athletic, service, and other extracurricular activities. They have spent most of their years of schooling learning how to play this game the right way to achieve academic success. This right way is mutually constituted, whereby students both shape and are shaped by the rules of this game (Grenfell & James, 1998). It is within and through the dialectic between the game and the players that hierarchies of power are played out and students' relative positionings are determined.

Like most other African American students at the four schools, Janora believes that she is on the "losing team" in the school game. As she explains, "It sure is a game all right, but we're the underdogs. … [The whites] are on the team that wins all the time." She goes on to explain that the "right way" of playing the school game reflects a "white way" of knowing and doing. She explains, "Everything runs the way that white people do things," and African American students must "act white" in order to be successful (or even "survive") in the school game. Ms. Johnson similarly points out during the parent group discussion that white values and ideals dominate the culture of her son's school. Ms. Daniels adds that these values and ideals are often in conflict with those of African Americans. Most of the African American parents in the discussion believe that their children's schools respect only white ways of knowing and doing and, by so doing, place their children at a disadvantage. African American students remain at a decided disadvantage in a game where the rules are controlled by whites.

Not only are the rules of the game not as fair for students of color as for white students, but they also send powerful messages to all students that white cultural understandings are superior to other cultural groups' ways of knowing and doing. White notions determine the standard for academic success, and this standard encourages narrow-mindedness by providing little room for respecting and learning other ways of knowing and doing. Students keep too occupied with following the "right way" to build the capacity to imagine other ways. The power of this certain way regulates identities, knowledge, and practices. It is through this "right way" of identifying, knowing, and doing that the social transmission of privilege is itself legitimized (Lamont & Lareau, 1988). This version of how things ought to be establishes a set of class-based dispositions, perceptions, and appreciations that reinforce and regenerate privilege.

Success comes from being superior to others. Mr. Thornton's statement, "Competition is not a dirty word," about McLean represents the general attitude at the four schools in this study. To varying degrees, the schools promote a competitive culture within and outside the classroom context to prepare their students for the "harsh realties and demands of the world outside school" and "to give them the skills necessary to have a competitive edge in life." Outside the classroom, all the schools except for Oakley require students to participate in their athletic programs in order to hone their competitive attitudes and skills. Instead of a requirement, Oakley strongly encourages participation in sports "to give students a more appropriate venue to be competitive than the classroom." Similar to the other schools, Oakley's athletic program is a site for students to strengthen their competitive character.

Students carry their competitive attitudes that are valued and reinforced on playing fields with them into the classroom context. In fact, all but Oakley have designed their overall educational program in ways that encourage students to use skills and attitudes in the classroom that they have learned and developed on playing fields in order to gain higher levels of academic success. Most of the students in this study do act in similar ways in the classroom as they do on playing fields. They are playing to win and do what it takes to achieve academic success. Although Oakley students are less competitive in the classroom than students at the other three schools, the increased focus in recent years on gaining admission to selective colleges has spurred competitive attitudes in order to stand out among others. At all four schools, the college-oriented desires and expectations of students and their families provide further encouragement for competition. Students and their families are competing for the college prize.

The competitive environments at these four schools promote individual student achievement over the value of cooperation and group success.

Students are taught that academic success is gained by being better than others, or as I heard numerous times over the course of my research, "standing out above the rest." Although all four schools claim to promote a strong sense of community and emphasize the value of community in their mission statements and school publications, their competitive environments disrupt connection, making closeness among students and educators impossible (hooks, 2003). Their emphasis on competition precludes collaboration, which limits the opportunities for students to learn what it means to build and sustain meaningful relationships with others. In an environment where competition is the order of the day, there is little room for arousing collective concern for anything other than self-interests.

Do whatever it takes to win. Most students in this study explain that they are playing the game of school to win and will do what it takes to gain academic success. In their pursuits of academic success, they regularly act in ways to prove that they are "the fittest," such as putting other students down to make themselves look better, dominating class discussions to get the attention of their teachers, getting on the good side of the adults in their lives, and, at times, cheating on assignments. Often these strategies successfully give them the advantage in the game. Although I observed students cheating only a few times over the course of my research, several students in these studies, except those at Oakley, claim that cheating is a common practice at their schools. Even at Oakley, Kevin explains that cheating is acceptable "when teachers put too much or unfair amount of pressure on [students]." Similar to what I heard from several students at the four schools, Kevin believes that cheating is "a survival thing" and "something that you're forced to do." Students believe that cheating is justified in a competitive environment.

Similar to what Pope (2001) found in her study of five students "doing school," behaviors such as cheating, however, contradict "the very traits and values many parents, students, and community members expect schools to instill" (p. 150). By encouraging (and, more importantly, rewarding) success over others, the four schools described in this book, some more than others, promote win-at-all-costs behaviors and attitudes. Students learn to value winning above all else, even if this means acting in ways that go against other values that the adults in their lives have attempted to instill in them. Instead of fostering traits such as cooperation and honesty, the schools' competitive environments promote the opposite and provide little room to uphold more important and meaningful values than winning.

Fulfillment is gained by accumulating. Parents in these studies place a tremendous amount of pressure on their children to achieve the level of academic success necessary to gain admission to highly selective colleges. They claim that the reason for this pressure is to make sure their children have fulfilling lives. They describe fulfillment as a sense of happiness and accomplishment, and believe that "going to a good college will make this [fulfillment] more possible. It sets them on the right path," as a Parker parent explains. Parents are acutely aware that a degree from a highly selective college often leads to careers providing wealth and power, which allows their children to maintain their class advantages. Parents believe that their children will feel fulfilled in life if they achieve a level of success that allows them to keep "the comforts of life that they're accustomed to," as a Bredvik mother explains.

Only a few parents mention the cachet associated with their children attending highly selective colleges. A mother at Parker admits, "Every parent wants to be able to tell others that their child goes to Harvard or Yale or colleges like those. … If your child goes to a top-notch college, then you know you're a good parent. You've done your job as a parent." Consistent with what Brantlinger (2003) found in her study of affluent mothers, most of the parents' "self-definitions extended to and incorporated their offsprings' success," and a source of parents' "positive identity was attributing their children's achievement to their child rearing" (p. 40). Some teachers at the four schools, however, argue that the primary source of parents' college-oriented desires and expectations for their children is associated more with status than their feelings about themselves as parents. A Bredvik teacher claims that "[parents] want the status that comes along with their kids going to good schools like they want other things that represent status. I'm not saying it's completely the same as a fancy car, but it's close. If your kid gets into Harvard, then it's like everything else in their lives that shows how successful they are." Symbolic markers of both parents' sense of self and class privilege are figured prominently in parents' ambitious aspirations for their children. Their understandings of what it means to be fulfilled in life are constructed around these markers.

Students feel an intense pressure to achieve the goals that their parents have set for them. The majority of students at these schools believe that their "parents are the biggest factor in what [they] do to get into a good college," as a student at Bredvik explains. A student at Oakley elaborates, "It's never been really an option not to go to college. My parents have been talking about going to college since I was in kindergarten. I've always been told that's what I have to do after high school to be successful later on." These two students' sentiments reverberated throughout my conversations with other students. In striving to meet the expectations of their parents, they do what they have to do to get good grades and high test scores, and they participate in the right number of activities to secure admission to selective colleges. Their schools mediate their parents' expectations by making their "primary responsibility … to get their students into top colleges," as a teacher at Parker explains. The four schools provide the institutional culture, the college counseling, and the college preparatory programs necessary for students to gain entrance into high-status colleges. Everything about all four schools conveys that all students will continue on to college, and most likely to "good" colleges.

The interaction of family and institutional influences places students at these schools on the ambitious track toward gaining admission to high-status colleges and acquiring the educational credentials necessary to secure and maintain their class privilege. They keep jam-packed schedules that often begin early in the morning (earlier than most adults begin their workdays) and end late at night. After school hours, they are involved in sports, service projects, committee meetings, homework, and for a very few, paid job responsibilities. They study, read, and complete what their teachers assign to get high grades and select courses based on college requirements. They spend most of their time inside and outside school doing what they have to do, or what they think they have to do, to win the college prize, not because they find what they do necessarily engaging. Although not all of what students do is entirely motivated by "transcript packing" (Peshkin, 2001), they are "always thinking about how [what they do] will benefit [them] in getting into college," as Nicole at Parker explains. The ever-present reality in their choices, activities, and schoolwork is how what they do helps them fulfill their and their parents' college-oriented desires and expectations. Being engaged in what they do takes a back seat to their drive to accumulate the credentials necessary to keep them on the "right path" to a selective college and, as their parents claim, to fulfillment in their lives. They have learned to associate fulfillment with accumulation.

Others are too different from us to relate. One of the striking qualities that all four schools share is their exclusive nature. They promote and emphasize their distinctive, exclusive, and superior qualities to set them apart from others. They are closed off from others and, in various forms, are gated communities. The incredible beauty and abundance of the campuses of McLean and Parker, for example, are a far cry from their surrounding communities. Both schools sit on top of hills detached from their neighbors. Quite the opposite, Oakley and Bredvik share a close relationship with their local communities, but these communities are themselves exclusive. Like McLean and Parker, they are isolated from communities different from themselves.

Oakley is the only school in this study for which this isolation goes against the school's ideals and values. In fact, school officials at the three private schools work hard at promoting their elite status; they want others to know that they are above the rest. They promote their exclusivity, in part, because they are private and have to "sell their school to families. We have the job of convincing them that they're getting their money's worth," as Parker's admission counselor explains. As a public school, Oakley has a similar form of pressure that comes from the need to demonstrate educational excellence to local citizens for financial support; they have to "sell their school" to their community. Similar to the private schools, Oakley's officials work hard at making sure that people, both within and outside their community, know that they stand above other schools, even though this attitude runs counter to the school's liberal character. The pressure to secure financial support overrides their liberal ideals. In various ways, all four schools promote their differences from, and pit themselves against, others in expressing their excellence. They regulate "others" to a lesser status to justify and legitimate and thus protect their interests. The class segregation of their school communities is a deliberate choice to maintain their superiority over those perceived as other.

All four schools do emphasize, however, the importance of their students going outside the "bubble" of their privileged environments to be involved in service. Even though the schools place a value on service (and all but Bredvik even require their students to do service), their service projects and activities operate by the "charity model," which allows their students to "give back"—that is, help those who are less fortunate—without promoting social transformation. In fact, the goals of the charitable model of service reinforce privileged ways of knowing and doing by embracing certain unpleasant assumptions about people, especially those different from the service providers. One basic assumption is that any community would function better if only it would act like the service provider. Another assumption is that there are no connections between those who provide service and those who receive service, that they are more different than they are similar. This assumes that their lived experiences, hopes, dreams, and aspirations are so profoundly different that difficulties can be resolved only by finding the one right answer. In this context, service is mainly about the nature of the activity and the work of the service provider. Students are not provided the necessary conditions to step outside their privileged positions to learn from others in the population at large in order to understand and appreciate different ways of knowing and doing. The charity model of service provides little room for students to develop meaningful, mutual, and respectful relationships with individuals outside their closed communities. Even though they are physically stepping outside their "bubble" and crossing lines in social interactions through these service activities, they are not provided the types of experience that allow them to become sensitive to the nature and needs of other social classes and other cultural groups (Brantlinger, 2003). Students continue to be isolated from "others."

Instructional Settings That Interrupt Privilege

For the most part, these five lessons are not "officially" taught as part of the formal curriculum at the four schools. Instead, they are part of the hidden curriculum; that is, "the norms, values, and belief systems embedded in the curriculum, the school, and classroom life, imparted to students through daily routine, curricular content, and social relationships" (Margolis, Soldatenko, Acker, & Gair, 2001, p. 6). There is an extensive body of literature on the hidden curriculum. Phillip Jackson (1968) is generally recognized as the originator of the term *hidden curriculum*. In his observations of public elementary classrooms, Jackson identified aspects of classroom life that were inherent in the social relations of schoolings. He found that particular values, dispositions, and behavioral expectations led to rewards for students and shaped their learning experiences. Furthermore, he found that these features of school life had little to do with the stated educational goals but were essential for success in school.

Since then, several scholars (e.g., Anyon, 1980; Apple, 1982, 1988, 1993; Giroux, 1983b) have explored the complex ways that the hidden curriculum powerfully influences the educational experiences of students and transmits important lessons to them about particular ways of knowing and doing that correspond to their social class. For example, Jean Aynon's study of five elementary schools in contrasting social class settings documented how the hidden curriculum works in ways to perpetuate social class stratification of the larger society. School experience of the students at the five schools differed qualitatively by social class. Anyon found class distinctions not only in the physical, cultural, and interpersonal characteristics of each school, but also in the nature of instruction and schoolwork. These differences, as she explained, "not only may contribute to the development in the children in each social class of certain types of economically significant relationships and not others, but would thereby help to *reproduce* this system of relations in society" (p. 90). Anyon argued that classroom practices have theoretical meaning and social consequences that contribute to the reproduction of unequal social relations.

Consistent with this body of research, the lessons that are a part of the hidden curriculum of the four schools hide in plain view the cultural processes that reinforce and regenerate privilege. These lessons send powerful messages to students about their place in the world, who they are and should be, and their relations with those outside of their world. Unacknowledged, these lessons often teach students unintended knowledge, values, dispositions, and beliefs. In fact, most of these lessons are in direct contradiction to the schools' stated goals, which aim to teach students high moral character, integrity, respect for others, and responsible participation in the world. These lessons instead prepare students to lead their lives guided by distinctive ways of knowing and doing that overshadow these more positive, productive goals. They contribute to establishing the taken-for-granted sets of ideas for how things ought to be and the frame of reference for what is considered common sense that function to reinforce and regenerate the cultural meanings students use to construct their identities. As conduits for learning privilege and power, these lessons assist students in constructing privilege as a central component of their identities.

Identities, however, are neither constant nor stable. They are constantly shaped and reshaped by the complex interactions of everyday realities and lived experiences. As students mediate their sense of self-understanding, they can be offered the necessary cultural tools and resources that can interrupt privilege. Students can be taught alternative lessons about themselves, their place in the world, and their relations with others; lessons not only that are more aligned with (purportedly) intended goals for student learning, but that also offer alternatives to privileged ways of knowing and doing. Over the course of my research, I observed only a few moments when instructional settings offered students the necessary tools and resources to interrupt privilege. These moments challenged the everyday, commonsense nature of the lessons that reinforce and regenerate privilege. These instructional settings, often created by the adults in students' lives but sometimes facilitated by the students themselves, shared particular qualities in imagining beyond the taken-for-grantedness of privilege.

One of these qualities was honesty. Students were provided opportunities in their pursuits of academic success to learn ways to deal with, and work through, failure in healthy ways. Students were provided safe spaces to make mistakes and then learn from them. During these moments, the adults in students' lives served as important models by being honest about what they knew and didn't know, honest about moments in their lives when they wished they had made different decisions, and honest about moments when they "messed up." These role models were upholding natural human qualities in their work with students or in their roles as parents. They provided their students/children opportunities to learn from these qualities—even the imperfect ones. By so doing, these adults taught students important lessons about dealing with failure.

These instructional settings also encouraged openness by expanding the scope of what was considered "the real fudge," to use the words of Ms. Perry at Parker, or in other words, what knowledge was acknowledged as legitimate (Apple, 1999). Curricula, however, are not simply a collection of facts; they tell a story, from which students learn some important (often unintended) lessons. These lessons emerge from what is and what is not included in curricula. As Kumashiro (2002) points out, "What educators do *not* do is as instructive as what they do" (p. 82). When instructional settings encouraged openness, teachers included different, conflicting stories in their curricular choices. They offered their students opportunities to learn from others outside their own cultural group and to learn that there was not just one way of seeing things, or even two or three—there were multiple perspectives on every issue and every story. During these moments, teachers encouraged students to open their minds to others' points of view and to the complexity of the world and the many perspectives involved (Nieto, 2002).

These instructional settings also engaged students in what they were doing and learning. When a student at Parker spent her free time during the school day painting, a group of aspiring writers at Bredvik published a zine of their creative work once a month, another Bredvik student shared her poetry regularly on open mike nights at a local coffee shop, and an Oakley student devoted hours a day on his computer designing a virtual reality game, they were not thinking about how these activities would help them get into a good college. They also were not focused on accumulating. Instead, they were doing what they loved and were passionately committed to doing their best. In these moments, students stepped outside materialistic ways of knowing and doing to find a more meaningful purpose for their activities and pursuits. Even though these moments of engaged learning and doing occurred mostly outside the classroom context, there were a few occasions when students during class discussions and activities struggled for understanding, wanted to learn and work with others, and found fulfillment in what they were doing. These moments allowed students to establish a more intimate connection with their learning (hooks, 1994).

These instructional settings encouraged collaboration and emphasized the value of community. Over the course of my research, I witnessed moments when students worked together on their train ride to school, in the hallways, at lunchtime while grabbing a bite to eat, and on campus during their breaks. In these moments students were going against the competitive nature of their schools in order to learn from each other. Rather than trying to outdo each other, they were engaging with each other in meaningful ways that recognized the value of cooperative learning. Students in these instructional settings learned how to work with others. While doing so, they were building their capacity to imagine someone else's point of view, what Kohn (1992) calls "perspective taking," and learning what it took to establish and maintain supportive, healthy, and positive relationships with others.

Finally, these instructional settings encouraged students to develop the habits of heart and mind necessary for working toward critical awareness. In these settings, a few teachers at Parker and Oakley, for example, used such practices as journal writing, reading, writing, reflection, research, analysis, and observation to develop their students' awareness of the world around them and to urge students to live more meaningfully and justly. These teachers taught students to see through versions of truth that teach people to accept unfairness so that their students were able to envision, define, and identity ways they could work toward a more humane society. In this process, an encounter was created between students and their capacity to imagine beyond privileged ways of knowing and doing. Students were encouraged to make decisions to live their lives as if the lives of others truly mattered. Students were provided opportunities to develop an awareness of the world around them and to learn what it meant to live more meaningfully and justly.

These characteristics do not translate into easy prescriptions for interrupting privilege. They do not serve as easy, quick, or certain alternatives to the ways that privilege is perpetuated, re-created, and regenerated in schools. Moreover, there are other characteristics that could be added. My purpose has been not to be exhaustive but to illuminate the primary ways that educators, students, and parents at the four schools worked toward interrupting privilege. Their efforts serve as examples of the possibilities for redefining, reenvisioning, and reimagining how things ought to be.

A Critically Hopeful Vision

Efforts toward interrupting privilege extend beyond the here and now and the taken for granted "to the terrain of hope and agency, to the sphere of struggle and action" (Arnowitz & Giroux, 1985, p. 19). In these efforts, educators must cultivate a spirit of hopefulness about their own capacity and that of others to change the conditions that reinforce and regenerate privilege. These efforts must be steeped in a hopeful vision for the capacity of human agency. Inden (1990), as cited in Urrieta (2005), defines human agency as:

> The realized capacity of people to act upon their world and not only to know about or give personal or intersubjective significance to it. That capacity is the power of people to act purposively and reflectively, in more or less complex interrelationships with one another, to reiterate and remake the world in which they live, in circumstances where they may consider different courses of action possible and desirable, though not necessarily from the same point of view. (p. 23)

Even though human agency exists within the contradiction between people as social producers and as social products (Holland et al., 1998), cultural meanings are neither imposed, hegemonic structures nor stable. Individuals mediate cultural meanings and have the capacity to transform these meanings in order to interrupt the cultural processes that these meanings validate and support. They have the agency to engage in political action to change the everyday practices and routines and the institutional structures that reflect and maintain social hierarchies of the larger society. In the context of affluent schooling, educators have the capacity to interrupt the cultural processes that regenerate and reinforce privilege.

Hope in the potentialities of individuals and possibilities of change is imperative for social transformation, yet in isolation is insufficient. As Freire (1994) points out, "Alone, [hope] does not win. But without it, my struggle will be weak and wobbly" (p. 8). Hope is an "ontological need" (p. 9), essential to both our being and our knowing, and integral to both epistemology and ontology. Freire argues that one of the tasks for educators is to "unveil opportunities of hope, regardless of the struggle" (p. 9) as they work toward critical consciousness.[3] Through critical consciousness, Freire believes that people should learn to question society, see through versions of "truths" that teach people to accept unfairness and injustice, and become empowered to define, envision, and work toward social justice. This process involves individuals becoming aware not only of the realities that shape their lives and the lives of others, but also of their own capabilities to transform those realities, an awareness of consciousness of something that achieves the power of two, a duality of consciousness.

Praxis, a process that involves continuous movement between reflection and action, is central to critical consciousness. For Freire (1970), praxis implies a balance and imbricate relationship between thinking and doing:

> Within the word we find two dimensions, reflection and action, in such radical interaction that if one is sacrificed—even in part—the other immediately suffers. ... When a word is deprived of its dimensions of action, reflection automatically suffers as well, and the word is changed into idle chatter, into verbalism, into an alienated and alienating 'blah.' It becomes an empty word, one which cannot denounce the world, for denunciation is impossible without a commitment to transform, and there is not transformation without action. (pp. 75–76)

Working toward critical consciousness requires moving from knowledge and theoretical understanding to action. Critical consciousness is an ongoing, purposefully motivated process of reflecting, critiquing, affirming, challenging, and acting that ultimately transforms individuals' collective understandings of the world (Darder, 2002).

In this process, as McLaren (1989) urges, "Educators must begin candidly and critically to face our society's complicity in the roots and structures of inequality and injustice. It means, too, that as teachers we must face our own culpability in the reproduction of inequality in our teaching, and that we must strive to develop a pedagogy equipped to provide both intellectual and moral resistance to oppression [and, I would add, to privilege]" (p. 21). In working against oppression and privilege, the educator's task is not to force students to merely repeat their expectations, which, as Kumashiro (2002) points out, "is a process that denies students their agency and limits the possibilities of change to what is imaginable within the partial knowledge of the teacher" (p. 79). Because knowledge is partial and partisan, one version will always be problematic because, as Lather (1998) points out, it assumes "the rhetorical position of 'the one who knows' " (p. 488), which positions those who offer an alternative version simply as "the ones who don't know. " Replacing one version of truth for how things ought to be with another one—even when offering an alternative to oppression and privilege—neither transforms nor liberates individuals from existing conditions; for, as Audre Lorde (1981) so aptly advises, "the master's tools will never dismantle the master's house" (p. 99). One version always closes off the infinite possibilities yet to be imagined and discovered. Educators, instead, should invite and encourage their students to explore many possible ways of knowing and doing—ways that come, as Ellsworth (1997) argues, "elsewhere to provoke something else into happening—something other than the return of the same" (as quoted in Lather, 1998, p. 492).

This is not to suggest that educators do not share their own critically hopeful vision of what ought to be with their students. It is through this sharing that educators not only can be more certain about what lessons they are actually teaching their students, but also challenge their students' taken-for-granted, commonsense understandings of themselves and others. By sharing their own thinking, educators also encourage their students to join them in co-construction of knowledge that determines how students understand themselves and their relations with others. However, simply sharing new ideas and new ways of thinking and doing with their students does not always bring about change. As Kumashiro (2002) points out, "Students come to school not as blank slates but as individuals who are already invested in their thoughts, beliefs, and desires" (p. 73). Most often, students enter the classroom context with a well-established sense of self that continuously influences how they think and understand, and what they know and decide not to know. Thus, as Kumashiro continues to explain, "The problem that educators need to address is not merely a lack of knowledge, but a resistance to knowledge ... and in particular a resistance to any knowledge that disrupts what the students already know" (p. 73). It is through student resistance, however, that educators begin knowing their students for who they are instead of whom they want students to be.

However, as Ellsworth (1997) argues, there is always a space between the teacher/teaching and learner/learning; more specifically, a space between who the teacher thinks the students are and who they actually are. Educators are often threatened by this uncertain space and focus on maintaining control of it through content, instruction, classroom practices and rules, and the types of relationships they have with students. Rather than closing this "space between," educators "should work within that space, embrace that paradox, and explore the possibilities of disruptions and change that reside within the unknowable" (Kumashiro, 2000, p. 46; see also Lather, 1998). By working within this uncertain space, educators can move toward possibilities that are unforeseeable from the perspective of the present (Lather, 1998). It is within this space that what is considered normal and everyday can be contested and challenged in order to move toward a future yet to be imagined.

A Broader Agenda

Interrupting the cultural production of privilege requires intentional efforts on the part of educators to confront and transform lessons students learn about their place in the world and their relations with others. By creating instructional settings—in and outside of the classroom context—that interrupt privilege, we can be more certain about what lessons we are actually teaching students about themselves and others. We can begin imagining ways to work toward "the process through which students learn to critically appropriate knowledge existing outside their immediate experience in order to broaden their understanding of themselves, the world, and the possibilities for transforming the taken-for-granted assumptions about the way we live"

(McLaren, 1989, p. 186). By working toward this transformation, we can imagine the possibilities for changing the everyday practices and routines that miscommunicate the ways we want (or, at least, what we say and claim we want) our students to live their lives (Howard & EnglandKennedy, 2006).

We can, however, only imagine and work toward interrupting the cultural processes that reinforce and regenerate stratified structures in schooling. The effects of macroeconomic policies (see Anyon, 2005) and the social class divisions of the larger society overshadow efforts toward *disrupting*, rather than *interrupting*, these cultural processes in schools that perpetuate unequal relations. The United States not only is the most highly stratified society in the industrialized world but does less to limit the extent of inequality than any other industrialized democratic country. Class distinctions operate in virtually all aspects of American life. In the United States, democracy has become more of an economic metaphor than a political concept/ideal (Darder, 2002). It should not be surprising, therefore, that stratified schooling remains durable even with all the efforts over the years toward making American schooling more equal. Replete with uneven access and outcomes, schools continue to reflect the divisions of the larger society (Nieto, 2005). The efforts toward transforming stratified school structures will remain uncertain until democratic ideals are reflected and realized in the larger society. Working toward transforming stratified school structures and outcomes requires us to extend our efforts and attention beyond educational institutions. We must, in the end, develop a larger scope for our equality-seeking work.

However, comprehensive analyses of the reproductive nature of affluent schooling can elaborate and extend our understandings of the ways privileging systems are produced and reproduced. We can develop the necessary cultural script to extend beyond commodified notions that divert attention from, and protect, the concealed and sophisticated processes involved in the cultural production of privilege. By mapping out and exposing the contours of privilege, we can engage in the type of complicated conversation that is needed for understanding how the success of some relates to the failure of many. If social justice is at least one of the aims of scholarship and inquiry (Purpel, 1999), then we must work to unravel the cultural processes that reinforce and regenerate privilege. We must cast our scholarly gaze upward even when this means looking critically at ourselves and unmasking our own complicity with oppression and privilege. We can then hopefully develop a vision for American schooling that has yet to be imagined from the perspectives of our current theoretical frameworks.

Notes

Preface

1. See Brantlinger (2001) for an extensive review of research on the influence of social class on labeling disabilities.
2. In the most comprehensive study of how the poor make it to college, Arthur Levine and Jana Nidiffer (1996) found that the most influential factor in poor students' beating the odds of attending college was the positive influence of their mentors. They found that "[i]n the simplest terms, the recipe of getting to college is mentorship. … What mattered most is not carefully constructed educational policy but rather the intervention by one person. … It was the human contact that made the difference" (pp. 65, 139). These findings are consistent with my own experience.

Chapter 1

1. This is a pseudonym, as are all names of people and places in this book.
2. The school separated boys from girls (and vice versa) to provide students a safe space to talk about personal issues such as sex, puberty, body image, and so on. The educators who designed this advising program believed that students would talk more openly about these issues and act more appropriately in discussions and activities in single-gender settings.
3. Like many researchers who use qualitative methods, I view the research act as being far from value free (Denzin & Lincoln, 1994). As Horvat and Antonio (1999) explain, "Part of the research endeavor is the process of making meaning and not just observing but shaping, interpreting, and framing the research act" (p. 321). I viewed my subjectivity as "a garment that cannot be removed" (Peshkin, 1988, p. 17). I believe that my background (i.e., educational, professional, personal, and so forth) shapes my role as a researcher.
4. I conducted the study at McLean in 1995 and conducted the last study described in this book in 2001. There were some follow-up visits to two of the schools, Bredvik and Parker, in 2002 and 2003 to gather additional data about what the students who participated in these studies did after graduating high school.
5. I knew several school officials and teachers at all three schools before I conducted research. In fact, my relationship with the schools allowed me to gain access to these communities. Oakley, Parker, and Bredvik had never allowed outsiders to conduct research on their premises. It was beneficial for me not to be completely considered an "outsider" in these school communities in terms of gaining access to these sites—especially at the two private schools, Bredvik and Parker, which were very concerned about confidentiality. To respect their concerns, I use pseudonyms, and certain details about the schools and partici-

pants have sometimes been disguised. Similar to a technique Henry (1995) uses to protect participants' anonymity in her study, I also place certain events in settings different from where they occurred.

6. Before I began fieldwork at each site, I asked the principal (or, in the case of McLean, the headmaster) at each school to select a "typical" teacher to participate in my studies. I defined a typical teacher as one who did not have a reputation with students, colleagues, and parents for being extraordinarily bad or good or did not teach in a way that differed from the majority of his/her colleagues. When I began conducting my studies, it was not too difficult to conclude that these teachers were not "typical." I developed this conclusion primarily from the teachers' relationships with students, the faculty leadership roles they held, and how colleagues and students regarded them. I also concluded that their atypical status did not present a problem for my studies, since they all had similar status and positions within their individual communities.
7. More specifically, I visited schools in California, Georgia, Kentucky, New York, North Carolina, Massachusetts, Ohio, Virginia, and Texas. Most of these visits were arranged through my connections with other directors of nonprofit organizations in these states. I also had connections with some of the schools that I visited through Antioch College's cooperative education program.

Chapter 2

1. More specifically, the United States has nearly 22% of children living in poverty. To compare this with other industrialized countries, Scandinavian countries have 2–3%, Germany has 10%, and the United Kingdom has 16% (Shannon, 2006).
2. In the summer of 2005, the *New York Times* published a series on social class in America, titled *Class matters*. This series explores the various ways that social class influences Americans. It can be found at http://www.nytimes.com/indexes/2005/05/15/national/class.
3. For a deeper discussion on this point, see Peter Cookson's 1997 review of Powell's book in *American Journal of Education, 105*, 504–509.
4. The remaining sections in this chapter are a slightly modified version of a paper, "Privilege as Identity," that I cowrote with Mark Tappan in 2007 and presented at the Annual Meeting of the American Educational Research Association in Chicago, Illinois. I thank Mark for allowing me to use the paper for this chapter.
5. The study of adolescents' identity formation has traditionally fallen under the purview of developmental psychologists who have characterized this stage as pivotal in the transition to adult roles and identities (Erikson, 1968). However, recent poststructural, sociocultural, and sociological examinations of identity, for example, have questioned developmental models of adolescence in order to emphasize how material conditions, social constraints, interactions, and lived realities shape adolescents' identities (Fairbanks & Ariail, 2006; Lesko, 2001). Several scholars have argued that traditional developmental models do not account for the complexities in adolescents' negotiations of social expectations and structures, class and cultural affiliations, gender, and geography (Gilligan, 1982; Holland et al., 1998; Moje, 2002; Tappan, 2005).

6. Sleeter (1996) suggests that there are four interconnected concepts of this unawareness: historic roots or racist opportunity structures; the nature and impact of discrimination; the significance of group membership (i.e., color blindness); and misunderstandings of the nature of culture.

Chapter 3

1. John Gardner, who was head of the Carnegie Corporation, was one of the key builders of the American meritocracy. He published a book called *Excellence* in 1961 and argued that the United States must strive for both excellence and equality at every level of society. In this book, Gardner posed the question: Can America be both equal and excellent? He worried about the possible unfairness of using the education system to close down life options for many Americans. He ultimately concluded that we ought to wait "until as late as 18 or 19 years of age" before making final decisions in order to give the late bloomers a chance in this system.
2. A similar scenario of stratification of intelligence was raised more recently in Herrnstein and Murray (1994).
3. Patrick Brantlinger (1990) similarly argues that "[i]deologies are not simply false, they can be 'partly true,' and yet also incomplete [or] distorted. ... [They are not] consciously crafted by the ruling class and then injected into the minds of the majority; [they are] instead produced by specifiable, complex, social conditions" (p. 80). Because those who control the means of disseminating ideas have more opportunities to have their ideas become the ones that prevail, the ideas of dominant groups are the ruling ideas. Members of the dominant groups have traditionally been the winners in meritocracies and therefore interested in preserving/defending these systems. Dominant groups are interested in emphasizing the grain of truth in these myths/ideologies.
4. In describing the communities where the schools in this book are situated, I was influenced by Sara Lawrence-Lightfoot's method of portraiture (Lawrence-Lightfoot & Davis, 1997). Although I do not follow this method faithfully, I was interested in capturing "the complexity, dynamics, and subtlety of human experience and organizational life" (p. xv) in these larger school communities. I was interesting in constructing "portraits" of Watercrest and the other communities in this book.
5. The description of Mr. Perkins' class, as well as the descriptions of Ms. Perry's class in chapter 4 and Mr. Linn's class in chapter 5, is a composite of the classroom observations I conducted during my fieldwork (approximately 30 per classroom). To develop these composites, I performed a frequency count to identify reoccurring activities and practices. I eliminated activities and practices from the composite that had occurred in only three or fewer classes of the thirty. After identifying frequent activities and practices, I constructed a narrative for each class.
6. Most African American students enter Bredvik in the seventh grade. The student population in the Lower School is almost completely white.
7. They did know that I was a private schoolteacher as well as a researcher. At the beginning of my fieldwork, students acted toward me the way they would have around their teachers. Then, there was a pivotal moment in the fourth month of my fieldwork, when Mr. Perkins was out of the room and Keegan was not

completing his work but was instead socializing. One of his friends turned to him and warned him that "he better cut it out because Mr. Perkins is going to find out." His friend believed, and I would later find out that most other students shared his belief, that I was telling Mr. Perkins what I was observing. Keegan assured the group that I was not a "spy" for Mr. Perkins. He then proceeded to share some of what he had told me during our interviews and discussions that would have gotten him in trouble if I had shared this information with Mr. Perkins and/or other teachers. From that point on, the students viewed me less as an authority figure. In fact, they began paying less attention to me at all.

8. This is consistent with Ellsworth's (1997) argument that there is a "space between" the teacher and the student; more specifically, between who the teacher thinks the student is and who the student actually is. In Janora and Keegan's perspective, there is also a "space between" the parent and the child.

Chapter 4

1. Moreover, elite schools have a particular "organizational habitus" (McDonough, 1998) that places students at an advantage. Horvat and Antonio (1999) explain that an organizational habitus is "the set of class-based dispositions, perceptions, and appreciations transmitted to individuals in a common organizational culture" (p. 320). This concept takes into account the fluid interaction between individuals and social structures. There is interplay between students making decisions about their lives (in this case, college decisions) and school structures that influence these decisions.
2. The title of this section is a variation of John Knowles' *A Separate Peace*, which was inspired by his experiences attending Phillips Exeter Academy in Exeter, New Hampshire. This novel was influenced by Knowles' experiences growing up in the hills of West Virginia and then entering Phillips Exeter in his adolescent years. I use a variation of this novel's title to emphasize the distinction between Parker's campus and the community where Parker is located.
3. Girls take up a position in this storyline through a discursive process (Davies, 2000). Even though girls have access to a variety of positions through this process, schools and classrooms tend to reinforce conventional or stereotypical positions that both define and limit the positions available to girls (Enciso, 1998).
4. In a national survey, Alt and Peter (2002) found that 68% of private school teachers said they had a lot of influence on establishing curriculum, compared with 44% of public school teachers. Moreover, private school teachers were more likely to say that they had a lot of influence on setting student performance standards (63% versus 38%).
5. For a discussion of the advantages of, and other issues related to, private college counseling, see McDonough, Korn, and Yamasaki (1997).

Chapter 5

1. In a discussion about this chapter, Bill Pinar brought to my attention that none of the guests on these two shows were educators or experts in the field of education. This serves as an example of the ways that educators are excluded from

discussions about the current state of American education. This also supports a point that I make later in this chapter about the lack of respect and distrust for educators in this country.

2. The *Oprah Winfrey Show/Time* magazine poll was conducted by telephone between March 28 and 30, 2006, among a national random sample of 1,000 adults, age 18 and older throughout America. The margin of error for the entire sample is approximately ±3 percentage points. The full *Oprah Winfrey Show/Time* questionnaire and trend data may be found at: http://www.oprah.com/tows/pastshows/200604/tows_past_20060411_c.jhtml.
3. It would take years before the Coleman Report would be studied carefully enough for it to be realized that many of the claims in the report were not supported by evidence. See Berliner and Biddle (1995), pp. 116–125, for an analysis of the Coleman Report.
4. In my dialogue with Deborah Meier on issues that came up during my research at Oakley (Howard, 2005b), she points out that because the outcomes are predictable, "schools that have predominantly rich students can treat testing as a game and continue doing their own thing. They can direct their attention elsewhere. It is the schools that have poor kids that feel the pressure of high-stakes standards" (p. 23).
5. Meier (2002) argues that this is one of the main benefits of small schools.
6. It is important to note that this is a very white way of defining and understanding diversity. One could certainly argue that this way of framing diversity allows "progressive" individuals at Oakley to "feel better" about the lack of diversity within their community in terms of social class and race.

Chapter 6

1. Although I did not have access to the private space of the male locker room, I triangulated data gathered from informal and formal interviews with teachers, parents, and students to construct the details of the incident. I gathered information from different individuals with different roles in the school community. As a participant observer, I had access to public and semiprivate discussions (e.g., in the teacher's workroom, in parent meetings) about the incident and had several informal conversations with parents, teachers, and students to understand the different ways the incident was framed within the community.
2. A slightly modified version of the following sections on this incident at Bredvik appeared in Howard and EnglandKennedy (2006).

Chapter 7

1. For 20 years, *Forbes* magazine has published an annual list of the world's wealthiest people. In their first ranking, there were 140 billionaires. In 2006, they identified the top 400 of the 793 billionaires in the world.
2. For information about the Bill and Melinda Gates Foundation, see the organization's website at http://www.gatesfoundation.org/default.htm.
3. Quoted from a C. J. Loomis, June 25, 2006, article, "A conversation with Warren Buffett." Found at: http://money.cnn.com/2006/06/25/magazines/fortune/charity2.fortune/index.htm.

4. Independent Sector is a nonprofit, nonpartisan coalition of more than 700 national nonprofit organizations, foundations, and corporate philanthropy programs, collectively representing tens of thousands of charitable groups in every state across the nation. This group's mission is to promote, strengthen, and advance the nonprofit and philanthropic community to foster private initiative for the public good.
5. The program's director explained to me that it would hurt their relationships with the public schools where they recruit students for the program if they were viewed as "taking the cream of the crop" out of the public school system. Administrators at the school and program make it a point to emphasize that Pathways is not a recruitment program for the school.
6. The belief held by the program administrators was that they had to pay racial minorities a higher salary than they paid the rest of the staff. They maintained that students of color (both at the high school and college levels) who applied to the program were not typically as affluent as the white staff members. The administrators reported that students of color "could not afford to spend the summer volunteering," as the director explained. One could certainly question their explanations for not having a diverse staff.
7. I want to thank Erik Malewski for bringing this to my attention and helping me sort out some of my thinking about Galvin and Claire's resistance. I would also like to thank Alan Block for his critical questions and comments on an earlier draft of this section.
8. It is important to note that Galvin and Claire do not want to give up their wealth. As I have framed privilege throughout this book, I am referring here to privilege as an identity.

Chapter 8

1. The title of this chapter is a phrase borrowed from Collins (1986).
2. My focus on African Americans is not to suggest that other racial minority groups within these school communities did not have their own set of problems. At the four schools, African Americans were the largest racial minority group, which is the primary reason that I focus on this group. Since there were more African Americans, I had more opportunities to witness during my research the struggles they faced within these environments. Asian Americans were the second largest group. However, I did not observe Asian American students having the same social and academic problems as African American students. Again, this is not to suggest that they did not have these problems; I simply did not witness them during my research. There were a few Latinos/as (less than 1% of the student population) at two of the schools, McLean and Bredvik, and these students did seem to face similar difficulties as African Americans. However, they were not directly involved in my research studies.
3. It is important to note that seven of the nine parents had at least one child attending either Bredvik or Parker. Moreover, one of the parents (Mrs. St. John) who did not have a child attending one of these two schools served on a committee at Bredvik. All but one parent had some association with one or both of these schools.
4. See the National Association of Independent Schools at http://www.nais.org.

Chapter 9

1. I originally conducted this research to explore the ways that affluent and poor schools understood the concept of academic achievement. Like many others, I designed this study to compare affluent schools with poor schools. The findings of this comparative study are reported in Howard (2001).
2. During the course of my research, Nicole and Scott were very interested in my research at Reed High School and became "fascinated" with Jason. However, even when I would discuss Jason's circumstances with them, they never gave an opinion about Jason specifically. Instead, they made general statements about poor people; they rarely talked about specific individuals—even when they discussed members of their own social class group. They avoided talking about individuals but instead made generalized statements about groups of people. In other words, they avoided personalizing the characteristics that they were assigning to poor and affluent students.

Chapter 10

1. I realize that the word "unintentional" has some limitations in describing these contradictions. For example, these unintentional lessons, in the context of affluent schooling (as I argue later in this chapter), protect class interests and reinforce privileged ways of knowing and doing. It certainly could be argued that individuals are very intentional in protecting their interests and reinforcing privilege. I use the term "unintentional" to emphasize the point that individuals are often unaware of the unintentional outcomes of these lessons. In fact, these unintentional outcomes are often in direct contradiction with stated (intentional) outcomes.
2. It is appropriate that the elephant in this analogy is white, since whiteness, part of what I am discussing, is often ignored.
3. To add to this point, Freire said, "It is imperative that we maintain hope even when the harshness of reality may suggest the opposite" (as quoted at the beginning of bell hooks's *Teaching Community, 2003*).

References

Aggleton, P. (1987). *Rebels without a cause? Middle class youth and the transition from school to work.* London: Falmer Press.

Allan, E. J., & DeAngelis, G. (2004). Hazing, masculinity, and collision sports: (Un)becoming heroes. In J. Johnson & M. Holman (Eds.), *Inside the world of sports initiations and hazing* (pp. 169–178). Toronto: Canadian Scholars' Press.

Alpert, B. (1991). Students' resistance in the classroom. *Anthropology and Education Quarterly, 22*, 350–366.

Alt, M. N., & Peter, K. (2002). *Private schools: A brief portrait.* Washington, DC: National Center for Education Statistics.

Anderson, G. L., & Irvine, P. (1993). Informing critical literacy with ethnography. In C. Lankshear & P. McLaren (Eds.), *Critical literacy: Politics, praxis, and the postmodern* (pp. 81–104). Albany: State University of New York Press.

Ansalone, G. (2001). Schooling, tracking, and inequality. *Journal of Children and Poverty, 7*, 33–47.

Anyon, J. (1980). Social class and the hidden curriculum of work. *Journal of Education, 162*, 67–92.

Anyon, J. (1981). Elementary schooling and distinctions of social class. *Interchange, 12*, 118–132.

Anyon, J. (2000, April). *Political economy of an affluent suburban school district: Only some students get the best.* Paper presented at the American Educational Research Association Annual Meeting, New Orleans, Louisiana.

Anyon, J. (2005). What "counts" as educational policy? Notes toward a new paradigm. *Harvard Educational Review, 75*, 65–88.

Apple, M. (Ed.). (1982). *Cultural and economic reproduction in education: Essays on class, ideology and the state.* London: Routledge & Kegan Paul.

Apple, M. (1988). *Teachers and texts: A political economy of class and gender relations in education.* New York: Routledge.

Apple, M. (1993). *Official knowledge: Democratic education in a conservative age.* New York: Routledge.

Apple, M. (1995). *Education and power* (2nd ed.). New York: Routledge.

Apple, M. (1996). *Cultural politics and education.* New York: Teachers College Press.

Apple, M. (1999). *Power, meaning and identity.* New York: Peter Lang.

Apple, M., & Beane, J. (1995). Lessons from democratic schools. In M. Apple & J. Beane (Eds.), *Democratic schools* (pp. 101–105). Alexandria, VA: Association for Supervision and Curriculum Development.

Apple, M., & Weiss, L. (1983). Ideology and practice in schooling: A political and conceptual introduction. In M. Apple & L. Weiss (Eds.), *Ideology and practice in schooling* (pp. 3–25). Philadelphia: Temple University Press.

Arens, W. (1975). The great American football ritual. *Natural History, 84*, 72–81.

Armstrong, C. F. (1990). On the making of good men: Character-building in the New England boarding school. In P. W. Kingston & L. S. Lewis (Eds.), *The high status track: Studies of elite schools and stratification* (pp. 3–24). Albany: State University of New York Press.

Arnowitz, S. (1980). Science and ideology. *Current Perspectives in Social Theory, 1,* 75–101.

Arnowitz, S. (1992). *The politics of identity: Class, culture, social movements.* New York: Routledge.

Aronowitz, S., & Giroux, H. (1985). *Education under siege.* South Hadley, MA: Bergin & Garvey.

Artiles, A. J., & Trent, S. (1994). Overrepresentation of minority students in special education: A continuing debate. *Journal of Special Education, 27,* 410–437.

Asher, N. (2005). At the interstices: Engaging postcolonial and feminist perspectives for a multicultural education pedagogy in the South. *Teachers College Record, 107,* 1079–1106.

Badie, R. (1998, October 1). Private school boom: Growth drives demand for private schools as parents seek alternatives to public schools and their problems. *Atlanta Journal-Constitution,* p. JH1.

Bakhtin, M. (1981). *The dialogic imagination* (M. Holquist, Ed., C. Emerson, & M. Holquist, Trans.). Austin: University of Texas Press.

Banks, J. A. (1984). Black youths in predominantly white suburbs: An exploratory study of their attitudes and self-concepts. *Journal of Negro Education, 53,* 3–17.

Barton, L., & Oliver, M. (1997). Special needs: Personal trouble or public issue? In B. Cosin & M. Hales (Eds.), *Families, education and social differences* (pp. 89–101). New York: Routledge in association with The Open University.

Basso, K. H. (1990). *Portraits of "the Whiteman:" Linguistic play and cultural symbols among the Western Apache.* Cambridge, England: Cambridge University Press.

Bauman, R. (1986). *Story, performance, and event: Contextual stories of oral narrative.* Cambridge Cambridge University Press.

Bereiter, C., & Engelmann, S. (1966). *Teaching disadvantaged children in the preschool.* Englewood Cliffs, NJ: Prentice-Hall.

Bergin, D., & Cooks, H. (2002). High school students of color about accusations of acting white. *Urban Review, 34,* 113–134.

Berliner, D., & Biddle, B. (1995). *The manufactured crisis: Myths, fraud, and the attack on America's public schools.* Reading, MA: Addison-Wesley.

Bernstein, B. (1977). Social class, language, and socialization. In J. Karabel & A. H. Halsey (Eds.), *Power and ideology in education* (pp. 511–534). New York: Oxford University Press.

Bernstein, B. (1994). A rejoinder to Michael Huspek. *British Journal of Sociology, 45,* 103–108.

Bickel, R., & Chang, M. J. (1985). Public schools, private schools, and the common school ideal. *Urban Review, 17,* 75–97.

Bills, D. B. (1988). Educational credentials and promotions: Does schooling do more than get you in the door? *Sociology of Education, 61,* 52–60.

Bishop, A. (2002). *Becoming an ally: Breaking the cycle of oppression in people* (2nd ed.). Nova Scotia, Canada: Fernwood Publishing.

Blasi, A. (1984). Moral identity: Its role in moral functioning. In W. Kurtines & J. Gewirtz (Eds.), *Morality, moral behavior, and moral development* (pp. 128–139). New York: Routledge Falmer.

Bloom, S. G. (2005, September). Lesson of a lifetime. *Smithsonian,* 82–92.

Bogard, K. (2005). Affluent adolescents, depression, and drug use: The role of adults in their lives. *Adolescence, 40,* 281–306.

Bonilla-Silva, E. (2001). *White supremacy and racism in the post civil rights era.* Boulder, CO: Rienner.

Bonilla-Silva, E. (2003). *Racism without racists: Color-blind racism and the persistence of racial inequality in the United States.* Boulder, CO: Rowman & Littlefield.

Boudon, R. (1994). *The art of self persuasion: The social explanation of false beliefs* (M. Slater, Trans.). Cambridge, England: Polity Press. (Original work published 1990)

Bourdieu, P. (1977). *Outline of a theory of practice.* Cambridge, England: Cambridge University Press.

Bourdieu, P. (1984). *Distinction: A social critique of the judgment of taste.* Cambridge, MA: Harvard University Press.

Bourdieu, P. (1987). The forms of capital. In J. G. Richardson (Ed.), *Handbook of theory and research for the sociology of education* (pp. 241–258). New York: Greenwood Press.

Bourdieu, P. (1993). *Sociology in question.* Thousand Oaks, CA: Sage.

Bourdieu, P. (1994). *Language and symbolic power.* Cambridge, MA: Harvard University Press.

Bourdieu, P., & Passeron, J. C. (1977). *Reproduction in education, society and culture.* Beverly Hills, CA: Sage.

Bourdieu, P., & Wacquant, L. J. D. (1992). *An invitation to reflexive sociology.* Chicago: University of Chicago Press.

Bowles, S., & Gintis, H. (1976). *Schooling in capitalist America.* New York: Basic Books.

Brantlinger, E. (1985). What low-income parents want from schools: A different view of aspirations. *Interchange, 16,* 14–28.

Brantlinger, E. (1993). *The politics of social class in secondary schools: Views of affluent and impoverished youth.* New York: Teachers College Press.

Brantlinger, E. (2001). Poverty, class, and disability: A historical, social, and political perspective. *Focus on Exceptional Children, 33,* 1–19.

Brantlinger, E. (2003). *Dividing classes: How the middle class negotiates and rationalizes school advantage.* New York: Routledge Falmer.

Brantlinger, E., Majd-Jabbari, M., & Guskin, S. (1996). Self-interest and liberal educational discourse: How ideology works for middle class mothers. *American Educational Research Journal, 33,* 571–598.

Brantlinger, P. (1990). *Crusoe's footprints: Cultural studies in Britain and America.* New York: Routledge.

Brooks-Gunn, J., & Duncan, G. J. (1997). The effects of poverty on children. *Future of Children, 7,* 55–71.

Burton, R. L. (1999). A study of disparities among school facilities in North Carolina: Effects of race and economic status. *Educational Policy, 13,* 280–295.

Butler, J. (1990). *Gender trouble: Feminism and the subversion of identity.* New York: Routledge.

Butler, J. (1991). Decking out: Performing identities. In D. Fuss (Ed.), *Inside/out: Lesbian theories, gay theories* (pp. 13–29). New York: Routledge.

Carrington, V., & Luke, A. (1997). Literacy and Bourdieu's sociological theory: A reframing. *Language and Education, 11*, 96–112.

Carspecken, P. F., & Apple, M. (1992). Critical qualitative research: Theory, methodology, and practice. In M. LeCompte, W. Millroy, & J. Preissle (Eds.), *The handbook of qualitative research in education* (pp. 507-553). San Diego, CA: Academic Press.

Clay, M. M. (1975). *What did I write?* Auckland, New Zealand: Heinemann.

Clay, M. M. (1991). *Becoming literate: The construction of inner control.* Auckland, New Zealand: Heinemann.

Coleman, J. (1988). Social capital, human capital, and schools. *Independent School, 48*, 9–16.

Coleman, J., Hoffer, T., & Kilgore, S. (1981). *Public and private schools* (Final report to the National Center for Education Statistics, Contract No. 300-78-0208). Chicago: National Opinion Research Center.

Coles, R. (1977). *Privileged ones: The rich and well-off in America.* Boston: Little, Brown and Co.

Collins, P. H. (1986). Learning from the outsider within: The sociological significance of black feminist thought. *Social Problems, 33*, 14–32.

Collins, R. (1979). *The credential society.* New York: Academic Press.

The Commission on Excellence in Education (1983). *A nation at risk: The imperative for educational reform.* Washington D.C.: U.S. Department of Education.

Connor, M. H., & Boskin, J. (2001). Overrepresentation of bilingual and poor children in special education classes: A continuing problem. *Journal of Children and Poverty, 7*, 23–32.

Cookson, P. W., & Persell, C. H. (1985). *Preparing for power: America's elite boarding schools.* New York: Basic Books.

Cookson, P. W., & Persell, C. H. (1991). Race and class in America's elite preparatory boarding schools: African Americans as the 'outsiders within.' *Journal of Negro Education, 60*, 219–228.

Crosier, L. M. (Ed.). (1991). *Causalities of privilege: Essays on prep schools' hidden culture.* Washington, DC: Avocous Publishing Company.

Curry, T. J. (1998). Beyond the locker room: Campus bars and college athletes. *Sociology of Sport Journal, 15*, 205–215.

Curry, T. J. (2001). Reply to "a conversational (re)analysis of fraternal bonding in the locker room." *Sociology of Sport Journal, 18*, 339–344.

Damon, W., & Hart, D. (1988). *Self-understanding in childhood adolescence.* Cambridge: Cambridge University Press.

Darder, A. (2002). *Reinventing Paulo Freire: A pedagogy of love.* Boulder, CO: Westview Press.

Darling-Hammond, L. (2004). From "separate but equal" to "no child left behind": The collision of new standards and old inequalities. In D. Meier & G. Wood (Eds.), *Many children left behind: How the No Child Left Behind Act is damaging out children and our schools* (pp. 3–32). Boston: Beacon Press.

Davies, B. (2000). *A body of writing, 1990–1999.* Walnut Creek, CA: AltaMira Press.

De Civita, M., Pagani, L., Vitaro, F., & Tremblay, R. E. (2004). The role of maternal educational aspirations in mediating the risk of income source on academic failure in children from persistently poor families. *Children and Youth Services Review, 26*, 749–769.

Delpit, L. (1988). The silenced dialogue: Power and pedagogy in educating other people's children. *Harvard Educational Review, 58*, 280–298.

Delpit, L. (1995). *Other people's children: Cultural conflict in the classroom*. New York: New Press.

Denzin, N. K., & Lincoln, Y. S. (1994). Entering the field of qualitative research. In N. K. Denzin & Y. S. Lincoln (Eds.), *Handbook of qualitative research* (pp. 1-17). Newbury Park, CA: Sage.

Devins, N. E. (Ed.). (1989). *Public values, private schools*. London: Falmer.

Dewey, J. (1916). *Democracy and education*. Carbondale: Southern Illinois University.

Dimitriadis, G. (2001). *Performing identity/performing culture: Hip hop as text, pedagogy, and lived practice*. New York: Peter Lang.

Doane, A. W., & Bonilla-Silva, E. (Eds.). (2003). *White out: The continuing significance of racism*. New York: Routledge.

Dolby, N. (2000). Changing selves: Multicultural education and the challenge of new identities. *Teachers College Record, 102*, 898–912.

Dolby, N. (2001). *Constructing race: Youth, identity, and popular culture in South Africa*. Albany: State University of New York Press.

Dolby, N. (2002). Making white: Constructing race in a South African high school. *Curriculum Inquiry 32*, 7–29.

Dolby, N., & Dimitriadis, G. (Eds.). (2004). *Learning to labor in new times*. New York: Routledge.

Douthat, R. (2005, November). Does meritocracy work? Not if society and colleges keep failing to distinguish between wealth and merit. *Atlantic Monthly*, 120–126.

Doyle, D. P. (1981). A din of inequity: Private schools reconsidered. *Teachers College Record, 82*, 661–673.

Du Bois, W. E. B. (1961). *The souls of black folk*. New York: Bantam Books.

Duckworth, E. (1987). *"The having of wonderful ideas" and other essays on teaching and learning*. New York: Teachers College Press.

Dyer, R. (1988). White. *Screen, 29*, 44–64.

Dyson, A. (1983). Reading, writing, and language: Young children solving the written language puzzle. *Language Arts*, 59, 204–214.

Eckert, P. (1989). *Jocks & burnouts: Social categories and identity in the high school*. New York: Teachers College Press.

Eder, D. (with C. C. Evans & S. Parker). (1995). *School talk: Gender and adolescent culture*. New Brunswick, NJ: Rutgers University Press.

Education Trust. (2001). *The funding gap: Low-income and minority students receive fewer dollars*. Washington, DC: Author.

Edward, R., & Hamilton, M. A. (2004). You need to understand my gender role: An empirical test of Tannen's model of gender and communication. *Sex Roles: A Journal of Research, 50*, 491–504.

Ellsworth, E. (1989). Why doesn't this feel empowering? Working through the repressive myths of critical pedagogy. *Harvard Educational Review, 59*, 297–324.

Ellsworth, E. (1997). *Teaching positions: Difference, pedagogy and the power of address*. New York: Teachers College Press.

Enciso, P. E. (1998). Good/bad girls read together: Pre-adolescent girls' co-authorship of feminine subject positions during a shared reading event. *English Education, 30*, 44–62.

Enos, S., & Troppe, M. (1996). Curricular models for service learning. *Metropolitan Universities, 7*, 71–84.

Erikson, E. (1968). *Identity: Youth and crisis.* New York: W. W. Norton.

Eyler, J., & Giles, D. W. (1999). *Where's the learning in service-learning?* San Francisco: Jossey-Bass.

Fairbanks, C., & Ariail, M. (2006). The role of social and cultural resources in literacy and schooling: Three contrasting cases. *Research in the Teaching of English, 40*, 310–355.

Falsey, B., & Heyns, B. (1984). The college channel: Private and public schools reconsidered. *Sociology of Education, 57*, 111–122.

Fay, B. (1987). *Critical social science.* Ithaca, NY: Cornell University Press.

Festinger, L. (1957). *A theory of cognition.* Evanston, IL: Row & Peterson.

Fine, M. (1991). *Framing dropouts: Notes on the politics of an urban public high school.* Albany: State University of New York Press.

Fine, M., Weis, L., Powell, L., & Wong, L. (Eds.). (1997). *Off white: Readings on race, power, and society.* New York: Routledge.

Foley, D. (1990). *Learning capitalist culture: Deep in the heart of Tejas.* Philadelphia: University of Pennsylvania Press.

Folmar, K. (1997, April 20). Education: Parents who shun public campuses cite smaller sizes and rigorous academics. *Los Angeles Times*, p. 2.

Fordham, S. (1991). Racelessness in private schools: Should we deconstruct the racial and cultural identity of African-American adolescents? *Teachers College Record, 92*, 470–484.

Fordham, S. (1996). *Blacked out: Dilemmas of race, identity, and success at Capital High.* Chicago: University of Chicago.

Fordham, S., & Ogbu, J. (1986). Black students' school success: Coping with the burden of acting white. *Urban Review, 19*, 176–206.

Frankenberg, R. (1993). *White women, race matters: The social construction of whiteness.* Minneapolis: University of Minnesota Press.

Freire, P. (1970). *Pedagogy of the oppressed.* New York: Seabury Press.

Freire, P. (1994). *Pedagogy of hope: Reliving pedagogy of the oppressed.* New York: Continuum.

Freud, S. (1960). *The ego and the id.* New York: W. W. Norton. (Original work published 1923)

Furco, A., & Billig, S. (Eds.). (2002). *Service-learning: The essence of the pedagogy.* Greenwich, CT: Information Age Publishing.

Fussell, P. (1983). *Class.* New York: Ballantine Books.

Gair, M., & Mullins, G. (2001). Hiding in plain sight. In E. Margolis (Ed.), *The hidden curriculum in higher education* (pp. 21–41). New York: Routledge.

Gamoran, A., & Berends, M. (1987). The effects of stratification in secondary schools: Synthesis of survey and ethnographic research. *Review of Educational Research, 57*, 415–435.

Gayles, J. (2005). Playing the game and paying the price: Academic resilience among three high-achieving African American males. *Anthropology and Education Quarterly, 36*, 250–264.

Geertz, C. (1988). *Works and lives: The anthropologist as author.* Stanford, CA: Stanford University Press.

Gegax, T. T. (2005, June 28). Not-so-hallowed-halls. *Newsweek, 143*, 45.

Gilbert, S. (1999, August 3). For some children, it's an after-school pressure cooker. *New York Times,* p. F7.

Giles, D. W., & Eyler, J. (1994). The impact of college community service laboratory on students' personal, social, and cognitive outcomes. *Journal of Adolescence, 17,* 327–329.

Gilligan, C. (1982). *In a different voice.* Cambridge, MA: Harvard University Press.

Gilligan, C., Brown, L. M., & Rogers, A. G. (1989). Psyche embedded: A place for body, relationships, and culture in personality theory. In A. Rubin, R. Zucker, R. Emmons, & S. Frank (Eds.), *Studying persons and lives* (pp. 86–147). New York: Springer.

Giroux, H. (1981). *Ideology, culture, and the process of schooling.* Philadelphia: Temple University Press.

Giroux, H. (1983a). *Theory and resistance in education: A pedagogy for the opposition.* South Hadley, MA: Bergin & Garvey.

Giroux, H. (1983b). Theories of reproduction and resistance in the new sociology of education: A critical analysis. *Harvard Educational Review, 53,* 257–293.

Giroux, H. (1992). *Border crossings: Cultural workers and the politics of education.* New York: Routledge, Chapman & Hall.

Giroux, H. (1997). Rewriting the discourse of racial identity: Towards a pedagogy and politics of whiteness. *Harvard Educational Review, 67,* 285–320.

Goffman, I. (1959). *The presentation of self in everyday life.* Garden City, NY: Doubleday Anchor.

Goodman, D. (2001). *Promoting diversity and social justice: Educating people from privileged groups.* Thousand Oaks, CA: Sage.

Gramsci, A. (1971). *Selections from the prison notebooks* (Q. Hoare & G. N. Smith, Eds.). New York: International Publishers.

Grenfell, M., & James, D. (1998). *Bourdieu and education: Acts of practical inquiry.* London: Palmer.

Griffin, C. (2001). Imagining new narratives of youth: Youth research, the "new Europe" and global youth culture. *Childhood, 8,* 147–166.

Griffin, S. (1992). *A chorus of stones: The private life of war.* New York: Doubleday.

Guynn, K. (2002). *Hazing in public and private schools: An analysis of legal responses to hazing.* Unpublished doctoral dissertation, Cleveland State University.

Haberman, M. (1991). The pedagogy of poverty versus good teaching. *Phi Delta Kappan,* 73, 290–294.

Hall, S. (1996). Who needs "identity"? In S. Hall & P. du Gay (Eds.), *Questions of cultural identity* (pp. 1–17). London: Sage Publications.

Hardiman, R., & Jackson, B. (1997). Conceptual foundations for social justice courses. In M. Adams, L. A. Bell, & P. Griffin (Eds.), *Teaching for diversity and social justice: A sourcebook* (pp. 16–29). New York: Routledge.

Harkavy, I., Puckett, J., & Romer, D. (2000). Action research: Bridging service and research. *Michigan Journal of Community Service Learning,* Special Issue, 113–119.

Harker, R., Mahar, C., & Wilkes, C. (1990). *An introduction to the work of Pierre Bourdieu: The practice of theory.* New York: St. Martin's Press.

Hauser, R. N., Simmons, S. J., & Pager, D. I. (2000). *High school dropout, race/ethnicity, and social background from the 1970s and the 1990s* (Working paper no. 2000-12). Madison: University of Wisconsin-Madison, Center for Demography and Ecology.

Haymes, S. (1995). White culture and the politics of racial difference: Implications for multiculturalism. In C. Sleeter & P. McLaren (Eds.), *Multicultural education, critical pedagogy, and the politics of difference* (pp. 105–128). Albany: State University of New York Press.

Hays, K. (1994). *Practicing virtues: Moral traditions of Quaker and military boarding schools.* Berkeley and Los Angeles: University of California Press.

Heath, S. B. (1983). *Ways with words.* New York: Cambridge University Press.

Helms, J. (1990). Toward a model of white racial identity development. In J. Helms (Ed.), *Black and white racial identity* (pp. 49–66). Westport, CT: Greenwood Press.

Hemmings, A. (1996). Conflicting images? Being black and a model high school student. *Anthropology and Education Quarterly, 27,* 20–50.

Henry, J. (1995). *If not now: Developmental readers in the college classroom.* Portsmouth, NH: Heinemann.

Herrnstein, R., & Murray, C. (1994). *The bell curve: Intelligence and class structure in American life.* New York: The Free Press.

Hill, D. (1989, September/October). Fixing the system from the top down. *Teacher Magazine,* 50–55.

Hinchey, P. H. (2001). *Finding freedom in the classroom: A practical introduction to critical theory.* New York: Peter Lang.

Holland, D., & Eisenhart, M. A. (1990). *Educated in romance: Women, achievement, and college culture.* Chicago: University of Chicago Press.

Holland, D., Lachicotte, W., Jr., Skinner, D., & Cain, C. (1998). *Identity and agency in cultural worlds.* Cambridge, MA: Harvard University Press.

Hollmann, B. B. (2002). Hazing: Hidden campus crime. *New Directions for Student Services, 99,* 11–23.

hooks, b. (1994). *Teaching to transgress: Education as the practice of freedom.* New York: Routledge.

hooks, b. (2000). *Where we stand: Class matters.* New York: Routledge.

hooks, b. (2003). *Teaching community: A pedagogy of hope.* New York: Routledge.

Horvat, E. M., & Antonio, A. L. (1999). "Hey, those shoes are out of uniform": African American girls in an elite high school and the importance of habitus. *Anthropology and Education Quarterly, 30,* 317–342.

Horvat, E. M., Lareau, A., & Weininger, E. B. (2002, April). *From social ties to social capital: Class differences in relations between schools and parent network.* Paper presented at the annual meeting of the American Educational Research Association, New Orleans, Louisiana.

Howard, A. (2000). Pedagogy for the affluent. *Encounter: Education for Meaning and Social Justice, 13,* 34–40.

Howard, A. (2001). Examining poor and affluent students' perceptions of academic achievement. *Academic Exchange Quarterly, 5,* 95–100.

Howard, A. (2002). Students from poverty: Helping them make it through college. *About Campus, 6,* 5–12.

Howard, A. (2005a). Lessons of poverty: Towards a literacy of survival. *Journal of Curriculum Theorizing, 21,* 73–82.

Howard, A. (2005b). Standardized solutions?: A dialogue with Deborah Meier. *Encounter: Education for Meaning and Social Justice, 18*, 22–28.

Howard, A., & EnglandKennedy, E. (2006). Breaking the silence: Power, conflict, and contested frames within an affluent high school. *Anthropology and Education Quarterly, 37*, 347–365.

Howard, A., & Tappan, M. (2007, April). *Privilege as identity*. Paper presented at the Annual Meeting of the American Educational Research Association, Chicago, Illinois.

Hubbard, R. S., & Power, B. M. (1999). *Living the questions: A guide for teacher-researcher*. York, ME: Stenhouse Publishers.

Inden, R. (1990). *Imagining India*. Oxford, England: Blackwell.

Independent Sector (2001). *Deducting generosity: The effect of charitable tax incentives on giving*. Washington, DC: Author.

Ingersoll, R. (1999). The problem of underqualified teachers in American secondary schools. *Educational Research, 28*, 26–37.

Jackson, P. W. (1968). *Life in classrooms*. New York: Holt, Rinehart, and Winston.

James, T., & Levin, H. M. (1988). *Comparing public and private schools* (Vol. 1). New York: Falmer.

Jencks, C. (1972). *Inequality: A reassessment of the effect of family and schooling in America*. New York: Harper & Row.

Jensen, A. R. (1969). How much can we boost IQ and scholastic achievement? *Harvard Educational Review, 39*, 1–123.

Jensen, R. (2005). *The heart of whiteness: Confronting race, racism, and white privilege*. San Francisco: City Lights.

Jimerson, J. B. (2001). A conversational (re)analysis of fraternal bonding in the locker room. *Sociology of Sport Journal, 18*, 317–338.

Johnson, A. G. (2001). *Privilege, power, and difference*. Mountain View, CA: Mayfield Publishing Co.

Kao, G., Tienda, N., & Schneider, B. (1996). Racial and ethnic variation in academic performance. *Research in Sociology of Education and Socialization, 11*, 263–297.

Katz, M. B. (1975). *Class, bureaucracy, and the schools: The illusion of educational change in America*. New York: Praeger.

Keating, A. (1995). Interrogating "whiteness," (de)constructing "race." *College English, 57*, 901–918.

Kendall, J. C. (1990). Combining service and learning: An introduction. In J. C. Kendall (Ed.), *Combining service and learning: A resource book for community and public service* (Vol. 1, pp. 1–33). Raleigh, NC: National Society for Experiential Education.

Kimmel, M. S., & Ferber, A. L. (Eds.). (2003). *Privilege: A reader*. Boulder, CO: Westview Press.

Kingston, P. W. (1981). The credential elite and the credential route to success. *Teachers College Record, 82*, 589–600.

Kingston, P. W., & Lewis, L. S. (1990). *The high status track: Studies of elite schools and stratification*. Albany: State University of New York Press.

Kivel, P. (1996). *Uprooting racism: How white people can work for racial justice*. Philadelphia: New Society Publishers.

Kohn, A. (1992). *No contest: The case against competition* (rev. ed.). New York: Houghton Mifflin Company.

Kohn, A. (1998). Only for my kid: How privileged parents undermine school reform. *Phi Delta Kappan, 79*, 569–577.

Kozol, J. (1991). *Savage inequalities: Children in America's schools.* New York: Crown.

Kumashiro, K. K. (2000). Toward a theory of anti-oppressive education. *Review of Educational Research, 70*, 25–53.

Kumashiro, K. K. (2002). Against repetition: Addressing resistance to anti-oppressive change in the practices of learning, teaching, supervising, and researching. *Harvard Educational Review, 72*, 67–92.

Ladson-Billings, G. (1998). Just what is critical race theory and what's it doing in a *nice* field like education? *Qualitative Studies in Education, 11*, 7–24.

Lamont, M., & Lareau, A. (1988). Cultural capital: Allusions, gaps and glissandos in recent theoretical developments. *Sociological Theory, 6*, 153–168.

Langer, S. K. (2002). The logic of signs and symbols. In M. Lambek (Ed.), *A reader in the anthropology of religion* (pp. 136–144). Malden, MA: Blackwell.

Larrain, J. A. (1992). *The concept of ideology.* Hampshire, England: Gregg Revivals (Routledge).

Lather, P. (1998). Critical pedagogy and its complicities: A praxis of stuck places. *Educational Theory, 48*, 487–497.

Lather, P., & Smithies, C. (1997). *Troubling the angels: Women living with HIV/AIDS.* Boulder, CO: Westview Press.

Lawrence, S. (1997). Beyond race awareness: White racial identity and multicultural teaching. *Journal of Teacher Education, 48*, 108–117.

Lawrence-Lightfoot, S. (1983). *The good high school: Portraits of character and culture.* New York: Basic Books.

Lawrence-Lightfoot, S., & Davis, J. H. (1997). *The art and science of portraiture.* San Francisco: Jossey-Bass.

Lee, J.-S., & Bowen, N. K. (2006). Parent involvement, cultural capital, and the achievement gap among elementary school children. *American Educational Research Journal, 43*, 193–218.

Leistyna, P. (1999). *Presence of mind: Education and the politics of deception.* Boulder, CO: Westview Press.

Lemann, N. (1997, September). The SAT meritocracy. *Washington Monthly*, 32–36.

Leonhardt, D. (2005, May 14). A closer look at income mobility. *New York Times.* Retrieved from http://www.nytimes.com/pages/national/class/index.html

Lesko, N. (1988). *Symbolizing society: Stories, rites and structure in a Catholic high school.* New York: Falmer Press.

Lesko, N. (2001). *Act your age: A cultural construction of adolescence.* New York: Routledge Falmer.

Levin, J. (2003). White like me. In M. S. Kimmel & A. L. Ferber (Eds.), *Privilege: A reader* (pp. 189–194). Boulder, CO: Westview Press.

Levine, A., & Nidiffer, J. (1996). *Beating the odds: How the poor get to college.* San Francisco: Jossey-Bass.

Lienhardt, G. (1961). *Divinity and experience: The religion of the Dinka.* Oxford, England: Oxford University Press.

Loomis, C. (2006, June 25). A conversation with Warren Buffett. *Fortune.* Retrieved from http://money.cnn.com/2006/06/25/magazines/fortune/charity2.fortune/index.htm

Lorde, A. (1981). The master's tools will never dismantle the master's house. In C. Moraga & G. Anzaldua (Eds.), *This bridge called my back: Writings by radical women of color* (pp. 98–101). New York: Kitchen Table/Women of Color Press.

Luthar, S. S., & Becker, B. E. (2002). Privileged but pressured? A study of affluent youth. *Child Development, 73*, 1593–1610.

Lyman, P. (2004). The fraternal bond as a joking relationship: A case study of the role of sexist jokes in male group bonding. In M. Kimmel & M. Messner (Eds.), *Men's lives* (6th ed., pp. 169–178). Boston: Pearson Education.

MacLeod, J. (1987). *Ain't no makin' it: Leveled aspirations in low-income neighborhoods.* Boulder, CO: Westview Press.

Magolda, P. M. (2000). The campus tour: Ritual and community in higher education. *Anthropology and Education Quarterly, 31*, 24–46.

Mantsios, G. (2003). Media magic: Making class invisible. In T. E. Ore (Ed.), *The social construction of difference and inequality* (2nd ed., pp. 81–89). New York: McGraw-Hill.

Margolis, E., Soldatenko, M., Acker, S., & Gair, M. (2001). Peekaboo: Hiding and outing the curriculum. In E. Margolis (Ed.), *The hidden curriculum in higher education* (pp. 1–19). New York: Routledge.

Mark, P., & DeJong, F. (1998). Ritual and masking traditions in Jola men's initiation. *African Arts, 31*, 36–47.

McCarthy, C., & Crichlow, W., Dimitriadis, G., & Dolby, N. (Eds.). (2005). *Race identity and representation in education* (2nd ed.). New York: Routledge.

McDermott, R. P. (1977). Social relations as contexts for learning in school. *Harvard Educational Review, 47*, 198–213.

McDonough, P. M. (1998). Structuring college opportunities: A cross-case analysis of organizational cultures, climates, and habiti. In C. A. Torres & T. R. Mitchell (Eds.), *Sociology of education: Emerging perspectives* (pp. 181–210). Albany: State University of New York Press.

McDonough, P. M., Korn, J., & Yamasaki, E. (1997). Access, equity, and the privatization of college counseling. *Review of Higher Education, 20*, 297–317.

McFadden, M. G. (1995). Resistance to schooling and educational outcomes: Questions of structure and agency. *British Journal of Sociology of Education, 16*, 293–308.

McIntosh, P. (1988). *White privilege and male privilege: A personal account of coming to see correspondences through work in women's studies* (Working Paper 189). Wellesley, MA: Wellesley College Center for Research on Women.

McIntosh, P. (1990). White privilege: Unpacking the invisible knapsack. *Independent School*, Winter, 31–36.

McIntyre, A. (1997). *Making meaning of whiteness: Exploring racial identity with white teachers.* Albany: State University of New York Press.

McLaren, P. (1989). *Life in schools: An introduction to critical pedagogy in the foundations of education.* New York: Longman.

McLaren, P. (1995). *Critical pedagogy and predatory culture.* New York: Routledge.

McLaren, P. (1997). Unthinking whiteness, rethinking democracy, or farewell to the blonde beast: Towards a revolutionary multiculturalism. *Educational Foundations, 11*, 5–39.

McLaren, P. (1999). *Schooling as a ritual performance: Toward a political economy of educational symbols and gestures* (3rd ed.). Lanham, MD: Rowman & Littlefield Publishers.

McLoyd, V. (1998). Socioeconomic disadvantage and child development. *American Psychologist, 53,* 185–204.

McNeil, L. (1986). *Contradictions of control: School structure and school knowledge.* London and Boston: Routledge and Kegan Paul.

McNeil, L. (2000). *Contradictions of school reform: Educational costs of standardized testing.* New York: Routledge.

McRobbie, A. (1982). The politics of feminist research: Between talk, text and action. *Feminist Review, 12,* 46–57.

McRobbie, A. (1991). *Feminism and youth culture: From 'Jackie' to 'just seventeen.'* London: Macmillan.

Mehan, H. (1992). Understanding inequality in schools: The contribution of interpretive studies. *Sociology of Education, 65,* 1–21.

Meier, D. (2000). *Will Standards Save Public Education?* Boston: Beacon Press.

Meier, D. (2002). *In schools we trust: Creating communities of learning in an era of testing and standardization.* Boston: Beacon Press.

Meier, D. (2004). NCLB and democracy. In D. Meier & G. Wood (Eds.), *Many children left behind: How the No Child Left Behind Act is damaging our children and our schools* (pp. 66–78). Boston: Beacon Press.

Melchior, A., & Bailis, L. (2002). Impact of service-learning on civic attitudes and behaviors of middle and high school youth. In A. Furco & S. Billig (Eds.), *Service-learning: The essence of the pedagogy* (pp. 201–222). Greenwich, CT: Information Age Publishing.

Metz, M. H. (1998, April). *Veiled inequalities: The hidden effects of community social class on high school teachers' perspectives and practices.* Paper presented at the annual meeting of the American Educational Research Association, San Diego, California.

Mickelson, R. A. (1990). The attitude achievement paradox among black adolescents. *Sociology of Education, 63,* 44–61.

Mohanty, C. (1990). On race and voice: Challenges for liberal education in the 1990s. *Cultural Critique,* 179–208.

Moje, E. B. (2002). Re-framing adolescent literacy research for new times: Studying youth as resource. *Reading Research and Instruction, 41,* 211-228.

Morrow, R. A., & Torres, C. A. (1994). Education and the reproduction of class, gender, and race: Responding to the postmodern challenge. *Educational Theory, 44,* 43–61.

Mortimore, P., & Mortimore, J. (1999). The political and the professional in education: An unnecessary conflict? In J. S. Gaffney & B. J. Askew (Eds.), *Stirring the waters: The influence of Marie Clay* (pp. 221–238). Portsmouth, NH: Heinemann.

Nieto, S. (1996). *Affirming diversity: The sociopolitical context of multicultural education* (2nd ed.). White Plains, NY: Longman.

Nieto, S. (1999). *The light in their eyes: Creating multicultural learning communities.* New York: Teachers College Press.

Nieto, S. (2002). *Language, culture, and teaching: Critical perspectives for a new century.* Mahwah, NJ: Lawrence Erlbaum.

Nieto, S. (2005). Public education in the twentieth century and beyond: High hopes, broken promises, and an uncertain future. *Harvard Educational Review, 75,* 43–64.

Noguera, P., & Akom, A. (2000, June 19). The significance of race in the racial gap in academic achievement. *Motion Magazine*. Retrieved from www.inmotionmagazine.com/pnaa.html

Nuwer, H. (2000). *High school hazing: When rites become wrongs*. New York: Grolier Publishing.

Nuwer, H. (Ed.). (2004). *The hazing reader*. Bloomington: Indiana University Press.

Oakes, J. (1985). *Keeping track: How schools structure inequality*. New Haven, CT: Yale University Press.

Oakes, J. (1988). Tracking: Can schools take a different route? *National Education Association, 6*, 41–47.

Oakes, J. (1990). *Multiplying inequalities: The effects of race, social class and tracking on opportunities to learn math and science*. Santa Monica, CA: RAND Corporation.

Oakes, J., & Guiton, G. (1995). Matchmaking: The dynamics of high school tracking decisions. *American Educational Research Journal, 32*, 3–33.

Oakes, J., & Lipton, M. (1999). *Teaching to change the world*. Boston: McGraw-Hill.

Obeyesekere, G. (2002). An essay on personal symbols and religious experience. In M. Lambek (Ed.), *A reader in the anthropology of religion* (pp. 383–397). Malden, MA: Blackwell Publishers.

O'Connor, C. (2002). Black women beating the odds from one generation to the next: How the changing dynamics of constraint and opportunity affect the process of educational resilience. *American Educational Research Journal, 39*, 855–903.

Ogbu, J. U. (2003). *Black American students in an affluent suburb: A study of academic disengagement*. Mahwah, NJ: Lawrence Erlbaum Associates.

Oliff, H. (2002). Lifting the haze around hazing. *Education Digest, 67*, 21–27.

Olson, C. P. (1983). Inequality remade: The theory of correspondence and the context of French immersion in northern Ontario. *Journal of Education, 165*, 75–98.

Orfield, G. (2000, April). *What have we learned from school reconstitution?* Paper presented at the annual meeting of the American Educational Research Association, New Orleans, Louisiana.

Ortner, S. (1973). On key symbols. *American Anthropologist, 75*, 1338–1346.

Ortner, S. (1991). Reading America: Preliminary notes on class and culture. In R. G. Fox (Ed.), *Recapturing anthropology: Working in the present* (pp. 163–189). Santa Fe, NM: School of America Research Press.

Penuel, W. R., & Wertsch, J. V. (1995). Vygotsky and identity formation: Sociocultural approach. *Educational Psychology, 30*, 83–92.

Persell, C. H. (1997). Social class and educational equality. In J. A. Banks & C. A. M. Banks (Eds.), *Multicultural education: Issues and perspectives* (3rd ed., pp. 87–107). Boston: Allyn & Bacon.

Peshkin, A. (1988). In search of subjectivity: One's own. *Educational researcher, 17*, 17–21.

Peshkin, A. (1991). *The color of strangers, the color of friends*. Chicago: University of Chicago Press.

Peshkin, A. (2001). *Permissible advantage? The moral consequences of elite schooling*. Mahwah, NJ: Lawrence Erlbaum Associates.

Phelen, P., Davidson, A. L., & Yu, H. C. (1998). *Adolescents' worlds: Negotiating family, peers, and school*. New York: Teachers College Press.

Phillips, M., Brooks-Gunn, J., Duncan, G., Klevanov, P., & Crane, J. (1998). Family background, parenting practices, and the black/white test score gap. In C. Jencks & M. Phillips (Eds.), *The black/white test score gap* (pp. 229–272). Washington, DC: Brookings Institution Press.

Pinar, W. F. (2004). *What is curriculum theory?* Mahwah, NJ: Lawrence Erlbaum Associates.

Pinar, W. F. (2006, October). *The racial and gender politics of contemporary curriculum reform in the United States.* Paper presented at Hanover College Department of Education, Hanover, Indiana.

Pope, D. C. (2001). *"Doing school": How we are creating a generation of stressed out, materialistic, and miseducated students.* New Haven, CT: Yale University Press.

Powell, A. (1996). *Lessons from privilege: The American prep school tradition.* Cambridge, MA: Harvard University Press.

Powell, R. (1996). Confronting white hegemony: Implications for multicultural education. *Multicultural Education,* Winter, 12–15.

Proweller, A. (1998). *Constructing female identities: Meaning making in an upper middle class youth culture.* Albany: State University of New York Press.

Proweller, A. (1999). Shifting identities in private education: Reconstructing race at/in the cultural center. *Teachers College Record, 100,* 776–808.

Puka, B. (1993). The liberation of caring: A different voice for Gilligan's "different voice." In M. J. Larrabee (Ed.), *An ethic of care: Feminist and interdisciplinary perspectives* (pp. 215–239). New York: Routledge.

Purcell-Gates, V. (1988). Lexical and syntactic expectations held by well-read-to kindergartners and second graders. *Research in the Teaching of English, 22,* 128–160.

Purcell-Gates, V. (1995). *Other people's words: The cycle of low literacy.* Cambridge, MA: Harvard University Press.

Purpel, D. (1999). *Moral outrage in education.* New York: Peter Lang.

Rappaport, R. (2002). Enactments of meaning. In M. Lambek (Ed.), *A reader in the anthropology of religion* (pp. 446–468). Malden, MA: Blackwell Publishers.

Reay, D. (2001). "Spice girls," "nice girls," "girlies," and "tomboys": Gender discourses, girls' cultures and femininities in the primary classroom. *Gender and Education, 13,* 153–167.

Reed-Danahay, D. (2005). *Locating Bourdieu.* Bloomington: Indiana University Press.

Riessman, F. (1962). *The culturally deprived child.* New York: Harper & Row.

Ricoeur, P. (1986). *Lectures on ideology and utopia.* New York: Columbia University Press.

Ripple, C. H., & Luthar, S. S. (2000). Academic risk among inner-city adolescents: The role of personal attributes. *Journal of School Psychology, 38,* 277–298.

Robinson, L. (2004). Hazing—a story. In J. Johnson & M. Holman (Eds.), *Making the team: Inside the world of sports initiations and hazing* (pp. 169–178). Toronto: Canadian Scholars' Press.

Robinson, T. (2000). Dare the school build a new social order? *Michigan Journal of Community Service Learning, 7,* 142–157.

Rocha, C. J. (2000). Evaluating experiential teaching methods in a policy practice course: The case for service-learning to increase political participation. *Journal of Social Work Education, 36,* 53–60.

Rockquemore, K. A., & Schaffer, R. H. (2000). Toward a theory of engagement: A cognitive mapping of service learning. *Michigan Journal of Community Service Learning, 7,* 14–23.

Rodkin, P. (2003). Bullies and victims in the peer ecology: Four questions for psychological and school professionals. *School Psychology Review, 32,* 384–400.

Rosenblum, K. E., & Travis, T.-C. M. (2003). *The meaning of difference: American constructions of race, sex and gender, social class, and sexual orientation* (3rd ed.). New York: McGraw-Hill.

Rothenberg, P. S. (Ed.). (2002). *White privilege: Essential readings on the other side of racism.* New York: Worth Publishers.

Rothstein, R. (2004). *Class and schools: Using social, economic, and educational reform to close the black-white achievement gap.* Washington, DC: Economic Policy Institute.

Sacks, P. (2001). *Standardized minds: The high price of America's testing culture and what we can do to change it.* Cambridge, MA: Perseus Books.

Sadkar, M., & Sadkar, D. (1994). *Failing at fairness: How our schools cheat girls.* New York: Simon & Schuster.

Sanday, P. (1990). *Fraternity gang rape: Sex, brotherhood, and privilege on campus.* New York: New York University Press.

Sandy, J. (1989). The choice of public or private school. *Social Science Journal, 26,* 415–431.

Scales, P., & Roehlkepartain, E. (2004). *Community service and service-learning in U.S. public schools, 2004.* St. Paul, MN: National Youth Leadership Council.

Scott, J., & Leonhardt, D. (2005, May 15). Shadowy lines that still divide. *New York Times.* Retrieved from http://www.nytimes.com/pages/national/class/index.html

Scheurich, J. (1993). Toward a white discourse on white racism. *Educational Researcher, 22,* 5–10.

Schiefflin, E. L. (1985). Performance and the cultural construction of reality. *American Ethnologist, 12,* 707–724.

Schwarz, J. E., & Volgy, T. J. (1992). *The forgotten Americans.* New York: W. W. Norton.

Seller, M., & Weis, L. (Eds.). (1997). *Beyond black and white: New faces and voices in U.S. schools.* Albany: State University of New York Press.

Seyfried, S. F. (1998). Academic achievement of African American preadolescents: The influence of teacher perceptions. *American Journal of Community Psychology, 26,* 381–402.

Shannon, P. (2006). *Educational equity, politics and policy in Texas.* Keynote address delivered at the annual meeting of International Reading Association, Chicago, IL.

Shujaa, M. (Ed.). (1994). *Too much schooling, too little education.* Albany: State University of New York Press.

Shumer, R., & Belbas, B. (1996). What we know about service learning. *Education and Urban Society, 28,* 208–223.

Sklar, H., Collins, C., & Leondar-Wright, B. (2003). The growing wealth gap: The median household net worth matches the sticker price of the new Ford Excursion. In T. E. Ore (Ed.), *The social construction of difference and inequality* (2nd ed.), pp. 90–95. New York: McGraw-Hill.

Sleeter, C. E. (1996). *Multicultural education as social activism.* Albany: State University of New York Press.

Sleeter, C. E. (2000, April). *Keeping the lid on: Multicultural curriculum and the organization of consciousness.* Paper presented at the annual meeting of American Educational Research Association, New Orleans, Louisiana.

Sleeter, C. E. (2005). *Un-standardizing curriculum: Multicultural teaching in the standards-based classroom.* New York: Teachers College Press.

Sleeter, C. E., & Grant, C. A. (2003). *Making choices for multicultural education: Five approaches to race, class, and gender* (4th ed.). New York: John Wiley & Sons.

Sleeter, C. E., & McLaren, P. (Eds.). (1995). *Multicultural education, critical pedagogy, and the politics of difference.* Albany: State University of New York Press.

Solórzano, D. G., & Delgado-Bernal, D. (2001). Examining transformational resistance through a critical race and latcrit theory framework: Chicana and chicano students in urban context. *Urban Education, 36*, 308–342.

Spencer, M. B., Noll, E., & Stolzfus, J. (2001). Identity and school adjustment: Revisiting the "acting white" assumption. *Educational Psychologist, 36*, 21–30.

Spring, J. (1972). *The rise and fall of the corporate state.* Boston: Beacon Press.

Stipic, D., & Ryan, R. (1997). Economically disadvantaged preschoolers: Ready to learn but further to go. *Developmental Psychology, 33*, 711–723.

Suitor, J. J., Powers, R. S., & Brown, R. (2004). Avenues to prestige among adolescents in public and religiously affiliated high schools. *Adolescence, 39*, 229–241.

Swartz, D. (1997). *Culture and power: The sociology of Pierre Bourdieu.* Chicago: University of Chicago Press.

Swartz, E. (1993). Multicultural education: Disrupting patterns of supremacy in school curricula, practices, and pedagogy. *Journal of Negro Education, 62*, 493–506.

Tannenbaum, S. C., & Brown-Wiley, S. (2006). Tandem pedagogy: Embedding service-learning into an after-school program. *Journal of Experiential Education, 29*, 111–125.

Tappan, M. (1992). Texts and contexts: Language, culture, and the development of moral functioning. In L. T. Winegar & J. Valsiner (Eds.), *Children's development within social contexts: Metatheoretical, theoretical, and methodological issues* (pp. 93–117). Hillsdale, NJ: Erlbaum.

Tappan, M. (1997). Language, culture, and moral development: A Vygotskian perspective. *Developmental Review, 17*, 78–100.

Tappan, M. (2000). Autobiography, mediated action, and the development of moral identity. *Narrative Inquiry, 10*, 81–109.

Tappan, M. (2005). Domination, subordination, and the dialogical self: Identity development and the politics of "ideological becoming." *Culture and Psychology, 11*, 47–75.

Tappan, M. (2006). Reframing internalized oppression and internalized domination: From the psychological to the sociocultural. *Teachers College Record, 108*, 2115–2144.

Tatum, B. D. (1987). *Assimilation blues: Black families in white communities: Who succeeds and why?* New York: Basic Books.

Tatum, B. D. (1997). *"Why are all the black kids sitting together in the cafeteria?": And other conversations about race.* New York: Basic Books.

Thompson, B., & Tyagi, S. (1996). *Names we call home: Autobiography on racial identity.* New York: Routledge.

Thompson, C. E., & Carter, R. T. (1997). *Racial identity theory: Applications to individual, group, and organizational interventions.* Mahwah, NJ: Lawrence Erlbaum Associates.

Thompson, J. B. (1984). *Studies in the theory of ideology.* Berkeley and Los Angeles: University of California Press.

Thompson, J. B. (1990). *Ideology and modern culture: Critical social theory in the era of mass communication.* Stanford, CA: Stanford University Press.

Turner, V. (1967). *The forest of symbols: Aspects of Ndembu ritual.* Ithaca, NY: Cornell University Press.

Turner, V. (1974). *Dramas, fields, and metaphors.* Ithaca, NY: Cornell University Press.

Turner, V. (1985). *On the edge of the bush.* Tucson: University of Arizona Press.

Urrieta, L. (2005). "Playing the game" versus "selling out": Chicanas and Chicanos relationship to whitestream schools. In B. K. Alexander, G. L. Anderson, & B. P. Gallegos (Eds.), *Performance theories in education: Power, pedagogy, and the politics of identity* (pp. 173–196). Mahwah, NJ: Lawrence Erlbuam Associates.

U.S. Census Bureau. (2004). Historical income tables: Households. Retrieved from http://www.census.gov/hhes/income/histinc/h0201.html

van Gennep, A. (1960). *The rites of passage* (M. Vizedom & G. Caffee, Trans.). Chicago: University of Chicago Press.

van Manen, M. (1991). *The tact of teaching: The meaning of pedagogical thoughtfulness.* Albany: State University of New York Press.

Varenne, H., & McDermott, R. (1998). *Successful failure: The school America builds.* Boulder, CO: Westview Press.

Vygotsky, L. (1978). *Mind in society: The development of higher psychological processes.* (M. Cole, V. John-Steiner, S. Scribner, & E. Souberman, Eds.). Cambridge, Massachusetts: Harvard University Press.

Wahl, G., & Wertheim, L. J. (2003, December 22). A rite gone terribly wrong. *Sports Illustrated, 99*, 68–76.

Walkerdine, V. (1990). *Schoolgirl fictions.* London: Verso.

Walsh, M. (2000, September 6). Hazing is widespread, student survey shows. *Education Weekly, 20*, 14–16.

Waterman, A. S. (1997). An overview of service-learning and the role of research and evaluation in service-learning programs. In A. S. Waterman, (Ed.), *Service-learning: Applications from the research* (pp. 1–11). Mahwah, NJ: Lawrence Erlbaum Associates.

Watt, J. (1994). *Ideology, objectivity, and education.* New York: Teachers College Press.

Weber, M. (1978). *Economy and society.* Berkeley and Los Angeles: University of California Press.

Weiler, K. (1988). *Women teaching for change: Gender, class and power.* New York: Bergin & Garvey.

Weisberg, J. (2006, June 28). Wealthy and wise: Warren Buffett's lesson to the rich. *Slate.* Retrieved from http://www.slate.com/id/2144668

Wertheim, L. (2003, December 22). A rite gone terribly wrong. *Sports Illustrated, 99*, 68–76.

Wertsch, J. (1995). The need for action in sociocultural research. In J. Wertsch, P. del Rio, & A. Alvarez (Eds.), *Sociocultural studies of mind* (pp. 56–74). New York: Cambridge University Press.

Wertsch, J. (1998). *Mind as action.* New York: Oxford University Press.

Wexler, P. (1992). *Becoming somebody: Toward a social psychology of school.* London, England: Falmer Press.

Wildman, S. M. (1996). *Privilege revealed: How invisible preferences undermine America.* New York: New York University Press.

Willie, S. (2003). *Acting black: College, identity, and the performance of race.* New York: Routledge.

Willis, P. (1977). *Learning to labor: How working class kids get working class jobs.* New York: Columbia University Press.

Winfrey, O. (Executive Producer). (2006, April 11, 12). *The Oprah Winfrey Show* [Television broadcast]. Chicago: Harpo Productions, Inc.

Wingate, B. (Ed.). (1994). *An anthology of true hazing tales.* New York: The Outbound Press.

Wise, T. (2005). *White like me: Reflections on race from a privileged son.* Brooklyn, NY: Soft Skull Press.

Wood, G. (2004). A view from the field: NCLB's effects on classrooms and schools. In D. Meier & G. Wood (Eds.), *Many children left behind: How the No Child Left Behind Act is damaging our children and our schools* (pp. 33--50). Boston: Beacon Press.

Yair, G. (2000). Educational battlefields in America: The tug-of-war over students' engagement with instruction. *Sociology of Education, 73,* 247–269.

Zinn, H. (1980). *A people's history of the United States.* New York: Harper & Row.

Zweigenhaft, R. L., & Domhoff, G. W. (1991). *Blacks in the white establishment? A study of race and class in America.* New Haven, CT: Yale University Press.

Index

M

Made in the USA
San Bernardino, CA
11 July 2018